UP CLOSE AND PERSONAL

Methodology and History in Anthropology

General Editor: David Parkin, Fellow of All Souls College, University of Oxford

Volume 1
Marcel Mauss: A Centenary Tribute
Edited by Wendy James and N.J. Allen

Volume 2
Taboo, Truth and Religion
Franz B. Steiner
Edited by Jeremy Adler and Richard Fardon

Volume 3
Orientpolitik, Value, and Civilization
Franz B. Steiner
Edited by Jeremy Adler and Richard Fardon

Volume 4
The Problem of Context: Perspectives from Social Anthropology and Elsewhere
Edited by R.M. Dilley

Volume 5
Religion in English Everyday Life: An Ethnographic Approach
Timothy Jenkins

Volume 6
Hunting the Gatherers: Ethnographic Collectors, Agents, and Agency in Melanasia, 1870s–1930s
Edited by Michael O'Hanlon and Robert Welsch

Volume 7
Anthropologists in a Wider World: Essays on Field Research
Edited by Paul Dresch, Wendy James, and David Parkin

Volume 8
Categories and Classifications: Maussian Reflections on the Social
N.J. Allen

Volume 9
Louis Dumont and Hierarchical Opposition
Robert Parkin

Volume 10
Categories of Self: Louis Dumont's Theory of the Individual
André Celtel

Volume 11
Existential Anthropology: Events, Exigencies, and Effects
Michael Jackson

Volume 12
An Introduction to Two Theories of Social Anthropology: Descent Groups and Marriage Alliance
Louis Dumont

Volume 13
Navigating Terrains of War: Youth and Soldiering in Guinea-Bissau
Henrik E. Vigh

Volume 14
The Politics of Egalitarianism: Theory and Practice
Edited by Jacqueline Solway

Volume 15
A History of Oxford Anthropology
Edited by Peter Riviére

Volume 16
Holistic Anthropology: Emergence and Convergence
Edited by David Parkin and Stanley Ulijaszek

Volume 17
Learning Religion: Anthropological Approaches
Edited by David Berliner and Ramon Sarró

Volume 18
Ways of Knowing: New Approaches in the Anthropology of Knowledge and Learning
Edited by Mark Harris

Volume 19
Difficult Folk? A Political History of Social Anthropology
David Mills

Volume 20
Human Nature as Capacity: Transcending Discourse and Classification
Nigel Rapport

Volume 21
The Life of Property: House, Family, and Inheritance in Béarn, South-West France
Timothy Jenkins

Volume 22
Out of the Study and Into the Field: Ethnographic Theory and Practice in French Anthropology
Edited by Robert Parkin and Anne de Sales

Volume 23
The Scope of Anthropology: Maurice Godelier's Work in Context
Edited by Laurent Dousset and Serge Tcherkézoff

Volume 24
Anyone: The Cosmopolitan Subject of Anthropology
Nigel Rapport

Volume 25
Up Close and Personal: On Peripheral Perspectives and the Production of Anthropological Knowledge
Edited by Cris Shore and Susanna Trnka

UP CLOSE AND PERSONAL

On Peripheral Perspectives and the Production of Anthropological Knowledge

Edited by
Cris Shore and Susanna Trnka

berghahn
NEW YORK • OXFORD
www.berghahnbooks.com

First published in 2013 by

Berghahn Books

www.berghahnbooks.com

© 2013 Cris Shore and Susanna Trnka

All rights reserved. Except for the quotation of short passages for the purpose of criticism and review, no part of this book may be reproduced in any form or by any means, electronic or mechanical, including photocopying, recording, or any information storage and retrieval system now known or to be invented, without written permission of the publisher.

Library of Congress Cataloging-in-Publication Data

Up close and personal : on peripheral perspectives and the production of anthropological knowledge / edited by Cris Shore and Susanna Trnka.
  p. cm. — (Methodology and history in anthropology ; v.25)
  ISBN 978-0-85745-846-9 (hardback : alk. paper) —
  ISBN 978-0-85745-847-6 (institutional ebook)
  1. Anthropology—Methodology. 2. Knowledge, Sociology of. I. Shore, Cris, 1959– II. Trnka, Susanna.
  GN33.U6 2013
  301.01—dc23

2012032930

British Library Cataloguing in Publication Data

A catalogue record for this book is available from the British Library

Printed in the United States on acid-free paper

ISBN 978-0-85745-846-9 (hardback)
ISBN 978-0-85745-847-6 (institutional ebook)

CONTENTS

List of Illustrations — vii

Preface: Anthropologists Up Close and Personal — ix

Acknowledgements — xi

Introduction. Observing Anthropologists: Professional Knowledge, Practice and Lives — 1
  Cris Shore and Susanna Trnka

MICHAEL JACKSON — 34
Chapter 1. Suffering, Selfhood and Anthropological Encounters — 37

ANNE SALMOND — 56
Chapter 2. Anthropology, Ontology and the Maori World — 58

JOAN METGE — 73
Chapter 3. Building Bridges: Maori and *Pakeha* Relations — 75

GILLIAN COWLISHAW — 92
Chapter 4. 'Culture', 'Race' and 'Me': Living the Anthropology of Indigenous Australians — 94

NICOLAS PETERSON — 108
Chapter 5. Finding One's Way in Arnhem Land — 110

HOWARD MORPHY — 125
Chapter 6. Art as Action: The Yolngu — 127

DAVID TRIGGER — 140
Chapter 7. Rethinking Nature and Nativeness — 142

CHRISTOPHER PINNEY 158

Chapter 8. More than Local, Less than Global:
Anthropology in the Contemporary World 160

NELSON GRABURN 176

Chapter 9. Beyond Selling Out: Art, Tourism and Indigenous
Self-representation 178

NIGEL RAPPORT 195

Chapter 10. Sovereign Individuals and the Ontology of
Selfhood 197

SUSAN WRIGHT 213

Chapter 11. Hidden Histories and Political Transformations 215

MARILYN STRATHERN 231

Chapter 12. Gender Ideology, Property Relations and
Melanesia: The Field of 'M' 233

Conclusion. Looking Ahead: Past Connections and
Future Directions 247
   Cris Shore and Susanna Trnka

ILLUSTRATIONS

1. Michael Jackson with Jackamarra and Jampijinpa, at Paraluyu. Central Australia, 1990. (Photo courtesy of the author) — 53

2. Ritharrngu-speaking brothers, wives, children and affines gathered together to sing in memory of a deceased relative. Central Arnhem Land, 1965. (Photo courtesy of the author) — 117

3. David Trigger playing a recording to Garawa men of a deceased Waanyi man singing a dreaming route. Gulf Country, Australia, 1990. Gerald Wollogorang (centre) and Lenin Anderson (left). (Photo courtesy of Richard Martin) — 150

4. Raghunath and the horse that cost Rs 70,000. 2010. (Photo courtesy of the author) — 165

5. Goddess factory, Guna, Madhya Pradesh. 2009. (Photo courtesy of the author) — 171

6. Nelson Graburn, in Kautchakuluk and Ikaujurapik's tent, Kimmirut village, Hudson Strait. 1960. (Photo courtesy of the author) — 181

7. Nelson Graburn, Ilisapi Kululak girl carrying her brother Jimmy in Kimmirut village, 1960. (Photo courtesy of the author) — 182

8. Nigel Rapport in the field, Cumbria. (Photo courtesy of the author) — 203

9. Susan Wright in her field site in Iran, 1976. (Photo courtesy of the author) — 217

10. Susan Wright and Iranian villagers collaborating on participatory research, 1996. (Photo courtesy of the author) — 224

11. Temporary accommodation for the visiting anthropologist, Kelua, Mt Hagen, 1964. (Photo courtesy of the author)   237

12. Marilyn Strathern with women and children at the edge of a ceremonial ground in Mbukl, Mt Hagen, 1964. (Photo courtesy of the author)   238

Preface

ANTHROPOLOGISTS UP CLOSE AND PERSONAL

This book originated from a series of conversations and debates about the nature of social anthropological enquiry and knowledge production with some of the discipline's leading and most innovative figures in New Zealand, Australia and the United Kingdom. What the volume offers are twelve highly personal yet structured accounts of anthropologists as authors and practitioners, their key discoveries, what attracted them to anthropology, how they have helped to shape the discipline, and in turn, how the discipline has shaped their works and lives. The result is a series of candid, first-person narratives that reveal something quite intimate and profound about the nature of the anthropological endeavour. In the pages that follow our contributors examine a range of key issues including the ethics and politics of activism; how anthropological knowledge is made (and what counts as 'anthropological' knowledge); what distinguishes anthropology as a way of seeing and engaging with the world; how anthropology's self-understanding and professional identity is changing; the nature of 'discovery' and how lived experience is transformed into ethnographic and scientific data; and how the discipline reproduces itself and the role of personalities and personal relationships in that process.

While each of the twelve individuals in this book offers a uniquely rich and personal account of what it means to be an anthropologist, taken as a whole these accounts shed light on wider epistemic and sociological forces that have defined, and continue to define, the past, present and future trajectories of social anthropology. Reflecting on these processes, the accounts offered up by the authors in this book provide a panorama of the life and times in which we live and the history of the discipline, particularly from the viewpoint of the antipodes.

In putting together this book, we have striven to capture a sense of the intimacy that characterised our initial conversations. Our aim is to offer the reader a somewhat different perspective on the work of anthropology than can normally be found in a textbook or academic article. We wanted to convey some of our authors' more personal and informal reflections to shed light on how major concepts in the discipline came into being and to give a sense of the personalities and subjective experiences that invariably underlie the typically more formal and polished products of ethnographic enquiry. Like Oliver Cromwell, we invited our authors to present a 'warts and all' portrait of their professional selves and lives. Whether they have lived up to that challenge is for the reader to judge.

Cris Shore and Susanna Trnka
Auckland, 2013

ACKNOWLEDGEMENTS

We would like to thank Dr Rolf Husman of Documentary Educational Resources, who helped us carry out some of the original interviews in Auckland. Thanks are also due to Richard Smith and Neil Morrison of the University of Auckland for technical assistance in the television studio's recording and editing room; to Alison Palmer for research assistance; and to Laura McLauchlan for transcription. We owe a particular debt of gratitude to John Michael Correll who managed to transform some of the archaic fieldwork photographs into digitally enhanced high quality images for this book. We also wish to acknowledge Dean Carruthers and Godfrey Boehnke for the portrait photographs of Anne Salmond and Joan Metge, respectively. We would also like to thank Elizabeth Berg at Berghahn for making the final production process so easy. Finally, we wish to thank our anthropology colleagues in New Zealand and in Denmark where some of the ideas for this book were presented as conference papers.

Introduction

OBSERVING ANTHROPOLOGISTS
Professional Knowledge, Practice and Lives

Cris Shore and Susanna Trnka

Anthropologists are experts at studying cultural 'others' and, in the process, elucidating hidden aspects of their own society. These twin perspectives have typically been seen as the aim of good ethnographic writing. This book reverses the analytical lens to focus on the anthropologists *themselves*: their works, lives and subjective encounters in the field and beyond. In doing so, it explores the relationship between personal experience and knowledge production, taking us behind some of the key concepts that have shaped the discipline, both its past and its present. The anthropological encounter not only changes our ideas about the world and provides a lens for understanding other people's worlds; as the narrative accounts in this book show, it can also fundamentally change who we are.

This book sets out to answer four key questions that are practical, political and epistemological in nature. First, what exactly is it that distinguishes anthropology as a professional practice and as a way of seeing and knowing the world? Second, how has the discipline changed in the past forty years, and does the geographical location of its practitioners affect the ways anthropology is practiced? Third, what are the most exciting innovations and directions that are reshaping anthropology today, and where have these ideas come from? And fourth, how do anthropologists engage with the urgent problems facing societies around the world, and how do they understand that engagement? In addressing these questions, we also hope to illuminate broader issues, including the constitution and reproduction of the discipline, the shifting identity of anthropology as a profession, its applications and its ethical entanglements.

There have been a number of works that have tried to shed light, in one way or another, on the practice of social anthropology. Many of these have highlighted the practice of fieldwork as the pillar of anthropology (Sanjek 1990: Borneman and Hammoudi 2009); others have explored anthropology as a form of writing, deconstructing the literary tactics and artifice of writing ethnography (Clifford and Marcus 1986; Geertz 1988). Still others, following the literary turn of the 1980s and calls for more self-reflexive accounts (Marcus and Cushman 1982), have adopted the genres of personal memoirs and 'confessional' writing (Nordstrom and Robben 1996; Coffey 1999; De Neve and Unnithan-Kumar 2006; Collins and Gallinat 2010). Most of these texts focus exclusively on fieldwork experiences. Sometimes they have been highly personal and often (embarrassingly) revealing; for example, Paul Rabinow's 'sensual interactions' with prostitutes in Morocco, which, he informs us, 'seemed to be too good to be true' (1977: 65, 69); Peter Wade's account (1993) of the sexual motivations that led him to do ethnographic research in Colombia; or Kenneth Good's (1991) romantic tale of 'going native' among the Yanomami in Venezuela. While these accounts have provided some valuable insight into the processes of anthropological knowledge formation, like most autobiographies, they tend to be selective and skewed towards the concerns of their authors. As observant critics have often noted, an autobiography typically reveals nothing bad except the author's memory and vanity. In a similar vein, there have been a number of fascinating anthologies of anthropologists' personal accounts of their relationships with key informants (Casagrande 1960; Watson 1999; see also Dumont 1978). Some of these accounts are humorous and self-deprecatory and are aimed at a more general public audience (Barley 1983); others are fictional narratives that set out to lampoon the practices of the anthropologist (Parkin 1986; Lodge 1991; McCall-Smith 2005, 2006a, 2006b; see also MacClancy 2005).

This book differs in three important ways. First, our concern is to examine the practice of anthropology in its wider sense. Anthropology as a profession is not simply a matter of 'doing fieldwork' or 'writing ethnography'; it also includes teaching, social activism and performing the role of public intellectual. These are not simply add-on components to practising anthropology; rather, in this book we demonstrate the close and dynamic relationship between these different dimensions, including how activism and teaching shape our fieldwork experiences and anthropological sensibilities. Second, our aim is to understand how the major theoretical tropes and paradigms that have influenced contemporary social anthropology have arisen not only through fieldwork, but as a result of other personal, historical and scholarly influences. And third, the process of creating these personal histories and narrative accounts is deliberately different from that of most of the works cited above. Rather than inviting contributors to send us their unmediated autobiographical musings and reflections on their own experiences, we met with them personally and led them through a set of semi-structured questions that sought to tease out the connections between personal history, intellectual influences and disciplinary formation. As a result, their answers were spontaneous and unrehearsed. Even though they later had a chance to revise their contributions, the resulting chapters strive to maintain the informality and conversational style of our interviews. Perhaps more important, this approach meant that our contributors were often asked to speak to topics that they may not have chosen themselves – sometimes putting people on the spot by asking questions that took them outside of their comfort zones. In a curious sense, our authors thus also became our 'informants'. Much like the collaborative process of ethnographic fieldwork, we engaged with them to elicit answers to the questions that we found most compelling. This represents a very different and perhaps uniquely 'hybrid' genre of anthropological writing – not quite an 'anthropology of anthropologists' (Kuper 1996) but somewhere between raw interview and reflexivity; autobiography and collaborative analysis (Fluehr-Lobben 2008); or between emic and etic perspectives on one's own professional practice. This also enabled us to look across the interviews to draw out unifying themes and key differences that highlight not only individual idiosyncrasies, but also generational patterns, national contexts and career trajectories.

The twelve individuals who are featured in this book have all dedicated a large part of their professional and personal lives to anthropology. Many of them are at the cutting edges of their respective fields: scholars whose work and writings have transformed anthropology as a discipline and who have inspired subsequent generations of students both nationally and internationally. Many of them have also had careers that span different countries, acting as public intellectuals and engaging in the major concerns that occupy anthropologists – and policy makers – in different settings. While not intended to be representative of particular national traditions, their work necessarily reflects some of the major intellectual currents and socio-economic and political changes that have occurred not only in New Zealand,

Australia and Britain, but in the discipline on a global scale. By exploring their individual works and lives, we aim to grasp some of the wider social and contextual changes that are occurring within the discipline, as well as within academia as a whole. Our authors also both reflect, and reflect upon, some of the generational shifts that have occurred in anthropology, from the 1950s, when Joan Metge and Nelson Graburn embarked on their studies, to the 1980s, when Christopher Pinney and Nigel Rapport received their doctorates. These accounts thus offer a glimpse into the ways in which the discipline produces and reproduces itself or, more precisely, how its practitioners remake the profession. Significantly, the early education and training of these authors reflects much more the influence of the British tradition of *social anthropology*, with its focus on social structures and social relations, than the North American tradition of *cultural anthropology*, with its characteristic concern with debates around meaning and symbolism (Kuper 1999; Spencer 2000). If one of our goals was to understand what has happened to that British anthropological tradition once it was exported to the colonies, another goal was to examine how practitioners in the so-called periphery have engaged with and redefined that legacy and the intellectual contributions that peripheries can make to challenging and rethinking the established normative orders and assumptions that emanate from the centre.

The Value of 'Peripheral Visions'

A major rationale for this book was to examine the relationship between knowledge production and anthropological location as understood in a broader sense than simply fieldwork (Gupta and Ferguson 1997). Our aim was to explore the extent to which the discipline of social anthropology in two post-colonial settler societies (Australia and New Zealand) differs from its counterparts in Britain's mainstream metropolitan centres. We have a personal stake in this question having both grown up and undergone much of our own professional training in anthropology in what could be described as the metropolitan centres of the discipline (Britain and the United States, respectively). Having both resettled in New Zealand in the last ten years, we continue to be struck both by the differences, yet more so by the *continuities* that define the discipline and practice of anthropology in these distinctive locales. Australia and New Zealand are often perceived to be on the periphery of global academic knowledge production. While the term 'periphery' may be viewed as a Eurocentric way of framing the issue, it is nonetheless useful for distinguishing between the financially well-endowed universities in the Northern Hemisphere's core metropolitan centres and universities in more marginalized sites. One important observation that arises from our authors' accounts is the rich intellectual *cross*-fertilization that occurs between core and peripheral sites in academia. This is partly a reflection of the increased movement of academics in the ever-more globalized world of academia, with New Zealand in particular having one of the most international academic labour forces in the world (Bonisch-Brednich 2010). The traffic works both ways, however. It would be impossible to attempt to draw national boundaries around the work and influence of antipodean anthropologists such as Raymond Firth, Roger Keesing, Bruce Kapferer, Michael Taussig, Michael Jackson or Anne Salmond. Moreover, most of these authors have spent substantial parts of their careers shifting to and from their countries of origin.

Nonetheless, New Zealand and Australia also provide specific contexts in which anthropology has developed, and they have given rise to several distinctive domestic concerns, from debates over post-colonial identities and subjectivities and the politics of indigeneity to applied anthropology and questions of ownership, appropriation and land rights (as we explore below). Antipodean perspectives have contributed more broadly to mainstream anthropology in various ways. As well as producing leading scholars, the Pacific region has given rise to many key concepts and distinctive disciplinary themes, including those of political leadership, chiefs and big men; gift-exchange and reciprocity; the politics of apology and post-colonial reconciliation; indigenous identity and rights; cultural genocide and the politics of forced assimilation; and theories of adolescence and childhood. As our contributors demonstrate, Australian and New Zealand anthropologists have contributed substantially to these debates, their development and, in particular, to their application.

Anthropology in New Zealand has also been the scholarly training ground for a number of leading Maori public figures, political and social activists, and intellectuals, including Robert Mahuta, Pita Sharples, Sir Hugh Kawharu, Ranginui Walker and Pat Hohepa. These leaders have all championed Maori rights and have been part of the movement that has gained wide public recognition for Maori culture with the result that *te reo Maori* (the Maori language) is taught in many public schools and that the New Zealand government now funds a Maori-language television station. There are also preschools (*kōhanga reo*), higher education institutions (*wānanga*) and alternative approaches to penal reform based on Maori cultural principles. While it has by no means overcome the inequalities created by its colonial legacy, New Zealand's Treaty of Waitangi partnership arrangement is often cited as an example of a more successful approach to indigenous-settler relations.

There is a long-held anthropological ideal of using voices from the margins to critique the core, or as Marcus and Fischer put it (1999: 138), bringing 'the insights gained on the periphery back to the centre to raise havoc with our settled ways of thinking and conceptualisation'. In the antipodes, the perspectives of indigenous peoples have gone a long way in challenging the assumptions of Eurocentric thinking. However, as Maori scholars and activists argue, this process could be taken much further, particularly in the areas of land rights and social justice (Smith 1999; Muru-Lanning 2010; Mutu 2011; Kawharu 2011). As Justice Eddie Durie notes (2011: 135), 'While both of New Zealand's founding cultures are passionate about property rights and expound the need to respect them, they differ on what those rights are.' He concludes that considerable work is still needed 'to close the gap in cultural comprehension'.

The subversive potential of peripheral perspectives may have an even greater transformative role. Using the metaphor of 'peripheral vision' in astronomy, June Nash (2001) has argued that sometimes the only way to see an object of study (like the cluster of stars known as the Pleiades) is to stare beyond it and catch a glimpse of the whole.

> If we look straight ahead with the tunnel vision of disciplines that concentrate on core institutions in the centres of global power, we miss the manifold processes known as globalization that occur on the margins. These core institutions are so intertwined with regional, national and local clusters that it is difficult, if not impossible, to perceive the macro formations. (Nash 2001: 15)

Like Nash, we suggest that an added dimension of the intellectual value of perspectives from countries like Australia and New Zealand arises precisely from their marginal positions. In much the same way as the 'upside-down' (or 'south-up') map compels us to recognize the taken-for-granted bias towards the Northern Hemisphere – and its attendant psychological effects (Meier et al 2011) – so views from the periphery can help to dislodge the normative values and assumptions inherent in Eurocentric perspectives. The value of peripheral viewpoints is borne out in much of the anthropological scholarship on the cultures of colonialism (Dirks 1992; Thomas 1995), and in the anthropology of post-colonialism (Werbner 2012, globalization and neoliberalization, and 'supply chain capitalism' (Tsing 2009) and citizenship (Partridge 2011). That process of foregrounding perspectives from the margins is largely what characterizes anthropology's keystone method of ethnographic fieldwork.

Professions and Identities: Anthropology as Seen from Within and Without

Ever since Malinowski, the most notable defining feature of social anthropology has been that of an individual embarking upon cross-cultural fieldwork. The idea of knowledge gained from empathetic understanding derived from long-term immersion in a different cultural milieu – be it in the Amazonian rainforest, a remote village in Africa or a small South Sea island on the brink of cultural extinction – has long been a central motif in both anthropological practice and representations of the discipline (Kuklick 2011). The romantic figure of Bronislaw Malinowski spending years living and working in seeming harmony with the Trobriand Islanders both epitomized and set the bar for what proper anthropological field research should entail – notwithstanding the disclosures about his personal life that came to light following the posthumous publication of his private diaries (Malinowski 1967).

All professions seem to acquire an external image which, however inaccurate it may be, substantially influences the people engaged in that field. In some cases this may also be a key factor in why individuals embark upon a career in that discipline. The allures of being a supermodel, famous musician, professional athlete – or nowadays a celebrity chef – are readily apparent; these careers appear to need little or no explanation. However misunderstood they may be in practice, these professions – like those of doctors, teachers and police officers – are instantly recognizable and enjoy a certain kudos. By contrast, those who work in what might be termed the 'knowledge industries' are harder to classify, as their work is neither particularly visible nor widely recognized. For example, most anthropologists can recount umpteen occasions when their response to the question 'So what do you do for a living?' has produced bafflement.

Anthropology as a profession seems to conspicuously lack serious public recognition. Or if it does enjoy notoriety, it is usually for the wrong reasons. The popular public image of anthropology has been shaped largely by negative stereotypes or romanticized caricatures. Among the most pervasive of these are the anthropologist as eccentric boffin and merchant in exotica; neo-colonialist and pith-helmeted butterfly collector; permanent tourist or deranged Westerner who sadly 'went native'; or government spy and intruder into other people's privacy. Perhaps a more appealing but equally problematic image is that of the anthropologist-as-hero. This trope includes popular figures such as Indiana Jones or the forensic scientists who feature prominently in popular television police dramas like *CSI*, *Bones* and *Cold Case*. Other less heroic but nonetheless appealing figures include Scarlett Johannson's rendition of the anthropologist-cum-accidental nanny in *The Nanny Diaries* or the young protagonist in the popular drama *Fierce People*, who models himself on his famous but distant anthropologist father by examining social relations among a rich and eccentric New Jersey family. These populist depictions invariably trade on images of anthropologists' engagement with the eccentric, the exotic and the seemingly 'primitive' Other. While these portrayals might seem unconvincing to most professional anthropologists, anecdotal evidence suggests that many students are drawn to the discipline by their allure. Indeed, a number of the contributors to this volume admit that their initial attraction to anthropology arose from its promise of exotica.

The question of what attracts individuals to anthropology – and what kinds of individuals are drawn to it – is important, because it raises issues that lie at the heart of this book, i.e. the sense in which anthropology entails a foray into other people's lives and worlds and the implications of that engagement for the people themselves, for anthropologists, and for the development of knowledge about our own and other cultures. How some of the leading practitioners in the discipline came to anthropology was one of the questions we wanted to answer, as it set the stage for understanding what anthropology is all about. To what extent have any of these external images influenced people to take up a career in anthropology?

The personal accounts in this book are not intended to be representative of the discipline as a whole, but they do, nonetheless, provide rich and instructive insights into the factors that have influenced people's decisions to devote their lives to this endeavour. What unites the authors in this book is the extent to which practicing anthropology is experienced as a vocation; i.e. not just an occupation and a profession but a mission and a passion. As Max Weber (1948: 84) famously wrote in his essay 'Politics as a Vocation', 'He who lives "for" politics makes politics his life, in an internal sense'. In similar vein, the authors in this book have shaped their lives around anthropology and have, in turn, had their lives reshaped by the discipline in a manner reminiscent of a 'calling'. And yet, for most of them, discovering anthropology came about largely by accident. Perhaps that itself is indicative of the ambiguity surrounding anthropology as a profession. This sense of the incidental and ephemeral nature of anthropology is well captured in Lévi-Strauss's autobiographical work, *Tristes Tropiques*. 'Anthropology', he wrote, is 'an ambiguous enterprise, oscillating between a mission and a refuge'. The ethnographer strives to understand other people's worlds both from intimate and distanced perspectives:

> The conditions of his life and work cut him off from his own group for long periods together; and he himself acquires a kind of chronic uprootedness from the sheer brutality of the environmental changes to which he is exposed. Never can he feel himself at home anywhere: he will always be, psychologically speaking, an amputated man. Anthropology is, with music and mathematics, one of the few true vocations; and the anthropologist may become aware of it within himself before ever he has been taught it. (Lévi-Strauss 1961: 58)

Many of our authors echo Lévi-Strauss's description of anthropology as something they felt attracted to even before they understood what it was (an entrée into other worlds or alien modes of thought? An escape from their own reality? A chance to discover – or remake – oneself?) Most anthropologists, however, would not share Lévi-Strauss's hyperbole or his pessimistic portrayal of the psychological impact of anthropological fieldwork. Nor would they share his assumption that anthropology can be discovered within oneself, even without any formal teaching or training. The reasons how and why people come to anthropology are both complex and subjective. Sociological factors also play an important role in drawing people to the discipline.

Coming to Anthropology

From the narrative accounts in this book we can deduce several distinct trajectories into anthropology. As mentioned, for several of our authors, discovering the discipline seemed to occur largely by accident. Part of the reason for that is almost certainly because anthropology is not taught in the mainstream school curriculum. It therefore retains a certain aura of mystery, as well as enticement about it. However, many were drawn to the discipline as a result of early childhood encounters with cultural 'others', experiences which had fuelled a fascination with different cultural worlds. For some, particularly Salmond, Jackson and Gillian Cowlishaw, those alternate worlds held out a promise of escape from their own seemingly dry and mundane cultural universes – even an opportunity to remake oneself. For others, particularly Marilyn Strathern and Susan Wright, it was about intellectual curiosity and dissatisfaction with the limitations of other subjects. There were those (such as Graburn, Wright and Salmond) who were attracted to the discipline through their personal encounters with charismatic teachers, while still others (like Rapport) initially came to anthropology to study archaeology or biological anthropology but migrated to social anthropology. For most of our authors, coming to anthropology entailed a combination of several factors.

The Accidental Anthropologists

The phrase 'accidental anthropologist' has been applied to a number of leading figures. Eric Wolf was famously described in his *New York Times* obituary as a biochemistry major at Queens College in New York who 'stumbled into an anthropology class one day and realized that the broad field embraced just about everything he was interested in, which was just about everything about every aspect of the human experience' (Thomas 1999: 10). Significantly, 'accidental anthropologist' is also the title of Jackson's memoir. As Jackson observes (in this volume), 'I stumbled on anthropology for reasons I can't fully fathom. And I remained in anthropology more by chance than design ...'

This metaphor of 'stumbling' is a far cry from that of the heroic adventurer who purposefully sets forth to discover the world and encounter exotic others. But in many respects the accidental nature of the encounter with anthropology is consistent with the discipline's methodology, i.e. the importance that 'serendipity' plays in anthropological fieldwork (Hastrup 1992). The contributors to this volume highlight the importance of the accidental and the contingent as a defining element of anthropological research: as Graburn observes when asked about his current projects, 'I generally don't have "projects" ... It's a little like that first fieldwork, [the research focus] just hits you'. Like many anthropologists, Graburn insists that none of his major research discoveries 'would have happened if I'd set out to plan them'. Most anthropologists relish the haphazard quality of anthropological engagement because of the unexpected – and sometimes unhoped for – insights it reveals. Indeed, as our authors vividly recount, a large amount of critical anthropological knowledge is acquired as a consequence of mistakes and blunders made in the field. But not all anthropologists 'stumbled' upon anthropology unawares; some actively seek out not only the discipline's promise of encountering difference but also the possibility of internalizing alterity.

Encountering Otherness

It has often been noted that anthropology attracts those who somehow feel themselves to be misfits or outsiders. It is precisely that sense of dislocation – and the realization of alternative social realities – that makes anthropology so appealing to some. Pinney, with characteristic panache, sums it up eloquently: 'I think my own experience fits a very common anthropological pattern. Many anthropologists – rather like brutal dictators – have marginal childhoods. They move in from the periphery to the centre and there's something in that dislocation which then makes them susceptible to anthropology as a practice.'

Equally striking is the fact that many of our contributors confess to having felt, even from a very early age, an attraction to other people's cultural worlds. For the New Zealand anthropologists, all of whom are *Pakeha* (i.e. New Zealand born and of British descent), the encounter with Maori was arguably the most important influence on their desire to step beyond the boundaries of what was defined as their 'own society'. Cowlishaw, Salmond, Metge and Jackson all speak to the importance of the Maori-*Pakeha* divide and its significance for their respective generations. All grew up in small towns which had, in Metge's words, 'Maori enclaves which were marginalized on the periphery of society'. For Salmond, '[T]here was no real way to participate [in Maori life] ... as the two communities were quite divided from each other. ... [T]hey coincided at *school* or in *sport*, but otherwise very little'.

Or as Jackson writes, 'It wasn't "apartheid", but in the bourgeois imagination there was an unspoken assumption that these people were not respectable enough to be true companions or neighbours.'

While for some this exotic and marginal status was a large part of the appeal, for others it was the richness and warmth of the 'Maori world' itself that was the main attraction. Jackson vividly recalls the shock of seeing 'exotic' elderly women 'with *moko* (traditional Maori tattoos) on their chins, smoking pipes' who 'inhabited a different world' and 'mysteriously came and went':

> Why did they live in this other place and where was it? What was it like? I gradually fantasized an identification with Maori as the embodiment of the misfit that I felt I was. I grafted my own sense of alienation onto these people who appeared to be living on the margins of society.

For Cowlishaw, the pull of Maoridom derived largely from a deep dissatisfaction with her own milieu and the 'restrained', 'repressed and boring cultural arena of dairy farming':

> As a *teenager* I had this sense of being in a very tight, closed and conventional world which I and other members of my family felt was like a prison, a prison of others' opinions and narrow moralism expressed in gossip. I was very conscious of the possibility of exploring the wide, varied and sophisticated world out there ...

For Salmond, Maoridom similarly offered the chance to step into an alternative reality:

> It gave me a different sense of the world ... I could walk out and look at a mountain or a hill that I've been looking at all my life, and all of a sudden, I'd see a totally different side to that place ... it's not 'Young Nick's Head,' a headland in Gisborne which was the first place named by Captain Cook, it's Te Kuri a Paoa, named after his dog by Paoa, one of the first Polynesian explorers to arrive in New Zealand. There's a 'double history' here, a double dimension to the landscapes that I was living in every day. Feeling like that about your own country all of a sudden is unsettling. It's not exactly *Alice in Wonderland*, but it's almost like that: i.e. everything I thought was stable and familiar started to take on radically new meanings.

Jackson took this even further, not only seeking to remake his social world but, more important, himself: first by identifying as a 'white Maori', symbolically severing ties to the *Pakeha* world of his parents, and subsequently by self-consciously placing himself in dangerous war-torn parts of the world in order to expose himself 'to extreme conditions of radical otherness' as a means of 'remaking' himself. For many anthropologists fieldwork encounters can result in radical, though sometimes equally subtle, realignments of their identities, moral values and outlooks on the world. Jackson may be unusual in consciously aiming for such a conversion, but, as our interviewees attest, being transformed by fieldwork is not a unique phenomenon.

Post-colonial social relations also captivated the interests of future anthropologists growing up in the metropolitan centres. Nicolas Peterson and Graburn, for example, both grew up in extraordinarily cosmopolitan households due to their family's close involvement with colonial and post-colonial enterprises. Peterson spent his childhood in an East London social and philanthropic settlement which was a magnet for visiting scholars. He describes how, 'As a boy, every day that I was at home I'd have lunch with ... a number of ... sociologists and intellectuals from across the British Commonwealth'. Similarly, Graburn's household included 'people who spoke foreign languages, talked about "the natives" and who enjoyed cuisines that were definitely not English'.

Talking to People Who Talk Back

Others took a more circuitous route to social anthropology; several of our authors were attracted to anthropology after first taking up either archaeology or biological anthropology. This includes Jackson and Rapport, as well as Strathern, who spent her teenage years going on archaeological digs unearthing Roman remains in southern England. For Strathern, the appeal of studying at Cambridge was that it offered a degree in both archaeology and anthropology:

> I thought this was absolutely perfect; it would allow me to indulge my passion for archaeology but then go on and be serious and do anthropology. Of course, I was eighteen years old and that now sounds really pompous!

While archaeology and biological anthropology held appeal, there were a number of factors that made social anthropology particularly alluring. A further factor that drew many of our other contributors was the influence of a charismatic teacher or practitioner. Edmund Leach was a particularly important influence on Strathern, Graburn and Rapport – as well as a whole generation of other students, including Fredrik Barth and Stephen Hugh-Jones. For Wright it was the 'transfixing' character of David Brookes ('dressed in a Bakhtiari robe [and] enacting a lot of dances and talking about Bakhtiari politics') that lit the fire. In New Zealand, Ralph Piddington shaped the careers of Metge, Salmond and Jackson.

Yet it was not only charismatic teachers, but the possibility of directly engaging with 'ordinary folk' as part and parcel of their intellectual enterprise that confirmed for many that anthropology was the right discipline for them. Some, like Wright, came to anthropology out of dissatisfaction with another discipline that they had originally chosen to study. For Wright, anthropology offered a way to explore the ordinary lives of those who had been largely eclipsed by the grand narratives of official history and connect their hidden histories to the major events that have shaped the world.

Indeed, what was often felt to be missing in other subjects were accounts of *ordinary* people's lives – in all of their complexity. Anthropology, as Ingold (1992: 696) observes, 'is philosophy with the people in'. This was something that Howard Morphy discovered after confiding to his geography schoolmaster that he wanted to study geography in order to better 'understand the needs of developing societies'. The reply he got was that 'human geography is the poor man's anthropology'.

In similar vein, Metge's original ambition had been to study archaeology, but she was told by the Auckland War Memorial Museum's education officer that she would do better 'to work with people who can talk back'. One of the distinguishing features of anthropology, as Metge's work testifies, is that it entails a constant conversation between 'informants' and researcher. Dealing with human subjects who have agency – and who are able to articulate their own thoughts and feelings – has profound implications for the production of anthropological knowledge. It makes the research process necessarily dialogic and open-ended, although as Metge points out, all too often people 'talk past' each other, and due to cultural misunderstandings their words fall on deaf ears (see also Metge and Kinloch 1978). Being receptive to those other voices and different ways of seeing is not only of crucial practical and political importance, it also expands the limits of our own thinking.

As Strathern also points out, anthropology is fortunate in that it is constantly challenged and renewed through its sustained dialogues with actors outside of academia who compel us to question our own disciplinary biases and assumptions. This makes anthropology arguably the most reflexive (some would say neurotically so) discipline in the social sciences. What we extrapolate from these encounters can be analyzed on at least two levels. First, what they reveal to us about humanity and the human condition in its widest sense, and second, what we can learn about specific societies and the cultural dynamics of particular locations. The art of anthropology lies in teasing out connections and mapping the myriad relationships between these domains.

Many anthropologists are drawn to the discipline precisely because of that challenge. If reading Rousseau first kindled Strathern's desire to explore the notion of 'society', it was Evans-Pritchard's vivid accounts of everyday Nuer life – 'the order of the descriptions and the details' – that convinced her to pursue anthropology. In contrast to Strathern, who was captivated by the minutiae (or 'imponderablia') of everyday life, Jackson had, by complete chance, picked up a battered copy of Lévi-Strauss's *Elementary Forms of Kinship* in the Congo and was struck by the notion of anthropology as the study of the human mind.

For others, the primary appeals were not only intellectual concerns but also a desire to engage with political issues and pressing social problems. As David Trigger reflects, '[A]nthropology's apparent alliance with the romance of tribal societies provided an alternative means of critiquing the establishment.' Despite criticisms of anthropology's supposed complicity in the colonial project, much of the discipline's attractiveness lies in its apparent associations with the perspectives of the subaltern, the marginal and the peripheral. As Pinney admits, anthropology seemed to offer a 'fourth international' version of politics that was both radical and internationalist. Metge, too, was drawn to anthropology out of a Christian-inspired commitment to social justice.

If the motivations for pursuing anthropology lie in a combination of learning about oneself and learning about our own and other people's worlds — and perhaps even being a catalyst for change and social justice — what are the possibilities for creating knowledge from such an enterprise? And what kinds of insights, understandings and knowledge does anthropology produce?

On the Production and Reproduction of Anthropological Knowledge

These questions beg a more profound issue of defining what exactly *is* anthropological knowledge. Following Plato, some philosophers would argue that knowledge is 'justified true belief', although this position is widely disputed by proponents of Continental philosophy. The Platonist approach holds that the basis for knowledge is reason and evidence, which enlighten us about the deeper abstract objects or concepts that are independent and timeless. By contrast, most anthropologists, wherever they may situate themselves on the spectrum between relativism and rationality, would probably ask *whose* reason and evidence? This recognition that concepts are always socially and historically situated is central to the anthropological sensibility or, to adapt C. Wright Mills's phrase, the 'anthropological imagination'. It is this *unsettling* of basic assumptions and categories — a constant questioning and contextualizing of common sense and received wisdom — that is the hallmark of anthropological thinking. This perspective is captured eloquently by Michael Herzfeld, when he writes:

> Social and cultural anthropology 'is the study of common sense.' Yet common sense is, anthropologically speaking, seriously misnamed. It is neither common to all cultures, nor is any version of it particularly sensible from the perspective of anyone outside its particular cultural context. (Herzfeld 2001: 1)

The anthropological sensibility derives largely from a concern to take seriously the multiplicity of different perspectives and practices across cultures. This recognition of our own and other people's modes of thinking — and the oscillation back and forth between them — generates discomfort and uncertainty. But from that disorientation there usually arise a series of insights that eventually culminate in anthropological knowledge.

If context is everything in anthropology, so too is comparison. In many respects comparison is an implicit component of anthropological practice. The most influential anthropologists have always been those who are especially adept at drawing out the comparative connections and making intellectual leaps across cultural fields. Strathern, for example, illustrates how our assumptions about what constitutes 'sharing', 'stealing' and 'borrowing' are radically undermined when viewed from the perspective of societies that operate a very different logic of property and ownership (see also Durie 2011). The concept of 'borrowing' in Western discourse usually suggests taking a possession that has been given willingly for a short period of time. However, at Xavier High School, in Chuuk, Micronesia, students regularly 'borrow' one another's possessions without permission and with no intention of returning them. In a context where 'persons deploy things to enhance their spheres of influence' such acts enable students to injure one other while deflecting the wrath of school authorities who would punish outright 'stealing' but tolerate supposedly 'local cultural practices of communal sharing'. 'Xavier borrowing' thus allowed students to influence one another's power and prestige while retaining a modicum of dignity before the foreign school authorities (Strathern 2011: 27–30).

Anthropological knowledge is reproduced along two main axes that are both mutually constituting and intersecting. The first is anthropological discourse in its broadest sense, which includes the various theories, debates, concepts and general principles that have shaped and defined anthropological thinking since the nineteenth century. While we would hesitate to label this a 'canon', there is, nonetheless, a body of literature, a way of framing our research problems and subjects, and a set of overarching concerns (which have traditionally included kinship, culture, social relations, symbolism, ritual, language and power) that most anthropologists are well acquainted with. The small size of the discipline, the impact of its key scholars (sometimes international but often more local), the influence of inspirational teachers and the uniqueness of its participatory method of research all combine to create ways of seeing and thinking that are distinctively anthropological. Each generation tends to be schooled (at least initially) in the theoretical approaches and debates specific to their time. For those trained in the 1950s (such as Metge and Graburn) the legacy of functionalism still hung heavily around the neck of the discipline; those trained in the 1960s (including Strathern, Jackson, Peterson and Salmond) found intellectual excitement in a number of new theoretical directions, from cultural ecology to structuralism. The 1970s generation (which includes Wright, Cowlishaw and Morphy) was particularly influenced by debates around Marxism, feminism and the critique of colonialism, whereas the post-1980 generation (including Pinney, Rapport and Trigger) contended with Orientalism, Gramscian and Foucauldian perspectives, post-modernism, cultural studies and the rise of indigenous activism.

Part of the anthropological sensibility, however, also includes sensitivity to the contingent nature of social events, to being open to changing circumstances and being willing to shift one's research focus, theoretical stance, or even one's entire research project, in response to events on the ground. Anthropological knowledge is generated largely through the dialectic between theoretical insight and ethnographic encounter. While all ethnographers may enter the field with research interests that are theoretically informed, most find their theoretical stance challenged, sometimes even totally undermined, by their informants and their fieldwork encounters.

The second axis to anthropological knowledge is disciplinary *practice*, which is largely shaped by ethnographic fieldwork, i.e. long-term participant observation in the everyday lives of peoples and cultures. The fieldwork encounter remains arguably the most central and distinctive means of generating anthropological knowledge and certainly the anthropologists' most recognizable professional practice. The expansion of fieldwork to include many previously unimaginable field sites and research topics – from the rituals of nuclear-weapons scientists (Gusterson 1998) and the cultures of biotech laboratories (Rabinow 1999) to the transnational worlds of corporate capitalists (Bourgouin 2007) and the practices of Wall Street traders (Ho 2009) – only serves to confirm the continuing utility and centrality of fieldwork based on face-to-face encounters as a defining anthropological method. Notwithstanding the critique of empiricism (i.e. the assumption that social reality can simply be deduced from immediate observation), the ontological imperative of 'being there' has not lost its importance – nor should it (Geertz 1988, but cf. Gupta and Ferguson 1997). The value of fieldwork is that it provides a corrective against disembodied theorizing (or 'armchair sociology') of the kind often found among the more scientific or positivistic disciplines. It also provides a creative arena for questioning our theoretical models and generating new theoretical insights.

Anthropological knowledge is therefore partially created through this restless shifting between the insiders' (or 'emic') viewpoint and the outsider ('etic') or analysts' perspectives; a constant tacking backwards and forwards, which, as Geertz (1985) argued, generates a sense of permanent motion central to hermeneutic understanding. Whether the outcome of such an understanding results in the ability to 'enter into' other people's lifeworlds or, to a more limited capacity, to engage in cultural mediation and translation, is an issue hotly contested among anthropologists themselves.

Another dynamism that helps to shape anthropological understanding is the constant movement between the universal and the specific, or as it is often framed, between global and local levels. There are at least two aspects to this jumping between scales. One is using observations of culturally specific events or processes to shed light on generalized understandings. For example, Serena Nanda's (1990) observation that in traditional Hindu society there is a recognition of three genders (male, female and *hijra*) was subsequently used to reflect critically on the socially constructed nature of Western gender dichotomies. The second aspect lies in showing how global processes are localized – or regionalized – and embedded. Anthropologists are particularly adept at tracking the way concepts travel, how certain discourses and practices take on unanticipated meanings as they cross boundaries and enter into new domains – as has been vividly demonstrated, for example, in the spread of new public management and the rise of 'audit culture' in higher education (Shore and Wright 1999; Strathern 2000; Shore 2008).

Given their engagement in this anthropological process characterized by the creative interplay between theory and fieldwork, local, global and intermediary scales, and emic and etic perspectives, what particular insights have our individual contributors produced?

Key Contributors to Anthropological Knowledge

The contributors to this volume, in many respects, have been witnesses to, and analysts of, some of the great transformations and major historical events that have occurred over the last five decades. These include Iran on the eve of the 1979 revolution (Wright); India as it underwent rapid industrialisation (Pinney); the post-1960s opening up of Papua New Guinea (Strathern); the dislocation of the Inuit (Graburn); the emergence of indigenous art as a commercial category (Morphy); the civil war in Sierra Leone (Jackson); the expansion of Jewish settlements in Israeli-occupied territories (Rapport); post-colonial race relations (Cowlishaw, Metge and Trigger) and the rise of indigenous activism over land rights in Australia and New Zealand (Peterson and Salmond).

Beyond the specificities of these particular events, their work has contributed to wider understandings of some of the major concepts of contemporary social science. The recognition of gender has become arguably one of the most important influences in reshaping social theory and the human sciences in the period of late modernity (Hall 1992: 285). Central to this has been the concept of 'gender ideology' and the ways that power is deployed through discourses around sex and gender. However, in the early 1970s, the concept of 'gender ideology' had not yet been articulated. It was Strathern, working in Papua New Guinea, who first brought this phenomenon to light: 'I had, as it were, discovered both gender and ideology', she muses, 'except that the term "gender" wasn't there yet'.

Similarly, the concepts of 'subject' and 'subjectivity' have been given fresh impetus thanks to the work of Foucault. The processes of neoliberalization have added further layers of complexity to the way in which modern political subjects are constituted. Wright's work has been pivotal in showing the linkages between neoliberal policies, government-inspired political technologies and the assemblage of new kinds of individuals such as the 'enterprising self' promoted by the Thatcher government in 1980s Britain. The work of Wright and Strathern have thus pushed anthropology to new understandings of the relationships between identity, personhood and discourse, opening up a major terrain for further scholarship on subjectivity and power.

The question over whether the proper focus for social sciences should be on individual actors, socio-cultural domains, or the universal dimensions of the human condition has long been a topic of heated debate within academia. Jackson and Rapport have each contributed their own unique perspectives on this issue. Rapport uses the term 'cosmopolitan anthropology' to describe his theory of the 'ontology of selfhood'. Anthropology's mission, according to Rapport, should be to recognize and promote the agency of individuals, as conventional sociological categories of 'nations, communities, ethnicities and classes' are merely 'epiphenomenal' when compared to the 'concrete realities of individual and species'. Equally uncomfortable with the conventional focus on culture and society, Jackson has pioneered 'existential anthropology' (Jackson 2005), a phenomenologically inspired approach that sees anthropology's aim as a striving towards greater understanding of the universal human condition, a marriage between raw experience and intellectual reflection. The positions espoused by Jackson and Rapport represent two extreme perspectives in the debate that all anthropologists, to a greater or lesser extent, engage with in their work.

In the broad fields of aesthetics, economics and production, Graburn's writings have brought to our attention the vital importance of tourism and indigenous art as social and economic practices – subjects that had previously been ignored by academia. Similarly, Pinney's work has opened up new ways of thinking about the relationship between aesthetics and culture, while Morphy has elucidated how art, far from being a static representation of culture, can constitute a mode of political action.

Dispossession, racism and the ways in which indigenous people and their worldviews have been marginalized in post-colonial settler societies are among the key themes reverberating through the work of Metge and Salmond. Both have made particularly significant contributions to foregrounding Maori voices and demonstrating what can be learned by listening to them. Whereas Metge has focused particularly on cross-cultural communication and the difficulties that arise when cultures 'talk past each other', Salmond's originality has been to look at history from an ethnographic perspective. Her rereading of Maoris' first encounter with Captain Cook in the East Cape of New Zealand invites us to acknowledge that the history of European exploration must be viewed from multiple perspectives.

In the Australian context, Cowlishaw, Trigger and Peterson have made significant contributions to understandings of race relations and indigenous rights, showing how anthropology can be successfully brought together with applied policy work. At the same time, each of these authors has helped to challenge the often one-dimensional and simplistic renditions of a static Aboriginal culture. Cowlishaw, like Salmond and Metge, was a pioneer in studying indigenous culture within an urban context and thereby highlighting the limitations of constructions of 'classic' Aboriginal culture. However, as these authors point out, anthropologists themselves have sometimes unfortunately encouraged such simplistic constructions, often in response to the legal imperatives of establishing 'traditional rights' to land as part of native title claims.

How Anthropologists Think – About Ownership and Appropriation, For Example

In bringing together these twelve accounts, our aim was to elicit deeper insights into the general processes involved in anthropological knowledge formation. Many of the key issues our authors highlight concern the different cultural concepts that shape other people's worldviews or cosmologies. Similarly, many of the topics they address (including property, the individual, concepts of the self, culture and society) are central theoretical themes in anthropological writing itself. These interviews offer a critical window onto the differing ways that contemporary anthropology deals with these issues. If anthropology is typically concerned with 'how natives think' (Sahlins 1995), these interviews show us something of the complexity of 'how anthropologists think'.

The issue of property rights is particularly sensitive in post-colonial settler societies. Not surprisingly, this theme features prominently in the lives and work of New Zealand and Australian anthropologists. In Australia, anthropologists have significantly influenced the judicial process by expanding the definition of what constitutes legitimate legal evidence of long-standing tribal relationships to specific territories. That evidence now includes cultural maps, songs, dances and material culture, as well as oral histories and genealogies (Strang 2000). Being called upon to give expert testimony in court in defence of indigenous title claims is another important aspect of the work of anthropologists in these countries and can have quite profound implications (Simons 2003; Sutton 2009). Both Peterson and Morphy were integral to the Blue Mud Bay native title claim, which resulted in Aboriginal ownership of 80 per cent of the inter-tidal zones of the Northern Territory. Similarly, Graburn proudly recollects how his ethnographic evidence helped to secure for the Canadian Inuit commercial fishing rights, resulting in their ownership of a $6 million (US) shrimp industry.

Property rights are just one aspect of the categories of 'ownership' and 'appropriation'. These concepts cover a range of different meanings and circumstances, from the conventional Western legal tradition of 'possessive individualism' and the more socio-centric conception of property typical of many Pacific cultures to contests over who has the authority to represent a particular culture or religion and questions over whether translating across cultures is necessarily an act of domination and appropriation rather than empathy and dialogue (Pállson 1993). A perennial concern amongst anthropologists, as well as indigenous scholars and activists, is the question of 'cultural survival' and whether commercialization of indigenous culture represents a form of 'cultural genocide' (Greenwood 1989). Graburn has long criticized this stance, arguing that there is nothing ethically wrong with indigenous groups commodifying aspects of their own culture in order to make a profit, 'which is something everybody has to do'. In similar vein, Morphy points out that the Yolngu of northeast Arnhem Land do not view the incorporation of their art into Australia's national self-representation as an act of 'appropriation': rather, they see it as making their culture more visible and placing their artwork on a par with European and other artistic traditions.

Politics of Representation: Culture, Society, Self and Other Sites of Contestation

A less obvious dimension of 'ownership' is ownership of *oneself*. This is a central concern for Rapport, who asserts that 'the only form of ownership worthy of that title is self-ownership' and who defines appropriation as the imposition of cultural categories upon the 'sovereign individual' or 'others telling me who I am and how my life should proceed'. For Rapport this is the foundation for what is both an intellectual and political project: namely, cosmopolitanism as the means of defending 'each individual's freedom to author' their own life according to their own standards 'of beauty or pleasure or duty ... or truth'. Anthropology, according to Rapport, begins 'from the ontology of selfhood'.

A very different concept of the 'self' emerges from Wright's analysis of neoliberal subjectivities. Wright shows how the self as 'individual project' is more a political rhetoric and tool of government (or, *pace* Foucault, a 'technique of the self') than an ontological fact. Not everyone is able to be author of their own lives. As Wright exemplifies through her fieldwork vignette of meeting a woman who announces, 'I've become one of Mrs Thatcher's individuals', this is a heavily politicized view of the self that forces people to become enmeshed in the state's project of neoliberalization and self-management – whether they choose to or not (see Rose 1999).

Representing other cultures is a central aspect of the anthropological project, although anthropologists have different understandings of the concept of culture. Salmond's work illustrates the perspective that cultures have distinct and sometimes irreconcilable worldviews. This is reflected, for example, in the seeming impossibility of finding a Western translation that does justice to the Maori term *tapu*. In part, this is because understanding and representing another culture is not just a scholarly or intellectual exercise; for Salmond it entails bringing 'my whole *self* to my scholarly practice and not just my head'. To truly come to know another culture, she warns, is a lifelong endeavour – 'It never ends: you're always learning, trying to enter into another language, to engage deeply with another philosophical tradition and another conception of the world'.

While Salmond's portrayal suggests a singular 'Maori culture', other anthropologists highlight the fact that even within an apparently unified cultural field there usually exists a multiplicity of perspectives, all of which are inflected by relations of power. Strathern exemplifies this in her account of Papua New Guinea on the eve of independence and how her initial view that the unpaid local magistrates were working for the public good was later disabused by the recognition that these individuals had their own, often tyrannical, interests at heart. The point here is the need to recognize that even in colonial and post-colonial contexts indigenous peoples do not have a singular cultural perspective or set of class interests (see Rata 2011).

The political nature of culture has been ably demonstrated by numerous scholars (see for example Dirks 1992; Thomas 1995; Kuper 1999). Cowlishaw gives a further twist on this theme by highlighting the political entanglements created when governments try to intervene to protect or 'restore' cultural forms and practices that are considered on the verge of extinction. In her case this involves suburban schoolteachers in Sydney taking it upon themselves to rediscover and teach Aboriginal children their 'ancient and unchanging culture'. This is complicated further by the fact that some indigenous people 'find iconic symbols of Aboriginal culture [as] irrelevant to their lives' when counter-posed against the needs for literacy and other skills for modern living. This highlights the familiar yet arguably irreconcilable anthropological dilemma of engaging in cultural difference without simplifying or essentializing other people's cultural perspectives or condemning indigenous peoples when they engage in strategic auto-essentialism (Spivak 1987; Turner 1991).

The need for indigenous people to define their own culture and identity and determine their own political agendas is particularly salient in post-colonial societies across the Pacific. The critique of colonialism, which developed within anthropology during the 1970s, was particularly acute in New Zealand and Australia, as our authors highlight. The authority of the anthropologist to represent the non-European other came under sharp attack. According to Linda Tuhiwai Smith (1999: 11), all Western disciplines are implicated in imperialism, but 'many indigenous writers would nominate anthropology as representative of all that is truly bad about research'. These tensions increased during the late 1980s, when a number of anthropologists took up the work of Hobsbawm and Ranger (1983) and began to analyze the 'invented' nature of aspects of indigenous cultures (Hanson 1989; Jolly and Thomas 1992; Thomas 1992; Van Miejl 2001). By the 1990s, a number of separate departments of indigenous studies, Maori studies and Pacific studies had been forged. This brought greater autonomy for indigenous writers but also resulted in the politics of gatekeeping and a fragmentation of ethnographic research on indigenous cultures (Webster 1998).

Ethics, Advocacy and Politics in the Academy

If representing peoples and cultures is contentious in anthropology, so too are the ethics of anthropological engagement and advocacy. Anthropologists who conduct long-term fieldwork usually become personally involved with the livelihoods and well-being of their informants. Indeed, according to the ethical guidelines of the American Anthropological Association, it is incumbent upon practising anthropologists to treat these as primary considerations. However, there may also be a tension between the requirements of scholarly objectivity and engagement in outright advocacy (Kirsch 2002). While the conventional anthropological stance is often deemed to be one of cultural relativism, some anthropologists become *less* willing to tolerate or accept various kinds of local cultural practices as their familiarity with a society increases. Pinney, for example, was moved to abandon his previously held relativist assumption that caste hierarchies in India are inevitable, through his attempts to establish a local village health clinic that would also assist Dalits and other marginalized social groups.

The issue of how to use anthropology not only to document and interpret other people's lives but to change them is particularly central to applied anthropology. Engagement with land-rights claimants and policy makers is particularly prominent in antipodean anthropology, given the importance of government-sponsored settlement processes, which often call upon the expertise of anthropologists. This can sometimes result in expert anthropological witnesses appearing on both sides of a legal dispute. It has also created a market for university master's programmes in applied anthropology geared towards creating a cadre of professionals who understand the cultural implications of both government and corporate policies across a range of areas, including development, aid, public health, human rights, refugees and migration. As it does in the United States (but not in the UK), applied anthropology enjoys a higher public profile in Australia and New Zealand – so much so that Peterson, Trigger and others argue for recognition of applied anthropology's contribution to anthropological theory.

Applying disciplinary skills and insights to policy and politics may require a willingness to take controversial stances. As Trigger argues:

> The way to handle politically and ethically *difficult* forms of engagement in the great world outside of the academy is not by sitting on the sidelines and refusing to get your hands dirty. It is *not* professionally responsible to say, 'I won't engage with government or industry – or indeed with community organizations – because I can take the higher moral ground within the academy, writing critiques of the Native Title Act or the environmental impact legislation that I can feel good about,

and publish in academic journals read by a small number of my professional colleagues'. We need to be a profession that can make compromises when compromises are needed. We need to focus more effort towards making practical contributions outside the academy, joining those efforts to our intellectual work inside the universities.

However, this can place anthropologists in a dilemma, as intervening to improve people's social and economic conditions may change their culture in unanticipated and arguably undesirable ways. As Peterson notes, it is basic anthropological knowledge that 'if the conditions of production, consumption and exchange are radically altered ... [y]ou cannot expect the cultural and ideational systems to remain unaffected'. The downside to advocacy, of course, is that one may misunderstand the local situation one is trying to observe (Low and Merry 2010). Whether it is better to be an advocate (and run the risk of getting it wrong) or to strive for noncommittal impartiality is a decision that most anthropologists are likely to face at some point during their professional lives.

The nature of ethnographic fieldwork necessarily entails close and intimate interaction with other people and therefore demands a particular sensitivity and respect on the part of the researcher. Nonetheless, it is almost inevitable that unforeseen events will arise that place the fieldworker in an ethical conundrum, such as being witness to the outbreak of ethnic cleansing (Bringa 1995) or a military coup (Trnka 2008); encountering community violence over witchcraft accusations (Strong 2004) or being obliged to take sides during an election campaign (Shore 1999); dealing with the grief of the death of a loved one (Rosaldo 1993; Watson 1999) or even falling in love (Blackwood 1995). One kind of ethical dilemma that can arise is the problem of disclosure if the ethnographic material could cause harm to one's informants. This may be particularly acute in situations of violence or political oppression. Wright's fieldwork on tribal groups in post-revolutionary Iran highlights some of these difficulties. Due to the ongoing tensions between the reforming Iranian regime and Iran's tribal minorities there was a potential danger that Wright's fieldwork data could be abused and therefore she took the bold decision not to publish her findings. Making choices about how to protect one's informants is something many anthropologists have to face, sometimes against a subpoena and at the cost of compromising one's career (see Brettel 1993).

If research entails protecting one's informants against potential harm, often the reverse is also true. Field researchers may themselves need defending by their informants. As Metge confides, *Pakeha* anthropologists working with Maori in the 1970s and 1980s were sometimes accused by Maori activists of 'building a career on the backs of Maori' or 'making money out of them'. In Maori society one does not normally defend oneself; if one's actions or person are worth defending, then someone else will stand up and do so. On most occasions, when subject to hostile criticism, Metge's Maori supporters would rally to defend her. But on one occasion her companions remained silent. That, for her, was a harrowing but instructive experience. Even more traumatic, perhaps, is for a fieldworker to find him or herself the target of another person's malice. As Trigger reflects, being 'ensorcelled' by an Aboriginal elder was a serious assault on his safety but one that, fortunately, mobilized his Aboriginal friends to take active steps to counteract that supernatural attack. One lesson he draws from this is that you know you have become fully integrated into a host society when people feel comfortable enough not only to defend you in public, but also to publicly vent their anger at you.

A more conventional measure of immersion is when members of the local community seek to adopt the fieldworker by treating him or her as a member of the village or family. For Salmond, her main informants were like surrogate parents – and became godparents to her children. Fictive kin relations of this kind can set the framework for lifelong ties and enduring obligations to support the family. These relationships both enrich the ethnographic fieldwork but can also impose severe limits on what kind of research and analysis is possible.

Another set of factors that both enable and constrain anthropological research are the institutional regimes and contexts under which most professional anthropologists work. There is a plethora of variables that shape what constitutes 'valid' anthropological research, from peer-review processes and journal publications to university boards, ethics committees, government-funding priorities or the criteria governing private research foundations and granting bodies. Arguably, the most significant of these are government policies towards the funding of universities and post-graduate education. But making one's research 'relevant' and keeping within the boundaries of what is considered 'appropriate' can be challenging. This is something that each generation of scholars has had to confront in one form or another. For example, Jackson recounts the poignant story of Ralph Piddington, the founding professor of anthropology at the University of Auckland, who as a PhD student in the early 1930s was sanctioned for writing polemical articles in socialist newspapers about the plight of the Karadjeri people of northwestern Australia. As a result of what was at that time deemed an unacceptable 'indiscretion' (Gray 1994;

Metge 2000), he was censured by the Australian National Research Council, which withdrew promises of future funding support, and was told he would never be find employment in any Australian university (Joan Metge, personal communication). Piddington, as Jackson observes, had 'stepped beyond the boundaries of what anthropology students were supposed to do. They were expected to do *academic* studies, not go out and bat for the people they were working with'.

Regrettably or not, having to adapt one's research to what governments or private funding bodies demand has always been a necessary exercise. In certain periods government research-funding policies have opened up, as well as closed down, opportunities to undertake innovative and independent ethnographic research. In the case of Morphy, it was only because universities in Britain were expanding during the 1960s and early 1970s, with increasing numbers of scholarships from the Economic and Social Research Fund (ESRC), that he was able to do a master's. However, that good fortune later became an obstacle, as the ESRC rules made it impossible to apply for further funding. Morphy eventually obtained a PhD scholarship from the Australian National University, and partly as a result of the scholarship's stipulation that he *had* to study Aboriginal art, he went on to become one of the foremost experts in this field.

While it is a truism to say that political and economic circumstances have always determined the conditions of academic existence, the current era seems to herald something different – a qualitative shift in the relationship between universities and government, as the state increasingly divests its responsibilities for funding higher education. As a result, university education has increasingly come to be perceived as a private investment rather than a public good (Marginson and Considine 2000; Wright and Rabo 2010). In this new environment academic knowledge is being redefined by government regulatory frameworks and bureaucratic requirements for demonstrating performance and productivity. In Britain, Australia and New Zealand, research-assessment exercises have been introduced to encourage greater competition and research output that is deemed more relevant for industry and commerce. The rise of so-called 'Third Stream' activities based on commercializing university knowledge and assets is radically redefining the meaning and the mission of the university in these countries (Hoffman 2011). Just as in the early 1980s, New Zealand and Australia once again have become laboratories for experimenting with neoliberal reform (Kelsey 1997; Shore 2010).

As Strathern notes in her chapter, this raises interesting questions about the conditions for knowledge production, which anthropologists are uniquely well placed to analyze. Unlike most other disciplines, anthropologists are trained to 'find out how things look from other points of view'. That is not only a valuable source of intellectual insight, it also enables its practitioners to 'have lives outside of their own conditions of reproduction', which then allows them to critically examine those conditions themselves. In short, anthropology's reflexivity includes reflecting on the conditions of its own existence, as well as oscillating between perspectives from the core and peripheries.

In many respects, those goals guide this volume. In presenting these twelve highly personal accounts, we hope to elucidate what distinguishes anthropology as a professional practice and a way of knowing – and engaging with – the world. We start with the 'periphery', foregrounding New Zealand and Australian anthropologists yet recognizing that many of these individuals have biographies that span the continents and should not be construed as exemplars of 'national traditions'. Most of these individuals have also conducted research in the antipodes and have anthropological expertise in the cultures of their 'home' (be it natal or adopted). These peripheral perspectives are counter-posed against those of four British anthropologists who teach in what are arguably more mainstream sites of anthropological knowledge production but who have also conducted fieldwork among people in more peripheral communities. However, most of these ethnographers have also shifted field sites during the course of their careers, which highlights another aspect of the fluidity and mobility that characterize anthropology as a discipline.

Above all, these accounts reveal the diverse ways in which ethnographic observations about how people conduct their lives can be used to generate much more profound insights into the principles that underlie contemporary social and cultural life. By combining rich vignettes of personal experience with more reflective philosophical musings on the nature of knowledge production, fieldwork and disciplinary practice, these chapters also take us behind the scenes of the anthropological endeavour to reveal some candid backstage views of how anthropologists conduct their professional works and lives.

References

Barley, N. 1983. *The Innocent Anthropologist: Notes from a Mud-Hut*. Harmondsworth: Penguin Books.
Blackwood, E. 1995. 'Falling in Love with an-Other Lesbian: Reflections on Identity in Fieldwork'. In *Taboo: Sex, Identity and Erotic Subjectivity in*

Fieldwork, eds. D. Kulick and M. Willson, 51–75. London/New York: Routledge.

Bonisch-Brednich, B. 2010. 'Migrants on Campus: Becoming a Local Foreign Academic'. In *Local Lives: Migration and the Politics of Place*, eds. B. Bonisch-Brednich and C. Trundle, 167–82. Farnham: Ashgate.

Borneman, J., and A. Hammoudi, eds. 2009. *Being There: The Fieldwork Encounter and the Making of Truth.* Berkeley: University of California Press.

Bourgouin, F. 2007. *The Young, the Wealthy and the Restless: Trans-national Capitalist Elite Formation in Post-Apartheid Johannesburg.* Lund: Lund University [Monographs in Social Anthropology No. 18.]

Brettell, C., ed. 1993. *When They Read What We Write: The Politics of Ethnography.* Westport, CT: Bergin and Garvey.

Bringa, T. 1995. *Being Muslim the Bosnian Way.* Princeton: Princeton University Press.

Casagrande, J., ed. 1960. *In the company of man: Twenty portraits by anthropologists*, New York: Harper.

Coffey, A. 1999. *The Ethnographic Self – Fieldwork and the Representation of Identity.* London: Sage.

Collins, P., and A. Gallinat, eds. 2010. *The Ethnographic Self as Resource: Writing Memory and Experience into Ethnography.* Oxford: Berghahn.

Clifford, J., and G. Marcus. 1986. *Writing Culture: The Poetics and Politics of Ethnography.* Berkeley: University of California Press.

De Neve, G., and M. Unnithan-Kumar, eds. 2006. *Critical Journeys: The Making of Anthropologists.* Aldershot: Ashgate.

Dirks, N., ed. 1992. *Colonialism and Culture.* Michigan: University of Michigan Press.

Dumont, P. 1978. *The Headman and I: Ambiguity and Ambivalence in the Fieldworking Experience.* Austin: University of Texas Press.

Durie, E. 2011. 'Cultural Appropriation'. In *Ownership and Appropriation*, V. Strang and M. Busse, eds., 131–48. Oxford/New York: Berg.

Fluehr-Lobban, C. 2008. 'Collaborative Anthropology as Twenty-first-Century Ethical Anthropology'. *Collaborative Anthropologies* 1:175–82.

Geertz, C. 1985. *Local Knowledge: Further Essays in Interpretive Anthropology.* New York: Basic.

———. 1988. *Works and Lives: The Anthropologist as Author.* Stanford: Stanford University Press.

Good, K. 1991. *Into the Heart: One Man's Pursuit of Love and Knowledge among the Yanomami.* Upper Saddle River, NJ: Prentice Hall.

Gray, J. 1994. 'Piddington's Indiscretion'. *Oceania* 64 (3), March: 217–45.

Greenwood, D. 1989. 'Culture by the Pound: An Anthropological Perspective on Tourism as Cultural Commoditization'. In *Hosts and Guests: The anthropology of tourism.* 2nd Ed., ed. V. L. Smith, 171–185. Philadelphia: University of Pennsylvania Press.

Gupta, A., and J. Ferguson. 1997. 'Discipline and Practice: "The Field" as Site, Method, and Location in Anthropology'. In *Anthropological Loca-*

tions: *Boundaries and Grounds of a Field Science*, eds. A. Gupta and J. Ferguson, 1–46. Berkeley: University of California Press.

Gusterson, H. 1998. *Nuclear Rites: A Weapons Laboratory at the End of the Cold War.* Berkeley: University of California Press.

Hall, S. 1992. 'The Question of Cultural Identity'. In *Modernity and Its Futures*, eds. S. Hall, D. Held and T. McGrew, 273–325. Oxford: Blackwell.

Hanson, A. 1989. 'The Making of the Māori: Culture Invention and Its Logic'. *American Anthropologist* 91: 890–902.

Hastrup, K. 1992. 'Writing Ethnography: State of the Art'. In *Anthropology and Autobiography*, eds. J. Okely and H. Gallaway, 116–33. London: Routledge.

Henderson, A. 1983. 'Submission of the Queensland Association of Professional Anthropologists to the Aboriginal Land Enquiry', unpublished m.s., University of Queensland.

Herzfeld, M. 2001. *Anthropology: Theoretical Practice in Culture and Society.* Oxford: Blackwell.

Ho, K. 2009. *Liquidated: An Ethnography of Wall Street.* Durham, NC: Duke University Press.

Hobsbawm, E., and T. Ranger. 1983. *The Invention of Tradition.* Cambridge: Cambridge University Press.

Hoffman, S. G. 2011. 'The new tools of the (scientific) trade: contested knowledge production and the conceptual vocabularies of academic capitalism', *Social Anthropology* 19: 439–62.

Howell, N. 1990. *Surviving Fieldwork: A Report of the Advisory Panel on Health and Safety in Fieldwork.* Washington, DC: American Anthropological Association.

Ingold, T. 1992. 'Editorial', *Man* N.S. 27(4): 693–96.

Jackson, M. 2005. *Existential Anthropology: Events, Exigencies and Effects.* Oxford: Berghahn.

Jolly, M., and N. Thomas, eds.1992. 'The Politics of Tradition in the Pacific'. *Oceania* 62(4), special issue.

Kawharu, M. 2011. 'In Search of Remedies and Reciprocity: Negotiating a Treaty Claim Settlement between Ngati Whatua or Kaipara and the Crown'. MA Thesis, Department of Anthropology, the University of Auckland.

Kelsey, J. 1997. *The New Zealand Experiment: A World Model for Structural Adjustment?.* Auckland: Auckland University Press.

Kirsch, S. 2002. 'Anthropology and Advocacy: A Case Study of the Campaign against the Ok Tedi Mine'. *Critique of Anthropology* 22(2): 175–200.

Kuklick, H. 2011. 'Personal Equations Reflections on the History of Fieldwork, with Special Reference to Sociocultural Anthropology'. *Isis* 102: 1–33.

Kuper, A. 1996. *Anthropology and Anthropologists: The British School*, third ed. London: Routledge.

———. 1999. *Culture: The Anthropologists' Account*. Cambridge: Cambridge University Press.

Lévi-Strauss, C. 1961. *Tristes Tropiques*. Translated by John Russell. New York: Criterion Books.

Lodge, D. 1991. *Paradise New*. Harmondsworth: Penguin.

Low, S. M., and S. E. Merry. 2010. 'Engaged Anthropology: Diversity and Dilemmas'. *Current Anthropology*, vol. 51, supplement 2 (October): S203–26.

MacClancy, J. 2005. 'The Literary Image of Anthropologists'. *JRAI*, 11 (3): 549–575.

Malinowski, B. 1967. *A Diary in the Strict Sense of the Term*. New York: Harcourt, Brace and World.

Marcus, G., and D. Cushman. 1982. 'Ethnographies as Texts'. *Annual Review of Anthropology* 11: 25–69.

Marcus, G., and M. Fischer. 1999. *Anthropology as Cultural Critique*. Chicago: Chicago University Press.

Marginson, S., and M. Considine. 2000. *The Enterprise University: Power, Governance, and Reinvention in Australia*. Melbourne: Cambridge University Press.

McCall Smith, A. 2005. *44 Scotland Street*. London: Little, Brown Book Group.

———. 2006a. *Espresso Tales*. London: Little, Brown Book Group.

———. 2006b. *Love over Scotland*. London: Little, Brown Book Group.

Meier, B. P., A. C. Moller, J. Chen and M. Riemer-Peltz. 2011. 'Spatial Metaphor and Real Estate: North-South Location Biases Housing Preference'. *Social Psychological and Personality Science* 2(5): 547.

Metge, J. 2000. 'Ralph Piddington'. In *Dictionary of New Zealand Biography, 1941–1960*, ed. C. Orange, 411–12. Wellington: Department of Internal Affairs and Auckland University Press.

Metge J. and Kinloch, P. 1978. *Talking Past Each Other: Problems of Cross-cultural Communication*. Wellington: Victoria University Press.

Muru-Lanning, M. 2010. '*Tupuna Awa* and *Te Awa Tupuna*: An Anthropological Study of Competing Discourses and Claims of Ownership to the Waikato River'. PhD thesis, Department of Anthropology, The University of Auckland.

Mutu, M. 2011. *The State of Māori Rights*. Wellington: Huia Publishers.

Nanda, S. 1990. *Neither Man nor Woman: The Hijras of India*. Belmont, CA: Wadsworth Publishing.

Nash, J. 2001. 'Globalization and the Cultivation of Peripheral Vision'. *Anthropology Today* 17(4): 15–22.

Nordstrom, C., and C. G. Robben, eds. 1996. *Fieldwork under Fire: Contemporary Studies of Violence and Survival*. Berkeley: University of California Press.

Pálsson, G. 1993. 'Introduction: Beyond Boundaries'. In *Beyond Boundaries: Understanding, Translation and Anthropological Discourse*, ed. G. Palsson. Oxford: Berg.

Parkin, F. 1986. *Krippendorf's Tribe*, New York: Atheneum
Partridge, D. J. 2011. 'Activist Capitalism and Supply-chain Citizenship: Producing Ethical Regimes and Ready-to-Wear Clothes'. *Current Anthropology* 52 (S3): S97–S111.
Rabinow, P. 1999. *French DNA Trouble in Purgatory*. Chicago: Chicago University Press.
———. 1977. *Reflections on Fieldwork in Morocco*. Berkeley: University of California Press.
Rata, E. 2011. 'Discursive Strategies of the Māori Tribal Elite'. *Critique of Anthropology* 31 (4): 359–80.
Rosaldo, R. 1993. *Culture and Truth: The Remaking of Social Analysis*. London: Routledge.
Rose, N. 1999. *Governing the Soul*. Cambridge: Cambridge University Press.
Sahlins, M. 1995. *How 'Natives' Think: About Captain Cook, for Example*. Chicago: Chicago University Press.
Sanjek, R., ed. 1990. *Fieldnotes: The Makings of Anthropology*. Ithaca, NY: Cornell University Press.
Shore, C. 1999. 'Fictions of Fieldwork: Depicting the "Self" in Ethnographic Writing'. In *Being There: Fieldwork in Anthropology*, ed. C. Watson, 25–48. London: Pluto.
———. 2008. 'Audit culture and Illiberal Governance: Universities and the Politics of Accountability', *Anthropological Theory* 8 (3): 278–299.
———. 2010. 'Beyond the Multiversity: Neoliberalism and the Rise of the Schizophrenic University'. *Social Anthropology* 18(1): 15–29.
Shore, C., and S. Wright. 1999. 'Audit Culture and Anthropology: Neoliberalism in British Higher Education'. *JRAI* 5: 557–75
Simons, M. 2003. *The Meeting of the Waters: The Hindmarsh Island Affair*. Sydney: Hodder.
Smith, L. 1999. *Decolonizing methodologie : research and indigenous peoples*. New York: Zed Books.
Spencer, J. 2000. 'British Social Anthropology: A Retrospective'. *Annual Review of Anthropology* 29: 1–24.
Spivak, G. 1987. *In Other Worlds: Essays in Cultural Politics*. London: Taylor and Francis.
Strang, V. 2000. 'Not So Black and White: The Effects of Aboriginal Law on Australian Legislation'. In *Mythical Lands, Legal Boundaries: Rites and Rights in Historical and Cultural Context*, eds. A. Abramson and D. Theodossopoulos, 93–115. London: Pluto Press.
Strathern, M., ed. 2000. *Audit Cultures: Anthropological Studies in Accountability, Ethics and the Academy*. London: Routledge.
———. 2011. 'Sharing, Stealing and Borrowing Simultaneously'. In *Ownership and Appropriation*, eds. V. Strang and M. Busse, 23–41. Oxford/New York: Berg.
Strong, T. 2004. 'Pikosa: Loss and Life in the Papua New Guinea Highlands', PhD dissertation, Department of Anthropology, Princeton University.

Sutton, P. 2009. *The Politics of Suffering: Indigenous Australia and the End of the Liberal Consensus*. Melbourne: Melbourne University Press.

Thomas, N. 1992. 'The Inversion of Tradition'. *American Ethnologist* 19(2): 213–32.

———. 1995. *Colonialism's Culture*. Cambridge: Polity Press.

Thomas, R. 1999. 'Eric R. Wolf, 76, an Iconoclastic Anthropologist'. *New York Times*, March 10. Available at http://www.nytimes.com/1999/03/10/us/eric-r-wolf-76-an-iconoclastic-anthropologist.html [accessed 27/10/2010].

Trnka, S. 2008. *State of Suffering: Political Violence and Community Survival in Fiji*. Ithaca: Cornell University Press.

Tsing, A. 2009. 'Supply Chains and the Human Condition'. *Rethinking Marxism* 21(2): 148–76.

Turner, T. 1991. 'Representing, Resistance, Rethinking: Historical Transformation of Kayapo Culture and Anthropological Consciousness.' In *Colonial Situations: Essays on the Contextualization of Ethnographic Knowledge: History of Anthropology*, vol. 7., ed. G. Stocking, 285–313. Madison: University of Wisconsin Press.

Van Meijl, T. 2001. 'Contesting Traditional Culture in Post-colonial Māori Society: On the Tension between Culture and Identity'. *Paideuma* 47: 129–45.

Wade, P. 1993. 'Sex and Masculinity in Fieldwork among Colombian Blacks'. In *Gendered Fields*, eds. D. Bell, P. Caplan and W. Karim, 199–214. London: Routledge.

Watson, C. W. 1999. 'A Diminishment: A Death in the Field (Kerinci, Indonesia)'. In *Being There: Fieldwork in Anthropology*, ed. C. Watson, 141–63. London: Pluto.

Weber, M. 1948. 'Politics as a Vocation'. In *From Max Weber: Essays in Sociology*, ed. H. H. Gerth and C. Wright Mills, 77–128. London: Routledge and Kegan Paul.

Webster, S. 1998. *Patrons of Maori Culture: Power, Theory and Ideology in the Maori Renaissance*. Dunedin: University of Otago Press.

Werbner, R. 2012. 'Anthropology and the Postcolonial'. In *Handbook of Social Anthropology*, eds. R. Fardon, O. Harris, T. Marchan, M. Nuttal, C. Shore, V. Strang and R. Wilson, 181–97. London: Sage.

Wright, S., and A. Rabo. 2010. 'Introduction: Anthropologies of University Reform'. *Social Anthropology* 18(1): 1–14.

Michael Jackson

Date of Birth: 1940
Place of Birth: Nelson, New Zealand. Grew up in Inglewood, Taranaki.
PhD: 'The Kuranko: Dimensions of Social Reality in a West African Society', 1971, Cambridge University, UK.

Fieldwork: northeast Sierra Leone, West Africa (Kuranko); southeast Cape York, Queensland, Australia (Kuku-Yalanji); Tanami Desert, Northern Territory, Australia (Warlpiri); Europe (African migrants and refugees)

Positions held: Michael Jackson's first position was as a senior lecturer (1973–77) and later reader (1977–82) in the Department of Anthropology and Maori Studies, Massey University, New Zealand. He subsequently held positions at the Australian National University in Canberra (March 1984 – June 1985) and at Indiana University (1989–1996); the University of Sydney (1996–97) and the University of Copenhagen (1999–2005). Since 2005 he has been the Distinguished Visiting Professor of World Religions, Harvard Divinity School.

Major works
- 2013. *Lifeworlds: Essays in Existential Anthropology.* Chicago: University of Chicago Press.
- 2013. *The Other Shore: Essays on Writers and Writing.* Berkeley: University of California Press.
- 2012. *Road Markings: An Anthropologist in the Antipodes.* Dunedin: Rosa Mira Books.
- 2012. *Between One and One Another.* Berkeley: University of California Press.
- 2011. *Life Within Limits: Well-being in a World of Want.* Durham: Duke University Press.
- 2009. *The Palm at the End of the Mind.* Durham: Duke University Press.
- 2007. *Excursions.* Durham: Duke University Press.
- 2005. *Existential Anthropology: Events, Exigencies and Events.* New York: Berghahn.
- 2004 (reprinted 2005). *In Sierra Leone.* Durham: Duke University Press.
- 2002 (reprinted 2006). *The Politics of Storytelling: Violence, Transgression, and Intersubjectivity.* Copenhagen: Museum Tusculanum Press.
- 1998. *Minima Ethnographica: Intersubjectivity and the Anthropological Project.* Chicago: University of Chicago Press.
- 1997. *The Blind Impress.* Palmerston North: The Dunmore Press.
- 1995. *At Home in the World.* Durham: Duke University Press.
- 1996, editor. *Things As They Are: New Directions in Phenomenological Anthropology.* Bloomington: Indiana University Press.

- 1990, co-editor with Ivan Karp. *Personhood and Agency: The Experience of Self and Other in African Cultures,* Uppsala Studies in Cultural Anthropology, 14. Stockholm: Almqvist and Wiksell
- 1989. *Paths toward a Clearing: Radical Empiricism and Ethnographic Inquiry.* Bloomington: Indiana University Press.
- 1986. *Barawa and the Ways Birds Fly in the Sky.* Washington: Smithsonian Institution Press.
- 1982. *Allegories of the Wilderness: Ethics and Ambiguity in Kuranko Narratives.* Bloomington: Indiana University Press.
- 1977. *The Kuranko: Dimensions of Social Reality in a West African Society.* London: Hurst.

Chapter 1

SUFFERING, SELFHOOD AND ANTHROPOLOGICAL ENCOUNTERS
Michael Jackson

You are well known in New Zealand as a poet as well as an anthropologist. Let us begin by asking you to explain how you came to discover anthropology as a discipline and as a way of thinking about the world?

That was probably when I was sixteen and living in a small Taranaki town. The country library service used to bring a selection of books to Inglewood every fortnight. A couple of those books impressed me a lot. One was Daryll Forde's *Habitat, Economy and Society* (1956), which intrigued me because it was about the impact of environment on human societies – a kind of environmental determinism – so it related to a school interest I already had in human geography. The other book which made an impact on me was William Howells's *Mankind So Far* (1944), a book about hominid evolution. I became fascinated by fossil skulls and questions about human origins. So when I went to the University of Auckland and saw that anthropology was an undergraduate option, those two books were in the back of my mind. But again, it wasn't social or cultural anthropology that really captured my imagination. It was Jack Golson lecturing on Sumeria and ancient Egypt. My interest in hominid evolution and economy and society shifted to an interest in early civilizations. For that course we used Gordon Childe's famous book, *Man Makes Himself.* Golson was an extraordinary lecturer and charismatic figure who went on to pioneer the prehistory of Papua New Guinea and, along with Roger Duff, was one of the archaeologists who gave us a clearer picture of pre-European Maori society. As students we would go on digs to the island of Motutapu, conduct salvage archaeology in Auckland's Mount Roskill, following Jack and inspired by him.

In New Zealand many anthropologists have spoken about the importance of the encounter with the Maori world in shaping their interest. Can you tell us about your own encounters with Maoridom and how it affected you?

Like a lot of *Pakeha* (New Zealanders of European, typically British, descent) who came to anthropology, I had a childhood fascination with Maori New Zealanders. One really didn't have much contact with them – it certainly was not encouraged. It wasn't 'apartheid', but in the bourgeois imagination there was an unspoken assumption that these people were not respectable enough to be true companions or neighbours. But I was a very much a loner as a kid and naturally wound up with other loners, people on the margins. I didn't interact with other people very much, but one of my closest childhood friends growing up in Inglewood was a Maori boy called Eddie Ngeru. This friendship met the approval of my parents if only because they were glad to see that their shy and reclusive son actually did have a social bone in his body. I vividly remember Eddie's house because of the hospitality his family showed me. They were very poor and the house was tatty: the linoleum on the floor was cracked; most of the matting consisted of old super phosphate bags; there was a coal range and the furniture was minimal and very battered. But it was a place of immense warmth, and I remember going there and feeling the homeliness of that poverty. That didn't just come from our friendship. The whole family had an emotional charge and vitality that I didn't find anywhere else, even though I was raised in a very loving family.

I was also intrigued by the Maori who came up from Waitara selling whitebait during the whitebait season. They were elderly women (*kuia*) with *moko* (tattoos) on their chins, smoking pipes like figures out of a Goldie painting.[1] Of course, that was very intriguing to a child, these very exotic people who mysteriously came and went. They didn't live in the town but sat on the street with their flax kits full of whitebait and *kai moana* (seafood). Nobody told me to avoid them, but I could see that they inhabited a different world to the one I inhabited. Why did they live in this other place and where was it? What was it like? I gradually fantasized an identification with Maori as the embodiment of the misfit that I felt I was. I grafted my own sense of alienation onto these people who appeared to be living on the margins of society. I remember a particular event when I was about sixteen and my father inducted me into his lodge – the Foresters' Masonic Lodge. I was instinctively repelled by this organization of men who got very drunk but talked at great length about the charitable work they were doing. I loathed their regalia, pomposity and pretentions. Much to my father's dismay, I resigned, using as my rationale the fact that Maori weren't admitted to the lodge and the fact that the lodge's charity did not extend to Maori. Where this came from, I haven't the faintest idea. Looking back I can't see any way of connecting the dots other than that my feeling of not wanting to be a member of that club found expression in my imagining that Maori could never be members of this club either. In a perverse but logical sense, I was a white Maori.

The lodge later informed me that they had framed my letter of resignation, because they'd never encountered such ingratitude. My father, of course, was deeply ashamed. I'm not sure if he ever went back to the Masonic Lodge after I'd spoiled it for him. But it was a sign of the burning sense of injustice I felt about what existed in this country. It haunted me, this sense that my grandparents had migrated to this place and never mentioned the fact that their migration had involved a brutal displacement of an indigenous people. How come these facts were never talked about?

Was this a kind of guilty secret shared by many New Zealanders?

Absolutely, and I remember it wasn't until I was in my twenties and began to do research to find out who were the *tangata whenua* in this part of Taranaki that I realized the depth of this. Such research was not easy, and even establishing the name of the *tangata whenua* ('people of the land') was difficult. They were Ngāti Maru, a sub-tribe of Ngāti Awa, who had lived in the upper reaches of the Waitara River. Their domain would have spread into the forests that originally covered the area of Inglewood. During the land wars of the 1860s, Ngāti Maru had given token allegiance to the Maori leader Wiremu Kingi, when he was defending the Waitara block against further encroachments by the British. For that token loyalty to Kingi they were subject to confiscations of their lands, and that is why they were no longer in the Inglewood area. But as children we were told – and I can clearly remember the story, since it was in broad circulation among *Pakeha* – that there *were* no Maori where we lived, because they had a superstitious dread that Mount Taranaki would one day walk back to rejoin its kith and kin, the other mountains in the Central North Island, as if Taranaki had gone into kind of exile. This kind of cock-and-bull story was a cover for what was basically a terrible series of historical injustices.

I became interested in this because I wanted to understand the historical quirks of fate that had resulted in my family being in this country. It wasn't as if the dispossessed poor from the British Isles were willing partners in this project of colonizing New Zealand. I imagine they were pretty ignorant of the situation they were coming to and the implications of their presence here. But the fact of the matter was that these questions were never addressed and for some reason I felt the need to address them. Even now I feel that need. Just last year, armed with the marvellously researched Taranaki report to the Waitangi Tribunal,[2] which detailed indigenous land claims in the Taranaki region, I found out more about the brutality of the colonization of Taranaki. I was struck by the meanness and the violence. Of course, there was another history of violence that preceded the arrival of Europeans here: inter-tribal warfare. All of that information can be readily accessed today. I drove around Taranaki last year, reconsidering all these questions and still wondering, 'how I can come to terms with being a child of this nation?' I don't feel comfortable here for a *lot* of reasons, but one of them is this unresolved sense that I really don't have the *right* to be here.

So fast-forwarding to your time at university, did any that sense of marginalization connect with the things that you studied as an undergraduate?

Yes. Our first year social anthropology courses were taught by Professor Ralph Piddington, who was a very unprepossessing individual by the standards of an eighteen-year-old New Zealander. He was palsied, he obviously drank to prime himself for teaching, and he was old. You know how intolerant you are at eighteen or nineteen of anyone who is old – let alone slightly doddery or frail. Even though his two-volume introduction to social anthropology still ranks as one of the finest introductions to the subject, it wasn't until I reread it in my fifties that I realized just how good it is. Reading between the lines, I discovered much of his biography buried in that book. And it's an extraordinary story. As a PhD student working at LaGrange Bay, in western Australia, among the Karadjeri, Piddington decided that these people were living under such appalling and persecuted conditions that he couldn't just study them, he *had* to advocate on their behalf. He therefore wrote an article exposing the injustices for *The World,* a Socialist newspaper in Sydney, and then again for a Socialist paper in London. As a result, his PhD grant was terminated and he had great difficulty finding the money to finish his PhD. I think he had a Fulbright grant. It was interesting that people like Elkin, who was professor of anthropology at the time, did not oppose the stripping of his grant, because Piddington had stepped beyond the boundaries of what anthropology students were supposed to do. They were expected to do *academic* studies, not go out and bat for the people they were working with. So Piddington's story is very compelling, and when I rediscovered it in my fifties I felt such regret for the fact that I had, at the age of eighteen, sat in his lectures and thought such disrespectful things about him. Here was a person I should have admired. If I'd read his book properly, I would have realized anthropology's implications for social action; i.e. it is not just about studying people but about getting involved in their lives, which may also include dealing directly with social injustices.

Looking back with hindsight, how has anthropology changed, and how has your own thinking about anthropology evolved?

As an undergraduate studying anthropology I had a passionate desire to change the world for the better. Isn't it everybody's passion at that age? So I was in revolt against the academy, which I considered out of touch with the real world. In those days it was relatively easy to spend half the year working outside the university. I worked on the waterfront all year round, not only for money but to strike the right balance between university life and what lay outside it.

I did 'seagulling' at the docks, i.e. temporary work in a sector that was strongly unionized. You'd go down to what's called the 'block' on one of the waterfront quays and wait to be allocated a job. Somebody would call out the name of a ship on a certain quay – what it was loading, whether the cargo was dirty or dangerous – and then you had the option of raising your hand and being assigned that job for so many hours. If you handled the dirty or dangerous cargo you would get considerable bonuses. I did that regularly.

But I was also committed to the idea of getting out into the world and doing some good. So as soon as I had finished university I went to Australia and eventually landed a job working in Aboriginal welfare in the state of Victoria. I got the job in spite of my youth and the fact that I was competing with more experienced people who had spent many years working in charity organizations like the Salvation Army. I got it because they were impressed by the fact that my degree included anthropology, and they thought this would help me understand Aborigines and be particularly relevant for this kind of work. But I became very disenchanted with 'Aboriginal welfare', as it was called in those days. I found that it was simply the benign face of Australia's assimilationist policies that were still in place. I subsequently went to London and worked in welfare for the London County Council, working with homeless people. Then, when I was about twenty-four, I picked up a job as a volunteer with a United Nations organization in the Congo. But again, that was a period of radical disenchantment, as I realized that the United Nations operations in that part of Africa were a kind of front for Cold War Euro-American political interests. I realized that these great piles of paper which accumulated in the offices of the UN's Department of Social Affairs did not represent real work being done on the ground, because working as a mere volunteer I would be dispatched to the interior to check out market-garden programmes, co-operatives or various other kinds community-development projects, only to find that there was nothing there. It was a bit like Marlow in *Heart of Darkness* going into these remote places and finding horror rather than development.

There was also an ongoing war in the Congo, which was profoundly disturbing to me. I've described this in my memoir (Jackson 2006a: 97–116). I was in Kasai Province, in a lakeside town called Luluabourg, which had been occupied by the rebels. I was there just after the so-called liberation and the town was still in a state of shambles. There were still unburied bodies. In the middle of this nightmare I was trying to visit villages in a little four-by-four jeep. It was at this time, in one of those villages, that I thought 'what the hell am I doing here, an agent of a civilizing mission?' And yet I was face-to-face with the most intriguing things. I was getting glimpses of masquerades and fetishes. Using my minimal French, I was engaging in conversations with villagers. Suddenly I realized, this is what anthropologists did. Rather than going to places to try and change everything, they try to understand everything. But something else interested me more at that time; I didn't only want to change the world, I wanted to be changed *by* the world. The idea of undergoing some sort of metamorphosis by exposing myself to these extreme conditions of radical otherness appealed to me as a way in which I could remake myself.

So I found my way, I don't know how, to an extraordinary community of Franciscan monks who had rehabilitated a ·coffee plantation that had fallen into ruins after the Belgians abandoned it following the secession of Kasai. The Franciscans had brought it back into production, and all the labour was provided by kids, most of whom were Baluba children who had lost their parents during the war. These kids were showing me around and talking to me about all manner of things. I guess I was having my first ethnographically informed conversations. I was very curious about them: where they came from, who they were. In the midst of this, one evening when I was looking for something to read, I came across a battered copy of Lévi-Strauss's book *Les Structures Élémentaires de la Parenté*. It was really dog-eared and some of the pages were missing, but I opened it up and *that's* when I discovered anthropology. Nothing I'd encountered as an undergraduate had so captured my intellectual imagination. I was really struck by the opening lines of the book, which stated that anthropology is the study of humankind not the study of a particular people: i.e. it's not about studying function or structure in the received sense of those words but about the study of the human mind. That, coupled with my desire to go into these villages and actually live in them, helped me conclude that anthropology might well be my path.

I was subsequently asked to leave the Congo, because I wasn't doing my job properly and the head of the UN Social Affairs Department asked me if I really wanted to be there. Of course, by this time, my mind was somewhere else, even though I was having a great time in Leopoldville, living at the heart of history, as I felt at the time. This was before the Rhodesian war for independence had begun and I was hanging out with members of Joshua Nkomo's freedom fighters, many of whom were in exile in the Congo and had found their way to Leopoldville. I was involved in things that engrossed me deeply. So I was ambivalent about leaving. But I was obliged to call it quits and went to France and then on to Greece, where I stayed for a while and taught English. When I returned to New Zealand I was in two minds about returning to university. I was gripped by this idea of going to dangerous places to further this metamorphosis and rebirth of myself. I didn't know much about the Vietnam War, which had escalated in the years I'd been away. I imagined myself as a correspondent, covering the war. At the same time, I explored the possibility of working in Maori welfare. I went down to Wellington for an interview and vividly remember being told that all my welfare experience was actually of little use if I wanted to go into Maori welfare. 'Maori', I was told, 'were not like Africans or Aborigines. Maori were superior to those people.' I didn't get the job, but a few days later I met the woman I would subsequently marry. Meeting Pauline changed the course of my life.

Rather than hit the road again, I decided to take a job relief teaching in a high school. The following year, because I had teaching experience, I got into Auckland Teachers' Training College. That then opened up the possibility of doing an MA in anthropology at Auckland and then, perhaps, a PhD and thereby getting back to Africa. In any event, this was my plan and these were the stepping stones. It all happened surprisingly quickly. Between leaving Congo at the end of

1964 and arriving in Sierra Leone at the end of '69, only four years had elapsed. And as soon as I got to Sierra Leone I felt that I was continuing my African life, only as an anthropologist. This worked out wonderfully well. Anthropology was the disciplined pretext for living in Africa in exactly the way that I'd always wanted to do.

Tell us more about your research interests and how these have developed since that time.

I got over my desire to change the world for the better and began to be interested in changing myself for the better. That I *was* changed for the better was partly having a clear vision of what I wanted to do, which was anthropology in Africa, and partly knowing Pauline, who, in the opinion of several of my friends, straightened me out. As for research, I had become interested in what Marshall McLuhan had written in *The Gutenberg Galaxy* about the impact of new communications technologies on human experience and human sociality. When I did my MA in Auckland with Hugh Kawharu as my supervisor, he asked me what I wanted to do, and I said that I wanted to look at the impact of literacy in early nineteenth-century New Zealand. Literacy impacted on Maori in unusual and dramatic ways, as I documented and explained in my MA thesis. My plan was to study at Cambridge with Jack Goody, who had just published his work on literacy in traditional societies (Goody 1968). I would focus my doctoral research on the impact of literacy in West Africa. In 1969, I went to Sierra Leone, worked in schools and researched the impact of reading and writing on both the experience and worldviews of people and on social relations. I looked at things like children's estrangement from their parents, changing attitudes to farming, the wild ideas that were associated with becoming educated for the first time, and the relation of schooling to social inequality. But I have never published this research. Other interests carried me away. I was greedy to know and understand everything going on in the village world; I wanted to live in remote farming communities, far from markets, roads and schools. My interests developed in many directions simultaneously, and I pursued them all to the extent that I could.

Looking back, the theme that came to preoccupy me was the amount of time people put into *dis*organizing, or *dis*membering their world and putting it all back together again. In my PhD I generalized from Kuranko to humankind, arguing that human beings were like Humpty Dumpty: you're a perfectly intact egg, you're sitting on a wall, you're well balanced, but periodically you pick yourself up and dash yourself to pieces, then put yourself back together again. But you do this collectively and deliberately. Life may be unmanageable, full of contingency and unpredictability, but in these trivial and prototypical ritual actions you preempt catastrophe, making and unmaking the world yourself, in your own time, in your own way.

I was really driven to understand what seemed to be a very perverse and needless cycle of destruction and re-creation that I saw unfolding in ritual, in storytelling and in everyday palaver: people seemed to pick quarrels with each other or inflate a minor bone of contention or prolong a court case, and I would be sitting there, thinking these matters could all be resolved in minutes if there was a will to do so. Why these rituals of playing around with reality? This riddle informed my writing. In Cambridge I looked for people who had theorized along these lines, but I really couldn't find much in the anthropological literature apart from references in Turner, Gluckman and Needham to role reversal and symbolic inversions. I took my bearings from the writings of existentialists. I felt that Jean-Paul Sartre and Maurice Merleau-Ponty did greatest justice to the ludic and theatrical phenomena I had encountered in the field. I went on to study phenomenological classics on embodiment, the imagination, and the emotions – topics that available models of culture and the social hardly touched upon.

Even though it was Lévi-Strauss who had inspired me initially, and as much as I loved his work, I began to find it too removed from the complex realities of conscious life and lived events. I wanted to study the structures of consciousness, not the unconscious. I wanted to complement social analysis with existential analysis. I was fascinated by how the human mind and the human imagination struggle to make life viable, personally and socially. Culture simply provides a repertoire of possibilities. However tried or true these may be, they never answer all the quandaries and questions that human situations present. One is constantly struggling not only to make sense of the world, but to articulate desires, act decisively, find a way in which one is not overwhelmed by life but has a hand in negotiating it, manipulating it, manoeuvring within it. These are the kind of existential issues I wanted to write about in a theoretical – as well as an empirical – way (Jackson 1977, 1982, 1989, 1998).

I also found a lot of inspiration in German critical theory, particularly Adorno. My discovery of Adorno, which I owe to Max Rimaldi, was a major turning point. Adorno's negative dialectics was the best articulation of the lack of fit between the way we represent the world to ourselves and the way the world is constantly pushing us beyond the boundaries of what we know, comprehend and can cope with.

This was around 1980 to 1981, when I was teaching at Massey University. It was right around the time that my first wife died.

The other important influence on my thinking was William James, whose *Radical Empiricism* echoes Adorno's negative dialectics. James emphasizes the transitive rather than the intransitive, looking at verbs rather than nouns, i.e. that which connects and bridges rather than that which appears to have an independent or substantive reality. From reading James I went on to John Dewey and American pragmatism and neo-pragmatism and realized that these authors were simply the American expression of phenomenology. James was in conversation with Husserl, and vice versa. At that point my thinking took a major step forward. I felt I had much firmer ground for articulating some of the ideas that anthropology failed to provide.

Throughout this period I was periodically unemployed. I was still doing anthropology, but I was also writing a lot of fiction and poetry. I wanted to find new ways of writing anthropology that could handle these phenomenological perspectives, that could integrate and interleave raw experience and intellectual reflection and not subvert or mask life with language.

Do you think that is an intrinsic shortcoming of anthropology, i.e. its inability to access or represent human subjectivity or interiority?

It's only an issue if you have interests like mine. If you're interested in the political economy of Vanuatu, you don't need to push the envelope too far. There are enough intellectual and empirical resources out there for you to write intelligently and insightfully in an objectivist vein. So it depends on what kind of anthropology you do. My interests lie in the human microsphere rather than in the politico-economic macrosphere, much as we tend nowadays to see the latter as determinative. The price I have paid is to be reminded from time to time, sometimes gently, sometimes harshly, that I am either writing behind the times or not really doing anthropology at all. I've had great difficulty getting work. And I've had difficulty getting my work accepted for publication. A recurring view is that I'm writing a curious form of literature. Or philosophy. That I regard fine, carefully crafted writing as a sign of clear thinking rather than a form of embellishment, or regard anthropology as a form of comparative philosophy using empirical methods, is often seen as eccentric, if not unprofessional (Jackson 2007). In recent years, in fact since coming to Harvard, the going has been easier. Not only because of the prestige of Harvard, but because I am working in religious studies and philosophy and spending far less time among anthropologists. But my commitment remains to rigorous empirical work, to ethnographic fieldwork, and to writing anthropology that does justice to the experiences of those with whom I have lived and worked, whose lives I have shared as a stranger and friend. Sound writing, in my view, means working with vernacular idioms and everyday metaphors, because these are our windows on to human consciousness. They're always opaque windows, the glass is never clear and the window is never wide open. But through vernacular language we get glimpses into what's going on in people's minds, what's going on in their thoughts, their imaginations and their lives.

Clifford Geertz, in his essay on the Balinese cockfight, has famously described having an 'aha moment', a fieldwork encounter when an aspect of the people or the self is made visible or understandable through a particular event. Can you recall any such experiences?

Perhaps those moments and events I mentioned before – in which people unmake the world only to remake it in their own ways. But this is nothing remarkable, unless you assume, like Clifford Geertz, that the main thrust of human endeavour is to render the world coherent and intelligible. My own view is that our struggle is to make life bearable and liveable, and to accomplish this we often flout convention, invite chaos, meditate on nothingness and retreat from the world. The human condition is multifarious, paradoxical and contradictory. Such a view is common to Homer, the great world epics, and so-called folktales. I've just finished rereading the Opies' wonderful book, *The Classic Fairy Tales.* It has a five-page introduction, a great anthropological essay. In talking about fairy tales they refer to the perennial struggles and pitfalls of being human. Nothing new is discovered in these tales, but we are reminded of questions that confront people everywhere in their everyday attempts to create viable families or communities, to keep body and soul together, to make ends meet, to find fulfilment in this life.

But on the other hand, Angela Carter's writing about German fairy tales, for example, shows us that these stories were collated at the time of the birth of German nationalism and you can see clear social dynamics at work in which the gathering of those tales was part of creation of the German national imaginary.

That's certainly an interesting view, but folktales existed long before nationalism found a use for them. Paul Ricoeur's distinction between *beginnings* and *origins* is useful here. You can date a beginning; you can say, 'on such and such a day, so and so was born' or 'on such and such a day, the French Revolution was initiated by such and such an event'. But Ricoeur points out that something always precedes the beginning, and this he calls the 'origin'. Every event is foreshadowed. And what is the nature of that foreshadowing? It is something in the nature of human existence that makes any event possible, perhaps even inevitable; it cannot enable you to determine at what moment, and in what form, and in what life the event will, as it were, make its appearance. And the same goes for discovery. Discovery is not like a beginning, it's more the disclosure of something originary, i.e. something that has always been there. You may discover how it finds expression in a new way, but it's an old reality that is being expressed. Or so it seems to me. What all of this means is that anthropology must recover its original impulse to have a unified conception of human life, of the human condition. It must not put the cart before the horse by beginning with a particular examination of a historical or cultural moment or a particular person's life. That exploration of the *particular* has got to be married to an understanding of the *general*. Of course, Lévi-Strauss was one of the last people I think to sustain that vision of anthropology.

Sometimes the lessons that we learn from our mistakes can also be a way of connecting the particular to the general. Were there any particularly memorable mistakes that you made during fieldwork that you learned from?

Well, it's hard to know if we learn from our mistakes. I really don't know whether I have. That's for other people to judge. But I have made my share of mistakes, ranging from errors in learning a new language to hurting people I love. Life is a series of mistakes, misunderstandings and misperceptions. I don't think that can be avoided, but it opens up questions about fallibility in science and perfectibility in our lives. One of my greatest inspirations has been the work of Hannah Arendt, whose work took on new meaning for me in post-war Sierra Leone (Jackson 2004, 2006b). The country was grappling with the question of how the terrible mistakes of the immediate past during the civil war could be addressed. Arendt's work resonated with what a lot of people in Sierra Leone were saying and doing: i.e. that you do it through forgiveness, which is a forward-looking response. It's not that you absolve the persecutor of what he or she did, but you give up on the idea that you can take your revenge on that person or that people can be changed or should be punished. You just rid your mind of that person and leave them in the past, so that your life is now fully reclaimed for yourself and for others to whom you owe something. That's the way in which you distance yourself from the past, in order to have a future.

The other component for Arendt is the promise. You make a promise that you will not do this again. Even though human beings make the same mistakes over and over, the ritual, public act of the promise is extremely important as a way of creating the possibility of the new – or what she calls 'natality' or rebirth. I think these are very profound insights. And they became very significant to me as I saw them being enacted in Sierra Leone. But it was only when I got back from the fieldwork in 2002 and reread her, that I suddenly thought, 'my gosh, she's talking about Sierra Leone!' Her comments were almost a word-for-word match of the things people were saying to me.

How has being in all this war-torn and traumatized society impacted on you emotionally and intellectually?

It's made me very interested in the nature of intervention. Post-war Sierra Leone was a space that foreigners could fill, managing the restoration of order, instilling the values of peace and human rights, bringing about reparation for damages, treating allegedly traumatized people, and facilitating the reconciliation process. But there was no consultation with local people as to whether these were their priorities – no discussion of what kind of reparation local people wanted or what kind of justice they sought. Kuranko people, with whom I'd worked for so long, chose silence. Most Westerners would take the view that you shouldn't shut up when you've been severely traumatized: you should tell your story, act it out, get it off your chest, and don't let it fester. But I've discovered that silence is not necessarily a bad thing. In the Kuranko imaginary silence is tied up with a sense of putting something behind you. It's a social choice you make, whether you're going to dwell on a bitter experience or let it go. If I've learnt anything from my Kuranko research, it is the importance of social judgement. We live in a culture where we don't always exercise sound judgement as to what we say and what we leave unsaid. There's a compulsion to speak about what's on our minds and to pursue our own preoccupations and obsessions, as people and as writers, regardless of whether there is any social profit in this for others.

But in Kuranko one is constantly measuring what one is inclined to say or do against the sense of what the ramifications or implications might be. What we would call 'memory' is for the Kuranko simply another aspect of what they call *miriye*, or thought. So somebody who has a spontaneous memory of something or a dream that incorporates a memory of someone they may have loved and who might have died – will exercise judgement, carefully considering the social appositeness of sharing that dream or memory with others. If Kuranko judge that sharing to be of no use to anyone else, or perhaps even harmful to others, then they will keep quiet about it. That degree of self-censoring might seem strange in our world.

When I first lived among Kuranko, older men would show me their tongues. They had blistering around the tongue from all the times they'd literally bitten their tongues to stop themselves blurting out something in an untimely and inappropriate way. These are things you learn and hopefully incorporate in your own life. But it's very hard for people who think thrice before venturing an opinion to deal with impatient foreigners who come in and say, 'we know what's good for you; we're going to build a store in your village' or 'we're going to put a dispensary here'. By the time Kuranko have thought through the implications and formed an opinion, the deed has been done.

What is your sense of the future of the discipline, or where do you hope to see anthropology going over the coming decade?

I have no more idea about the future of anthropology than the future of the planet. I mean, who knows? I try to live for the day ahead, not the years, putting my energy into the things at hand. Nor do I have an investment in the future of anthropology. I want to be a good teacher, to bring an ethnographic and comparative perspective to my students, to enlarge their horizons, to disabuse them of mistaken ideas about African societies (see Jackson 2005), but these are specific projects, and I do not think of them as necessarily identifiable with anthropology as a discipline or a profession.

Could you tell us why you titled your memoir The Accidental Anthropologist?

Because I stumbled on anthropology for reasons I can't fully fathom. And I remained in anthropology more by chance than design, because when you've got a degree in anthropology it's not going to be easy to find work in other fields. Besides, there have been periods in my life when I have been out of work and my involvement in anthropology has waxed and waned accordingly. The landscape of my intellectual life is an accidented one, like the Central North Island of New Zealand. It's chopped up, and there's little continuity or smoothness and no clear road that moves from place to place, project to project.

How is it that you were offered a post in a school of divinity?

I've had great luck in my life. My first job at Victoria University of Wellington was offered to me by Jan Pouwer, with whom I shared a passion for Lévi-Strauss's structuralism. My second job, at Massey University, was set up for me by Hugh Kawharu, who wrote [to] me in Cambridge shortly after I graduated in 1972 and he was appointed the first joint chair of social anthropology and Maori Studies.

After leaving Massey, I had some half-time, temporary work in Australia, followed by several years out of work. Then Michael Hertzfeld, who was teaching at Indiana University in Bloomington, and who I'd met in Canberra, contrived to get me a position at Indiana University, Bloomington. After eight years at IU I returned to Australia for family reasons and took a part-time temporary job at the University of Sydney. It was an eighteen-month renewable contract, but when the Howard government came to power, university funding was cut and I was unemployed again.

At that point I did something I'd never done before: I went to the American Anthropological Association Conference in Pittsburgh, Pennsylvania, and sought work. People kept telling me, 'You're overqualified. You'll never get any of these entry-level tenure-track jobs being advertised here'. I bumped into Susan Reynolds Whyte, who was teaching at the University of Copenhagen. We'd met in Uppsala, Sweden, some years earlier, at a conference of Africanists. She mentioned that she very much liked my book *Paths Toward a Clearing* and had been inspired by it in her own work. And she said, 'What are you doing here? I didn't think you went to these meetings?' I said, 'I'm looking for work.' And she said, 'Kirsten Hastrup, our head of department, is taking leave for a year. Would it be worth your while to come to Copenhagen for just a year?' At that point I had a wife and two small children to support, so I jumped at the chance. I managed to renew the contract annually and keep going the next six years. But in 2005 I was facing mandatory retirement.

As the date grew nearer, we were in a panic, thinking, 'where to now?' Then an old friend of mine from Indiana University in Bloomington who had moved to Harvard Divinity School visited me in Copenhagen. He found out I was about to be out of work and said, 'Well, what would you think about coming to Harvard?' And I said, 'It seems highly unlikely.' But he then went back and informed his dean. My book *The Politics of Storytelling* had apparently been distributed in the United States and had made an impact in religious studies, more so than in anthropology. So I had that going for me. I was flown to Harvard for an interview, which went very well, and I got the job. All these things happened serendipitously – which is another reason why my memoir explores the notion of the accidental and the contingent.

It's interesting how most retrospective accounts of life tend to connect all the dots and imply that our lives are shaped by continuity and determination rather than by serendipity. I love Gabriel Marcel's distinction between a 'problem' and a 'mystery'. He says a problem is something that stands before you in its entirety: if the problem is with a leaking tap, the solution is probably a washer, i.e. the problem is there and it's solvable. But he says a lot of things in life are not before us in their entirety and that makes them mysteries, because we can't know or grasp all the factors which bear upon that particular situation. Marcel reminds us that any account of life, even anthropological accounts, have to admit that there are areas which cannot be explained, named, or grasped. That's where the poetic comes in for me. Poetry is where the prosaic imagination stops, where it can't go any further except with a push from poetry. But then there's also a point that poetry itself is powerless to go. When there's only silence.

Finally, let me ask you what contribution has your work made beyond the academy? You said at the outset that you had once wanted to change the world. How has your work contributed to that aim?

As far as I know, it hasn't had any impact. I mean, whose life – let alone work – really has an impact on the life of the world? But I did try very hard to bring about some changes, particularly when I was in central Australia in the mid-1990s. During the Sierra Leone civil war I had to find somewhere else to do fieldwork. I had married again, and my wife and I wanted to be on a level playing field and she was very much interested in Aboriginal Australia. So we went into the unknown together and worked under contract for the Central Land Council, an Aboriginal organization in Alice Springs.

The book that emerged from this fieldwork experience was *At Home in the World* (Jackson 1995). I wanted to reach a non-Aboriginal Australian audience. I wrote in plain English. I wanted to paint a full picture of Aboriginal life as I had known it and was inspired partly

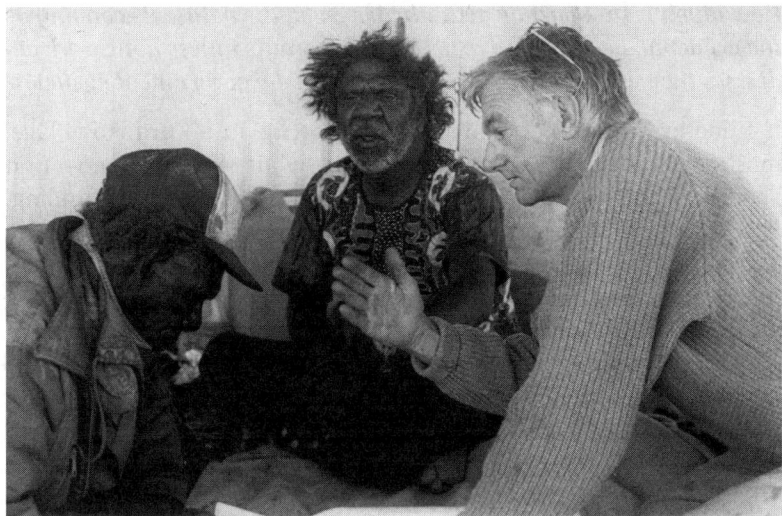

Illustration 1. Michael Jackson with Jackamarra and Jampijinpa, at Paraluyu. Central Australia, 1990. (Photo courtesy of the author)

by the fact that Bruce Chatwin's *The Song Lines* had enjoyed such a wide readership. Unfortunately the Australian edition of the book never found its way onto the market. HarperCollins was swallowed up by a larger publishing company, and all the copies of that book – and many others – were destroyed. I don't even know if any copies from the Australian edition exist anymore. So much for my first bid to influence the public. *Life Within Limits: Well-being in a World of Want (Jackson 2011)* is my other attempt to shape public opinion. It is an account of everyday life in my village in northern Sierra Leone. It's an attempt to write about well-being in the tradition of Amartya Sen. But to get away from the *a priori* assumption that Africa is a zone of desolation, corruption and misery. I wanted to present a more balanced picture of the struggles that exist there and the difficulties people have, but also of the joys and positive things in their lives, in order to develop a critique of our current notions of well-being or happiness. I have also written this book to reach an audience that would do well to rethink popular stereotypes about Africa. I also want to get away from the dominant anthropological discourse about Africa, which is basically framed in terms of the political economies of contemporary Africa and the impact of globalization, epidemic diseases like AIDS, and Pentecostal Christianity. There's a whole mode of writing about Africa in anthropology which doesn't touch upon the life worlds of rural Africa.

How much is that agenda actually driven by the political economy of the academy, i.e. is it hard to get research grants unless your work addresses themes that are considered 'relevant' by government agencies?

If I had proposed to go and study 'well-being' in a Kuranko village, most funding agencies would either say 'what on earth are you on about?' or else consider it too soft and amorphous to justify funding. If you are working in existential areas like well-being, storytelling and consciousness there is no way in which you can formulate these things in a fashion suitable for a grant.

I remember, when I was in Bloomington, I tried to get a National Science Foundation grant to work on migration. This was the time when transnationality was the emerging new paradigm for understanding shifting populations on a global scale. My interest was in Kuranko migration from country to city, but my emphasis was on the *experience* of the migrants. I did a huge library search and found just a handful of titles that even *touched* upon the experience of the migrant. So I constructed a proposal around this under-researched field. It was turned down for its methodological 'lack of rigour'. I remember the phrase precisely for its theoretical vacuity. So I gave up at that point and just went ahead and did the research using my own resources. However, there are now some brilliant studies being carried out along just these lines. In fact, two are from the University of Copenhagen. Hans Lucht, a PhD student of mine, did work on Ghanaian fishermen migrating to Italy, and Henrik Vigh, who worked in Guinea Bissau and followed people there as they moved to Lisbon. Both of these ethnographies really take you into the experience of these people, what they feel, think and struggle with at every step along the way. What you get is a wonderful picture of what is a stake life from *their* standpoint, not a set of suggestions for policy makers or administrators.

References

Forde, D. 1956. *Habitat, Economy and Society: A Geographical Introduction to Ethnology.* London: Methuen.
Goody, J., ed. 1968. *Literacy in Traditional Societies.* Cambridge: Cambridge University Press.
Howells, W. W. 1944. *Mankind So Far.* New York: Doubleday.
Jackson, M. 1977. *The Kuranko: Dimensions of Social Reality in a West African Society.* London: Hurst.
———. 1982. *Allegories of the Wilderness: Ethics and Ambiguity in Kuranko Narratives.* Bloomington: Indiana University Press.

———. 1989. *Paths Toward a Clearing: Radical Empiricism and Ethnographic Inquiry*. Bloomington: Indiana University Press.
———. 1995. *At Home in the World*. Durham: Duke University Press.
———. 1998. *Minima Ethnographica: Intersubjectivity and the Anthropological Project*. Chicago: Chicago University Press.
———. 2004. *In Sierra Leone*. Durham: Duke University Press.
———. 2005. *Existential Anthropology: Events, Exigencies and Effects*. New York: Berghahn.
———. 2006a. *The Accidental Anthropologist*. Dunedin: Longacre.
———. 2006b. *The Politics of Storytelling: Violence, Transgression and Intersubjectivity*. Copenhagen: Museum Tusculanum Press.
———. 2007. *Excursions*. Durham: Duke University Press.
2011. *Life Within Limits: Well-Being in a World of Want*. Durham: Duke University Press.

Notes

1. Charles Goldie was a late nineteenth-century New Zealand painter best known for his portraits of Maori chiefs (*ariki*) and women of rank (*kuia*). His paintings chronicled the traditional tattoos of these Maori men and women.
2. Established in 1975, the Waitangi Tribunal is a permanent commission of enquiry charged with making recommendations concerning claims made by Maori relating to alleged breaches by the Crown of promises made to Maori in the 1840 Treaty of Waitangi. –Ed.

Anne Salmond

Date of Birth: 1945

Place of Birth: Wellington, New Zealand. Grew up on the East Coast, in Gisborne.

PhD: University of Pennsylvania, 1972. Published in 1975 as *Hui: A Study of Maori Ceremonial Gatherings.* Wellington: Reed Publishers.

Fieldwork: New Zealand, Polynesia (Ontong Java, Tahiti, Hawaii)

Current affiliation: Distinguished Professor of Maori Studies and Social Anthropology, University of Auckland

Positions held: Professor Salmond's first position was in 1971, as a lecturer at the University of Auckland. She remains at Auckland as Distinguished Professor in Maori Studies and Anthropology. Her awards and distinctions include election as foreign associate, National Academy of Sciences (2009); recipient of the 2013 'Kiwibank New Zealander of the Year Award'; Corresponding Fellow, British Academy (2008); Founding Fellow, New Zealand Academy of the Humanities (2007); visiting professor, École des Haute Études (2006); Prime Minister's Award for Literary Achievement (2004); Fellow of Royal Society of New Zealand (1990); seventh Captain James Cook Fellow (1987); Nuffield scholar (1980); Elsdon Best Gold Medal (1976); Fulbright scholar (1968). Knighted in 1995 and CBE in 1988. She has also won many literary awards.

Major works

- 2011. *Bligh: William Bligh in the South Seas.* Berkeley: University of California Press / Auckland: Penguin NZ.
- 2009. *Aphrodite's Island: The European Discovery of Tahiti.* Berkeley: University of California Press.
- 2003. *The Trial of the Cannibal Dog: Captain Cook in the South Seas.* London: Allen Lane.
- 1997. *Between Worlds: Early Exchanges between Maori and Europeans, 1773–1815.* Honolulu: University of Hawaii Press / Auckland and London: Viking Press.
- 1991. *Two Worlds: First Meetings between Maori and Europeans, 1692–1772.* Honolulu: University of Hawaii Press.
- 1980. *Eruera: Teachings of a Maori Elder.* Wellington: A.H. and A.W. Reed.
- 1976. *Amiria: The Life Story of a Maori Woman.* Wellington: A.H. and A.W. Reed.
- 1975. *Hui: A Study of Maori Ceremonial Gatherings.* Wellington: Reed Publishers.

Chapter 2

ANTHROPOLOGY, ONTOLOGY AND THE MAORI WORLD
Anne Salmond

Let us begin by asking you about your intellectual biography and, in particular, how you discovered social anthropology.

Well, I'd have to go back a long way to the time when I was a little girl and I used to go down to Wellington to stay with my grandmother. I was taken off to the Dominion Museum to look at the model *pā* (Maori hill fort) that was built by my great-grandfather, James McDonald. My great-grandfather was a photographer and artist around the turn of the nineteenth century. He'd been riveted by Maori life; he loved it, could speak the language and participated in numerous projects led by the Dominion Museum, including some early expeditions to Maori communities. He worked with an early generation of New Zealand ethnographers, including Elsdon Best (whose books he illustrated with his photographs) and Te Rangi Hiroa (Sir Peter Buck), who were eager to record Maori custom before it disappeared. His particular interest was in making films and taking photographs to capture traditional aspects of Maori life.

He kept notebooks in which he recorded different customary practices. There was a carton of these notebooks in my grandmother's garage, and as a little girl, when I got really bored, I used to poke around and read through these notebooks, which also contained wonderful sketches of scenes from Maori life. So at the age of eight or nine I became curious about the intriguing stuff in these mysterious cartons.

I grew up in Gisborne, where the population was about fifty-fifty Maori-*Pakeha*. Because of my great-grandfather's work I was always curious about Maori life, but in those years there was no real way to participate in it, as the two communities were quite divided from each other. I mean, they coincided at *school* or in *sport*, but otherwise very little.

When I was in my teens I went to the States on an American Field Service scholarship and was asked to talk, among other things, about New Zealand and Maori life. I realized I was just talking off the top of my head, almost making it up. I had learnt some action songs, I could do the *poi*,[1] but I felt ashamed that I was talking about something that I didn't really understand. So I decided, 'okay, when I get home, I'm going to learn Maori and I'm going to find out about this part of my country.'

So, when I came back from the States, I went home to Gisborne, because I had six months before starting university at Auckland. I took a job in the local museum, cataloguing the Maori collection, and I started to learn the language, which I loved. I thought to myself that when I got to the university I should continue with Maori by studying anthropology, so that's what led me in that direction. For me, studying Maori and studying anthropology were always one and the same.

Anthropology at the University of Auckland was a very exciting field in which I could study linguistics, physical anthropology, archaeology and social anthropology, as well as Maori. We had magnificent teachers; there was Ralph Bulmer, an ethnobotanist who'd come to Auckland from Cambridge. There was Bruce Biggs, the Pacific linguistic expert, and Roger Green, a leading Pacific archaeologist. It was a *great* department.

This was in 1964 and I had just turned eighteen. It was as though everything happened at once. I joined the Maori club; I had a lot of close friends amongst the Maori students. Outside of the university I also met two senior elders, Eruera and Amiria Stirling, who were from the Te Whānau-ā-Apanui and Ngāti Porou *iwi* (tribes) and became my teachers and mentors for the next twenty years.

It was quite unusual in those years for *Pakeha* students to want to learn Maori. I think in the Maori Club there was just one other *Pakeha* member. For me, it became my passion. I was absolutely fascinated. I wanted to learn about everything Maori. The anthropology department was a great place to do that, because there was quite strong Maori involvement. One of the interesting things Ralph Piddington did was to introduce us to Maori ethnography and the possibility of thinking about Maori life in the contemporary environment.

People I was studying with included Pita Sharples, Hone Kaa, Donna Awatere, who later became prominent leaders in what became known as the 'Maori renaissance'. They weren't political activists at that time; it was almost *pre*-political when I first came to the University of Auckland. We went to rugby matches, had parties and had a fantastic time. It wasn't until a few years later that the Maori renaissance really took off with debates around the Treaty of Waitangi, land rights and the protests at places like Bastion Point. All that happened after I'd been around for a while, and my friendships were already pretty strong by then.

Thinking back to that time, who were the most important people or authors that shaped your thinking?

Above all, there were those great academics, my scholarly teachers who taught me a huge amount. But equally I would say Eruera and Amiria Stirling, because they also became my teachers. Eruera Stirling was a tribal historian, orator and scholar within the Maori tradition. He was one of the leading elders of his generation. He had very strong ideas about knowledge and about the responsibilities that went with it. He viewed knowledge as a treasure: he called it a 'blessing on your mind'. Scholarly activity was essentially a matter of how you live your life. It wasn't just gathering up information for your own enjoyment or pleasure; it was something to work with in the world.

It was very unusual for a Maori elder of such seniority – he was among the great elders of his time – to mentor a young _Pakeha_ girl, as I was then. He and Amiria took me under their wing and taught me over the next two decades, which was a real privilege.

It was a very different kind of education and I was thrown in the deep end. To teach me tribal history, Eruera would sit me down on the living room floor with very long sheets of paper and get me to record genealogies. He was trying to teach me how all the different New Zealand _iwi_ (tribal groups) were genealogically linked and the key marriages between them. This was so that when we went to the marae, I would know my way around. He did a lot of that kind of thing. Then they started taking me to marae and speaking Maori to me, so I was also learning Maori with them.

Amiria and I were terrific friends. She was a lot older than me; when we met she must have been in her late sixties, and yet we were really close. We had the same sort of sense of humour and enjoyed being together. She was a marvellous storyteller – and I was a fascinated audience. We laughed about a lot of the same things and we both liked growing flowers. It was curious how many things we had in common. I was in awe of Eruera. I looked up to him and was intimidated by him for quite a while, because he was this austere and quite reserved elder. He was a _tohunga_, someone who dwelt within the world of the ancestors, and that is a realm of the Maori world where you have to tread carefully. So I used to tiptoe around. But when he started teaching me, taking me to marae, I would drive him and Amiria to gatherings in my little blue VW, and in the car he'd spend the time rehearsing genealogies, telling tribal history and getting ready for what he'd say on the marae. We had this sort of 'travelling university' going for a long time. Over the years they took me into their family. I called him 'Koro' and Amiria 'Nanny', just like their grandchildren.

At the same time, I was meeting people such as Lady Lorna Ngata and Peggy Kaua. These dignified, glorious women had been very close to Sir Apirana Ngata, a former minister of native affairs and a visionary Maori leader from the East Coast. My great-grandfather knew him well – they had worked closely together on the Dominion Museum expeditions to record Maori customary life. Peggy and Lorna taught me action songs, and I was very impressed by them. I thought they were just amazing.

How did these encounters change your view of the world?

It gave me a different sense of the world. For example, I could walk out and look at a mountain or a hill that I've been looking at all my life, and all of a sudden I'd see a totally different side to that place. Now, I'd know its Maori name as well as its European name – it's not 'Young Nick's Head', a headland in Gisborne which was the first place named by Captain Cook, it's 'Te Kuri a Paoa', the dog of Paoa, one of the first Polynesian explorers to arrive in New Zealand, who claimed it by naming after his dog. There's a 'double history' here, a double dimension to the landscapes that I was living in every day. Feeling like that about your own country all of a sudden is unsettling. It's not exactly *Alice in Wonderland*, but it's almost like that: i.e. everything I thought was stable and familiar started to take on radically new meanings. That sense of wonder has never left me. It's awesome, but it's also difficult. I've been studying this stuff all my life and will probably continue till the day I die, because there's so much to learn. When you get immersed in tribal histories and genealogies, the subtleties of language, the art forms and the tribal landscapes out there, it's just such fun.

Tell us about your main research interests and how these have developed.

My first substantial scholarly work was as a linguist. When I was in my twenties I wrote a generative grammar of Luangiua, one of the

Polynesian outliers, an atoll off the coast of the Solomon Islands. This was under the supervision of Professor Bruce Biggs and Dr Andy Pawley, who gave us a rigorous training in generative linguistics, almost like the mathematics of language, based on the work of Noam Chomsky. I loved working with the language and had a great time when I went to work with the people from Luangiua in Honiara, the capital of the Solomon Islands. They told me all these amazing stories, which I would tape. We would spend hours sitting on the beach, learning seashell names. After three months, when I started writing this grammar of their language, I thought, 'what a strange way to represent this experience!'

I mean, for me it was like time-travelling back to pre-colonial times in Maori society, because many of these people couldn't speak English, couldn't speak pidgin, the women were still bare breasted, the people were tattooing their bodies, cooking in the ground, and death was happening in the village. When I wrote this quasi-mathematical grammar, which was published by Mouton, it was all very nice, but I thought, 'I'm not going to write like *that* again. Only ten people in the world will read this'. How could such an incredible experience be reduced to that kind of account?

After that, I decided to study sociolinguistics. I went to the University of Pennsylvania, because it had spectacular teachers in that field, including Dell Hymes, William Labov, Ward Goodenough and Erving Goffman. I spent a very concentrated period in Philadelphia, doing my PhD. With Eruera's encouragement, I decided that when I returned to New Zealand, I would write a sociolinguistic study of *hui* (ceremonial gatherings). However, once I started this work and began visiting marae with Eruera and Amiria, I thought to myself, 'I can't possibly write it this way. I need to respect the pattern of what's going on here. If I'm going to write this book, it has to be one that people can read and one that is true to these gatherings'. So in the end I structured it according to the major sequences in a *hui*. The book itself followed the ritual stages of the ceremonies that I witnessed taking place on marae (Salmond 1975).

I began my account with an historical examination of how these contemporary gatherings are both similar and different to the way they used to be. Then I went through, step by step, what happens in the ritual once you enter a marae. I had a lot of taped transcripts of speeches, chants and songs that I was able to include in the book. People in the Maori world really liked the book, because if you have to go to a *hui*, it's great to know what's going to happen and what resources you might need to perform creditably in those environments.

My next book developed out of my friendship with Amiria, and our time together on those marae (Salmond 1976). One day a friend of hers, Mrs Hoeft, came around and showed us a little book that she'd written called 'The Tale of the Fish', about growing up in Northland and Maori life in that part of the country. I remember Amiria looking at it and saying to me, 'Ani, I think we could do a bigger one than that' [laughs]. I said to her, 'Hmm, I bet we could.' This is how I got into oral history. As I said, Amiria was a fantastic storyteller, and I thought that the story of her life would make a great book and it would be fun for us to do it together. I had my daughter by then – also named Amiria. Amiria and Eruera were her godparents. She was just a little baby and sat on my lap while we filled some thirty tapes with stories. Because we knew each other really well, I would often just say, 'Nanny, tell me the one about ...', because I'd remember a particular story that she'd told me in the car or when we were bored in the middle of a *hui*. We sat there chuckling, laughing, even crying sometimes. My idea was that instead of putting an anthropological template on this and ramming her life into some kind of theoretical framework, why not let people share in her experience?

You have to edit the raw transcripts a little, because otherwise the language is ungrammatical or repetitive. But I wanted to capture her turns of phrase and the things that made her speech so charming and special, without making it look silly. My aim was to write it so that anyone could pick up that book and hear her voice and share what it was like to be in this other dimension of New Zealand society: what it was like to be a Maori woman, raising her children on the coast, going through tragedy and triumph, and then shifting to Auckland. In short, how did *she* experience *her* life? It seemed to work. People were able to read the book and feel 'This is what it's like to be in a Maori skin'. The book also won a literary award. Most importantly, Amiria loved it. She loved the personal relationships that came out of it; the people who read the book and rang her up to talk about it.

For me, another important goal was to break down social barriers. When I was travelling with the Stirlings I saw a lot of things happening that I hated. I saw people being disrespectful to Maori. There was a lot of raw prejudice in those years. People treated the Stirlings – whom I revered and loved like my own grandparents – as if they were a lower form of life. I couldn't bear it. I thought, we've got these two dimensions in this country, and I've started to explore the Maori one and found so much richness and depth. Yet other people are dismissing their world and saying ignorant things that don't make any sense at all. So part of my project was to shift *Pakeha* perceptions of Maori life.

It wasn't about preaching to them or being a polemicist, but sharing with them some of the riches of the Maori world so that we might change that dynamic.

How did all this connect with the wider shift and radicalization that was occurring in anthropology at that time?

The agenda that started to happen in the Maori world in the 1970s was even more radical. While Amiria and I were working on her book, things like the land marches and the occupation of Bastion Point were happening. Many of my friends from university such as Pita Sharples, Pat Hohepa, Ranginui Walker and Donna Awatere were leading the charge, followed by a younger generation including Taura Eruera and Nga Tamatoa, who were fighting for Maori land rights, the survival of the language and equality with *Pakeha*. The Maori critique was more sharp-edged than anything that was happening in anthropology.

I found it a struggle to bring together the anthropology I was learning with the political activism that was going on in New Zealand. Quite often, the stuff that was being written in the metropolitan capitals seemed a very long way away from the sorts of things I was dealing with as an anthropologist in my own country.

And anthropology at this time was often being accused of being the 'handmaiden of colonialism'.

Yes, but the curious thing was that many of my friends who were leading the charge on Maori issues were in fact trained as anthropologists: for example, Bob Mahuta, Pita Sharples, Sir Hugh Kawharu, Ranginui Walker and Pat Hohepa had all trained in anthropology. Given this situation, it was difficult to see anthropology as the handmaiden of colonialism in New Zealand, although Ranginui started to express that point of view. However, I'm not sure that any of the others did.

My focus at that time was on a new project that I'd started with Eruera. I had three kids under five and was working half-time at the university when he said to me, 'It's time for us to do my book now'. I had to put everything aside as much as I could – not the children obviously. It was the only time I've had student complaints, actually, for my essays not being marked on time! [laughs]. He had taught me so much that I couldn't say no. He also wasn't well and worried he may not have time to pass on his knowledge to a younger generation. So we just did it and he took me into his realm (Salmond 1980). Every time we taped, he would do a *karakia* (prayer). We had to follow strict rules of *tapu* (taboo): i.e. I couldn't tape if I had my period and we had stay away from food, so as not to break any *tapu* restrictions. He was from that world, where the ancestors were present and real, and he carried me a long way into it when we worked together. It was like being his student, but it was difficult, because I was a young *Pakeha* woman with children, and his world, with its power of *tapu*, can be quite frightening. *Tapu* is not just a thing you write academic papers about. It's a *force* in the world.

In Eruera's world, he would talk to his ancestors and things would happen. I was drawn into the Maori knowledge system in a serious way, because he was using me as a medium to convey some of his insights to the wider world. He was very selective about what he wanted to publish, and there were a lot of things that we didn't include in the book. Eruera had strong opinions about what was going on in New Zealand and the relationships between Maori and *Pakeha*. He was very involved in the land marches and Bastion Point protests and became a guide for young urban radical leaders, trying to steer them in ways that would be constructive. So by working with Eruera I became deeply saturated in *wānanga*, which is the Maori knowledgeable tradition, and straight after completing the book I went to Cambridge.

I had a *brilliant* time in Cambridge partly because I'd been struggling to bring together the things I was learning from Eruera with the whole scholarly 'Western episteme'. It was fabulous to be in Cambridge at that time and to have the space think, read and talk to the wonderful people there, people like Marilyn Strathern and Edmund Leach and the PhD cohort. There were times when I was with Eruera when I really did wonder whether it was possible to accommodate these two worlds in the same person. That is, in my own mind [laughs]. Because there are things that happen in the Maori world that shouldn't happen if you're thinking within the Western episteme. In *Te Ao Maori*, the Maori world, ancestors are real, and a power, and if you offend or cross them, it's dangerous. *Tapu* can kill people.

A lot of strange things happen when you spend time with someone like Eruera. I had three little kids to look after, and dealing with *tapu* is an intense experience. I managed to get the book together, read it through with him and make sure he was happy with it. Having completed that, it was a luxury to go to Cambridge and, for the first time in my anthropological career, if not in my life, to be free from all of those pressures and be in a place where I could just think. I could also talk about these issues with people who really cared about them and had fantastic insights to offer.

I started writing about knowledge systems at that time. I wrote a paper called 'Theoretical Landscapes', which was about semantics and knowledge, comparing Western and Maori approaches to knowledge and finding deep differences, as well as some similarities. I wrote about Maori semantics, grappling with words like *tapu* and *mana* as ontological words – words that hold a world – writing about them without domesticating or taming them and ripping away their power, which is what a lot of anthropological writing can do.

At what point did your research shift towards a focus on history?

I'd always been interested in oral history and still am now. The work I do draws on history all the time. Even though it might have been deposited in documents a hundred years ago, it's still oral history, i.e. talk that has been written down. Having worked intensively with speech, transcribing it into written text and creating documents of my own, I know that they don't have a final authority. Documents often record the discussion of recent or more remote events, and there's always the intervention of memory. Even a journal entry that's been written up by a sailor two days after an event is still highly crafted. Having been trained as a sociolinguist is really useful when you're working with these kinds of materials. I tend to read the sailors' logs and think of them in rather the same way as missionaries recording oral tradition from a Tahitian chief or a Maori elder. I don't see these as fundamentally different processes: I see the final document as an artefact of a process of communication.

When Eruera and Amiria died I had to stop and think, because we'd had this twenty-year journey together. Being at Cambridge, I'd started reflecting about different knowledge systems and the different rules, rituals and ceremonies that surround them. Perhaps because I was comparing Western and Maori forms of knowledge, I became interested in the relationship between Maori and Pakeha in New Zealand, and how it began. When I started thinking about the first meetings between Maori and Europeans, including Captain Cook's journeys and the arrival of the Endeavour at Poverty Bay and on the East Coast, I saw these episodes in a different light to most Western historians (Salmond 1991). I'd slept in marae at those places, and Eruera had told me the ancestral stories, so the ancestors who'd met Captain Cook were like people I knew.

So when I began writing about Captain Cook coming into Poverty Bay, one of the first questions I asked was, 'Who are those people on shore? What is going on there? Which iwi are involved? What are the tribal dynamics?' When Maori sent out challengers from one side of the Turanganui River to confront the strangers and one of them got shot, why did the people on the other side of the river not pick up his body? Well, now I know why, because I went into the tribal history and discovered that the Turanganui River was a boundary marker at that time. I began to realize that if I brought together the knowledge I'd learned with Eruera with the historical documents, the story totally changed. Instead of being a story about Captain Cook and the Endeavour, and the European exploration of the world, it became a two-sided history of encounter. Just as the landscapes have a double dimension, so do our early beginnings (Salmond 1997).

This gave me an entirely new perspective on the founding story of New Zealand – of Captain Cook 'discovering the country', which became one of the founding myths of race relations in New Zealand. For much of the last century, Captain Cook was greatly celebrated, and then 'villainized' in the nineteen seventies and eighties, when people began to say, 'You know, this bastard came and shot at us!' [laughs]. In Gisborne at that time they stopped having ceremonies on the beach to celebrate Cook's 'discovery' of New Zealand, because as local Maori pointed out, New Zealand had already been found and settled when Captain Cook stepped ashore; and they weren't very thrilled that their ancestors had been shot at. That debate recurs every year on the anniversary of Cook's arrival.

As we talk, I'm trying to think about the fundamental things I've learnt and one of the reasons why anthropology suits me and why I'm at home in the discipline. It's about our shared humanity. It's about the humanity of the journey that you make to come to terms with people who speak another language, who think about the world differently, but who are still people you can get to know – and often incredibly well. Yet you undertake that journey every time you talk to them. For me, learning to speak Maori, having that apprenticeship with Eruera and Amiria, has changed me a lot both as a person and as a scholar.

Have you had any memorable fieldwork experiences that particularly changed your view of the world?

I have memorable experiences all the time. One thing I would say is that as an anthropologist/historian/linguist, I almost never get 'out' of the field: the 'field' is my own country. Many of my closest friends and colleagues are Maori, and the younger generation of our family includes a lot of Maori members. So, where is 'the field'? Is it at home? Yes, it's at home. Any illuminations that come to me are not because I've 'gone into' the field and then come home to write about it. Probably the only time in my life that I've been 'out of the field' for any length of time was when I was in Cambridge, and in a way I treated that as a fieldwork experience. It taught me a great deal about Western knowledge, for example. And in my 'home' there are so many illuminating moments. There are times when I think I've understood something, then something else happens and I realize that I haven't grasped it at all.

For me, there are deeper experiences than simply intellectual ones. I don't see anthropology as a detached art. Within the Maori frame of reference, your relationships with other people matter more than anything else. You have to keep these alive forever, and you can't just take and not give back. Once you've engaged in one of those relationships, the obligations – but also the gifts – just keep on coming. It's the whole idea of the 'heart-mind', or in Maori, the *hinengaro*: i.e. heart and mind are not separate. It's like that for me as a scholar. I try and bring my whole *self* to my scholarly practice and not just my head, if you know what I mean. For Maori, the mind is not just in your head, the place where you think – it's located within the body. Some of the things that have taught me the most have been quite painful. Although I haven't been told to get lost very often, it did happen once or twice in the 1970s, when Maori-*Pakeha* relationships were really tense. Fortunately for me, I had people who stood up for me, elders who stepped in and told the critic to buzz off. When I was with Ererua and Amiria I had a complete cloak of protection. They had this *mana* that just enveloped me. So as long as I was with them, nobody was going to question my presence.

But it was very hurtful to be criticized. You think to yourself, 'is this worth it?' Then you think, 'Well, actually, yes it is. I have woven my life with these people; they are some of my closest friends, so I can't ever walk away.' It was then that I realized that I had no choice if I was going to remain true to the things I'd been taught. I've also learned from the experience of the power of things like *tapu* – but that is something I can't really talk about.

How important has teaching been for you?

Because I teach in Maori studies, I've always taught Maori courses and had many Maori students. It's really good. It keeps me on my toes. I can't make any false claims to authority. That's one of the things you can do when you're a metropolitan anthropologist – you're a long way away from the people who really know. But in my environment,

I can't say anything incorrect, because it's likely that there are people in the class who know more than me in some areas. I like it, because the most rigorous test of anything I'm thinking is to put it up in front of these students. About a month ago I made a slip up in somebody's name. There was a kid in the class whose ancestor that was and she put me right straight away – and in front of everybody! I said, 'You're right! Absolutely right, thank you for that!' So I learn from them the whole time.

But the Maori world is also very diverse; and there are probably quite a few Maori who haven't had some of the experiences of the Maori world that I've had by now. I can see that just with the contact I have today with students, many of whom are on a quest. They want to find out more about who they are, where their ancestors came from, what they were like and where they fit in the world. Teaching in that situation is brilliant.

What do you see as some of the most exciting developments within anthropology or between anthropology and other disciplines?

I'm interested in the relationship between anthropology and history. There've been developments across the disciplinary boundaries which I really enjoy. Obviously I have a long-standing interest in oral history, but in recent years my work has focused on the period of European exploration and discovery in the Pacific, and the micro-ethnographies of ships, islands, and communities in bays and harbours in New Zealand and across Polynesia (Salmond 2003, 2009). I draw inspiration from the work of Natalie Zemon Davis, a fabulous historian who works like an ethnographer. She uses historical documents but has a way of exploring societies in the past that I find inspiring.

The role I see for anthropology, and indeed for all of the humanities, is to encompass humanity itself. The humanities can't just be Western in orientation. If they're going to do their job properly, disciplines like philosophy, history, literary studies, etc. must move beyond Western assumptions about the world, what matters, and which traditions have something to offer. It has to become a true *humanity*, exploring the insights of the world. Anthropology's been a repository for a great deal of work in that area. It has been inspiring in various ways to other disciplines. But there's still a huge leap to be taken in the humanities themselves. It's difficult and it's demanding, because it means mastering other languages and coming to grips with the subtleties and complexities of other ways of thinking. But if Western scholars don't do this, their work runs the danger of being provincial.

Where do you see anthropology going in the future?

As you can probably tell, I'm not much interested in disciplinary boundaries [laughs]. For me, the disciplines are just that – ways of disciplining your thinking and enabling you to think in a rigorous fashion. Each of them has different ways of helping you to achieve that. History offers certain skills and approaches, and anthropology or linguistics offers others. It's the questions that you ask that are the real point. The disciplines are means of proceeding towards answers, insights and disclosures. What is distinctive about anthropology is that immersion in other ways of being. If I have any criticism of anthropology as a discipline, it is that sometimes it's not sufficiently demanding – the immersion in another way of being is too short and shallow. My experience would indicate that the task of anthropology is one of the most formidable scholarly challenges. It never ends – you're always learning, trying to enter into another language, to engage deeply with another philosophical tradition and another conception of the world. It entails engaging with other ideas about thought itself and the art forms that go with that. That takes time, and it takes a lot of work. It is not until you have learned to put some of your own deepest assumptions at risk that you can start asking really probing questions and contribute to wider discussions about what it is to be human in the world.

What would you say has been the main contribution of your work to public debates beyond the academy and beyond these disciplinary boundaries?

I've been active outside the university and that's probably because the realm of inquiry that I've been part of – trying to understand the Maori world and its interfaces with the West – is a source of burning public interest in New Zealand. People argue about these issues around dinner tables and on talkback radio.

I get pulled into all sorts of public activities. I spent six years as chair of the New Zealand Historic Places Trust, where the relationships between Maori and *Pakeha* heritage were being negotiated and debated. I've also had a lot to do with the science community in New Zealand and with university politics over the years, including almost a decade as pro vice-chancellor for equal opportunities at the University of Auckland. I've tried to engage with public issues as a writer. I regard myself as a writer as much as an anthropologist, because the art of communication is a critical part of what you do. If you learn something, you should share it. If you can write in a way that people can read and enjoy, they're more likely to enter into discussion or dialogue – and listen and think or be prompted to make enquiries of their own.

Since I write about New Zealand and the Pacific, a lot of people in this part of the world read my books. Different people draw different things out of them. Sometimes you're absolutely astonished at what they make of it! [laughs]. I find it lovely when an artist rings me up and invites me to a show because they were inspired by the images in one of my books and they've made an exhibition and want me to come and see what I think. That happens in various media. One of my books has even been turned into an opera!

This is all part of being in New Zealand and taking part in debates about what kind of country this is going to be: Where do Maori people and Pacific people fit into the wider society? How can this be conceptualized? How can people find fellow feeling across boundaries that sometimes appear pretty rigid? Are there ways in which you can communicate to break down some of those barriers? A key part of my relationship with Eruera and Amiria was about them wanting to reach out beyond those barriers to engage other people and letting them share something about what it was like to be in their world. Getting people to think in ways which are more charitable perhaps, or more open, and prepared to see that they might actually learn from Pacific or Maori worlds. For me, it's not so much learning *about* Maori life, it's actually learning *from* it.

This is where I think that anthropology has to be heading. It can't stay within the Western tradition for its key conceptions and insights. If the post-colonial debates have taught us anything, it is that people from other societies don't appreciate being objectified, turned into items of curiosity for detached inspection. The relational philosophies of Maori, for instance, insist that the partnerships in which anthropologists engage must be based on mutual exchange and learning, at an intellectual as well as a personal level. Too much of our talk about the discipline serve to distance us – talk about 'fieldwork' and 'data' and 'informants' – as though these people are simply resources for the production of anthropological information instead of thinkers in their own right, with insights to offer into what it is to be human.

I see anthropology as a form of comparative philosophy that helps us to bring to light our own unexamined assumptions – about the world and how best to inhabit it – and to generate new ideas and conceptions from this kind of fundamental rethinking. The arrogance of the past – the presumption that the West has a monopoly on 'advanced' ideas and knowledge, so that other ways of thinking become 'backward' exotica for inspection and classification by default, has rightly been attacked – the critique that anthropology is 'the handmaiden of colonialism', as you've mentioned. Some of the artefacts of the Enlightenment – possessive individualism, the 'invisible hand' of the market, and the assumption that shifts towards agricultural or industrial practices that reflect these ideas are invariably signs of 'progress' – are running up against their limits in the world at present. There is a need for new paradigms across a wide range of disciplines, radically different ways of thinking. I'd like to think that anthropology can help to inspire these conceptual experiments.

References

Salmond, A. 1975. *Hui: A Study of Maori Ceremonial Gatherings.* Wellington: Reed Publishers.
———. 1976. *Amiria: The Life Story of a Maori Woman.* Wellington: A.H. and A.W. Reed.
———. 1980. *Eruera: Teachings of a Maori Elder.* Wellington: A.H. and A.W. Reed.
———. 1991. *Two Worlds: First Meetings between Maori and Europeans, 1692–1772.* Honolulu: University of Hawaii Press.
———. 1997. *Between Worlds: Early Exchanges between Maori and Europeans, 1773–1815.* Honolulu: University of Hawaii Press / Auckland and London: Viking Press.
———. 2003. *The Trial of the Cannibal Dog: Captain Cook in the South Seas.* London: Allen Lane.
———. 2009. *Aphrodite's Island: The European Discovery of Tahiti.* Berkeley: University of California Press.

Notes

1. A *poi* is a traditional Maori dance using a ball of woven flax. –Ed.

Joan Metge

Date of Birth: 1930
Place of Birth: Auckland, New Zealand
PhD: 'The Changing Structure of Maori Society: A Study in Social Process in Urban and Rural Areas of Northern New Zealand', 1958, University of London.

Fieldwork: New Zealand

Current affiliation: Honorary Research Fellow, Anthropology Department, University of Auckland

Positions held: After a year as junior lecturer in geography at Auckland University College, Dr Metge spent two and a half years in the field studying Maori urban migration and then completed her PhD at the London School of Economics, under Professor Raymond Firth. In 1965, after more fieldwork and three years as lecturer in University Extension at the University of Auckland, she was appointed senior lecturer in anthropology at Victoria University of Wellington, and she held the position of associate professor (renamed reader) there from 1968 to 1988, including three years on leave as Captain James Cook Research Fellow (1981–83). After retiring in 1988 she continued writing and research as Honorary Research Fellow at Victoria and then Auckland Universities, in the fields of Maori-Pakeha relations and cross-cultural communication. Her awards and distinctions include: the Hutchinson Medal, London School of Economics, 1959; the Elsdon Best Memorial Medal, Polynesian Society, 1987; Knighted in 1987; Te Rangi Hiroa Medal, Royal Society of New Zealand, 1997; Honorary D Litt, University of Auckland, 2001; Asia-Pacific Mediation Forum Peace Prize 2006; and a social-science research medal bearing her name, awarded biennially by the Royal Society of New Zealand.

Major works

- 2010. *Tuamaka: The Challenge of Difference in Aotearoa New Zealand.* Auckland: Auckland University Press.
- 2001. *Korero Tahi: Talking Together.* Auckland: Auckland University Press.
- 1995. *New Growth from Old: The Whanau in the Modern World.* Wellington: Victoria University Press.
- 1992. *Cross Cultural Communication and Land Transfer in Muriwhenua, 1832–40.* Wellington: Submission to the Waitangi Tribunal.
- 1986. *In and Out of Touch: Whakamaa in Cross Cultural Context.* Wellington: Victoria University Press.
- 1978, co-author with Patricia Kinloch. *Talking Past Each Other: Problems of Cross Cultural Communication.* Wellington: Victoria University Press.
- 1976. *The Maoris of New Zealand: Rautahi.* London: Routledge and Kegan Paul. Republished 2004 as *Rautahi: The Maori of New Zealand.* London and New York: Routledge.
- 1964. *A New Maori Migration: Rural and Urban Relations in Northern New Zealand.* London: Athlone Press. Facsimile edition, 2004. Oxford: Berg.

Chapter 3

BUILDING BRIDGES
Maori and Pakeha *Relations*
Joan Metge

One of the unresolved issues in post-colonial societies like New Zealand and Australia concerns the expropriation of land and the question of cultural property. What has been your experience of this issue?

I began work as an anthropologist in the 1950s and – what was unusual for that time – I worked at home, in my own country, with the Maori people of New Zealand, as they moved into the city. In those days there was no formal association of anthropologists, no code of anthropological ethics. I developed my own rules of practice, guided by my professors' teaching and my own moral conscience. Questions about the ownership and appropriation of Maori knowledge weren't even asked – in fact, I found many Maori leaders eager to share such knowledge, in the hope of winning greater understanding and respect from 'the *Pakeha* in power'[1]. But times change. In the 1980s, young Maori seeking to recover their ancestral heritage protested against what they saw as exploitation by anthropologists and others. After that, I felt the time had come to tackle the issue head on, and in print (Metge 1995: 309–12; 2001:1–8; 2010: 7–8). It seems to me that a degree of appropriation is always involved when people of different cultures meet. As anthropologists we can't avoid it if we are doing our job properly. But such appropriation isn't necessarily all, or always, bad. It depends on how it is done. In my experience the key lies in treating people and their knowledge with respect – seeking their approval, involving them as far as possible as co-workers, acknowledging their contribution, giving – and giving back – as well as taking.

Tell us about the various positions you've held over the course of your career.

Well, the first was a summer position, as a student, when I worked at the Auckland War Memorial Museum as assistant to the ethnographer, Vic Fisher. Mostly it meant recording accessions, but there were occasional exciting tasks like choosing the flax and feather cloaks to be photographed for Te Rangi Hiroa's book *The Coming of the Maori*.[2] I spent 1952 as a junior lecturer in the Geography Department at Auckland University. Then it was straight into the field. I spent two years studying Maori migrants in Auckland city and six months in a Maori community in the Far North of the North Island. In 1955 I took a ship for London, where I spent another two years writing up my fieldnotes as a doctoral thesis at LSE [London School of Economics].

I came home in 1958 to find that the research fellowship I had been counting on had been scrapped, and there were no jobs in anthropology at Auckland, the only university in New Zealand that was teaching anthropology at that point. I filled in time doing odd research jobs for Professor Piddington, until the award of a Carnegie Social Science Research Fellowship saved my life – or my life in anthropology. So then I was able to get back into the field to explore Maori community life in depth. When the fellowship ran out there were still no jobs in anthropology, so I took one in 'University Extension'. For three years I worked closely with two Maori tutors, teaching nonexamination courses on 'Maori society and culture' and helping organize Young Maori Leaders' Conferences.

Then the professor appointed to head a new anthropology department at Victoria University of Wellington withdrew at the last minute and the post had to be readvertised. Victoria offered me the position of senior lecturer with responsibility for setting up Maori Studies. Of course, I accepted, and we had Maori Studies well under way when Professor Jan Pouwer[3] arrived to take over as head of department. Once enough Maori lecturers had been appointed, I pulled back from teaching in Maori studies courses. I insisted that I was a social anthropologist with a Maori specialty, *not* a 'Maori expert'. And when Maori Studies became a separate department I chose to stay in anthropology, where I could make sure that Maori topics continued to be included in general anthropology courses.

I stayed at Victoria for twenty-three years. I was promoted to associate professor in 1968 and had three years away on leave in the early 1980s as holder of the Fifth Captain James Cook Research Fellowship. It was great being back in the field. The harvest was so rich, writing it up for publication took years and still isn't finished (see Metge 1984, 1986, 1995). In 1988 I took early retirement from the university and embarked on a second career as an independent researcher and writer. Almost immediately I got involved with the claim that Te Runanga O Muriwhenua (representing the five tribes of the Far North) was pursuing before the Waitangi Tribunal.[4] I realized that some of the research I had done in the Far North in the 1950s and 1960s was highly relevant to the Muriwhenua claim and ended up writing three reports for the tribunal.

Let's go back to those early days in the 1950s and your initial encounters with anthropology. How did you first discover social anthropology as a discipline?

Well, I discovered archaeology first. Both my parents were teachers, and we had a lot of books at home, including Arthur Mee's *Children's Encyclopaedia*. I was fascinated with Crete, Ancient Greece and Rome – and above all, with Egypt. I also read all the books I could lay my hands on about the mythology of Scandinavian countries, Greece, Rome, the Irish, the Welsh and, of course, the Maori. We also had my grandfather's books on the Maori – books by Elsdon Best (1924), Edward Tregear (1904) and John Logan Campbell (1881) – and I knew those books inside out.

There were actually four strands in my discovery of anthropology. One was my reading which, as I said, was focused on archaeology to begin with. The second was the whole context of the time. I was born in 1930 and grew up through the Depression and the Second World War. That was the big picture. Then in the small country towns we lived in south of Auckland, Pukekohe and Matamata, there were Maori enclaves which were marginalized on the periphery of society. The third strand was my family circumstances. I had just one sister, no brothers, and our father was very supportive of us right from the beginning; he never made me feel that he would have preferred a son. He used to say, 'There's no sex in the brain.' He made me feel that girls could do anything. Another important aspect of my family upbringing was Christianity. My parents had – and practised – a very strong Christian faith, which I took on, of my own choice. That entailed a special emphasis on the equal value of all human beings and a feeling for the importance of social justice. In Pukekohe in those war years I saw that neither of those values was really given more than lip service. When we first moved to Pukekohe, houses were short and the only house we could get was outside the town limits, in the middle of the market gardens. Pukekohe was a *major* market-garden area. When we moved into the house we found that it had been a sly grog shop. In those days, there were paternalistic laws in place, which meant that Maori could not buy liquor legally. But of course there were *Pakehas* who were more than happy to capitalize on that and sell it illegally at high prices. We also saw there were no bylaws governing the conditions under which market-garden workers were housed. They were living all around us, in the most appalling circumstances. There was no social promotion in school in those days. At Pukekohe Primary School, most of the Maori children got no further than the primer classes and standard one; many of them didn't go to school a lot, and when they did, they were ostracized because they had skin problems due to the fertilizers used in the market gardens. As a child you absorb these things. You store up memories and those memories are a very powerful motivation.

There was also a fourth factor. Although we had very little contact with Maori, even the ones living across the road, there was one family in our community where the father was Chinese – and ran a market garden – and his wife was Maori. Their children attended school and their eldest daughter became my best friend. Now, as I recall, there was no hint of cultural difference there, but there were certainly physical differences. And that friendship was very important to me. Also, at church we had two ministers, one of whom was a young curate and one of the sunniest people I know. In many ways, when I think about or try to define the Maori concept of *aroha* (love, compassion and sympathy), I think of him. The other minister was a much older and very dignified man, and when I think of what *mana* means,[5] I think of him. So there were three people who I could relate to and who I held in deep respect, all from very different backgrounds to my own. They taught me, as I later realized, that it was possible to bridge the divide that I saw existing in that town and that that was what I wanted to do. But at that stage, I still hadn't heard of anthropology [laughs], so when I went to secondary school, I said I wanted to be an archaeologist, and the teacher said, 'Well, yes dear, but that's not possible. Archaeology happens on the other side of the world, and girls don't do it'. Stubbornly, I persisted in giving archaeology as my ambition, until my father sent me to the Auckland War Memorial Museum to talk to a friend of his, Dick Scobie, who was the museum's education officer and who later did some lecturing for Professor Piddington at Auckland University. Dick Scobie and I talked for a while and he looked at me and said, 'Wouldn't you rather work with people who can talk back?' And I thought, 'That's the most sensible thing I've heard!' He introduced me to social anthropology while I was still at school.

Tell us more about your intellectual journey and the major influences that have shaped your thinking.

When I started university in 1948, anthropology was on the books, but there was nobody to teach it, and each year I put it on my list of next year's courses. I ended up doing a BA and MA in geography. My MA thesis was on Maori migrations in northern New Zealand over the previous twenty-five years. It was based on census material and information supplied by helpful officers in the Department of Maori Affairs. The year I wrote my thesis was the year Ralph Piddington started teaching anthropology at Auckland. But I was already doing four papers as well as the thesis, and I had no time to take Anthropology One. However, the following year, while I was teaching as junior lecturer in geography, I took the second-year anthropology course. Ralph Piddington was my *real* introduction to anthropology.

In Anthropology Two we used Ralph Piddington's (1950) *Introduction to Social Anthropology*,[6] which must have been among the first truly 'student friendly' texts in anthropology. Piddington introduced us to British anthropologists like Meyer Fortes, Evans-Pritchard and Audrey Richards, and we read Raymond Firth's *We the Tikopia* (1936) and books by American authors, particularly Arensberg and Kimball (1940), the Lynds (1929) and Lloyd Warner (1952). Looking back years later, I realized that Piddington presented the work of all these writers through the lens of his own Malinowskian functionalism, but I simply picked up what made sense to me – like the idea of manifest and latent functions – and left behind what I found too complicated, like the 'Theory of Needs'. Piddington gave us a first-class education in fieldwork methods, drawing on his own experience among the Karadjeri for illustrations. I got a strong sense of his respect and affection for that people. Another great thing about Piddington was how supportive he was of his students. At that time it was taken for granted that you *had* to go overseas to do your PhD, you *could not* do it in New Zealand. Piddington fought for and got permission for me and one or two others to do our fieldwork in New Zealand, which for that era was a real breakthrough.

I chose to study under Firth at LSE because of the work he had done on nineteenth-century Maori economics (Firth 1929). I liked the way he balanced 'structure' and 'organization', belief and practice, and the way he attempted to deal with social change, even though he wasn't entirely successful. While in the UK I was most attracted to the work and personalities of Victor Turner, Max Gluckman and Mary Douglas.

When I started teaching at Victoria University of Wellington, I was still pretty much a functionalist, if a patchwork one. I was jolted out of that rut by the arrival of Jan Pouwer as professor. I am deeply grateful to Jan for introducing me to the study of language and the study of the brain, both of which became major interests of mine, but I couldn't make head or tail of his structuralist theory until I had read an array of books by and about Lévi-Strauss and made my own summaries, as I used to do as a student. Eventually I tumbled to the fact that Jan was a *Dutch* structuralist, closer to Josselin de Jong than Lévi-Strauss, but by then I had taken on board a number of Lévi-Strauss's ideas, in particular, structuring principles, deep-structure, mediation, transformation and bricolage. However, I reacted strongly against the way that Lévi-Strauss reduced the rich variation of real life stories to timeless 'structures' and became interested in studying real live Maori storytellers (see Metge 2010: 29–40).

Over the years since, I have been stimulated by the work of many other anthropologists, but I have steadfastly refused to commit myself to a single encompassing theory. If you do, it seems to me, you end up confirming your expectations, whereas, for me, the real reward lies in uncovering the *un*-expected.

How did you develop your interest in Maori issues?

Well, the roots of that go back to my childhood in Pukekohe. There was so much talk in newspapers and so on about the contemporary Maori situation and particularly about Maori migration to the city. It seemed to me that there was an awful lot of opinion floating around, but there wasn't really any solid grounding to back it up, because nobody had thought of talking to the people who were actually involved. I knew from my own background that there was a great deal of ignorance and misconceptions among *Pakeha* about Maori. For instance, in Pukekohe it was received wisdom that the workers on the market gardens were like flotsam and jetsam, rootless migrants who wandered from job to job. It was only years later that a colleague of mine, Bernie Kernot (1964), did research in Pukekohe and discovered that at least 50 per cent of the workers there were the descendants of the people who had been displaced by local land confiscations. There were all sorts of misunderstandings and I felt that it was important to get the views of the people themselves.

Your work challenged the prevalent assumption that the urban migration of Maori was a kind of an aimless drift, is that correct?

Yes. If there's one thing I'm proud of, it is being a major influence in banishing that word 'drift' from the New Zealand vocabulary [laughs]. That's why I called my book (1964) *A New Maori Migration,* because talking to the people themselves, both in the city and in one of the communities that they'd come from, I found they had perfectly rational reasons for moving into the city and these were much the same reasons that had brought rural workers into cities in Britain, brought British settlers to New Zealand, and brought their own Polynesian ancestors to Aotearoa. They came in search of a better quality of life and higher education for their children, and to escape from unemployment and lack of land. But there was also an element of adventurousness: people talked about the freedom, spreading their wings and escaping from small rural communities where everybody knows each other's business.

So your aim was to create a real empirical study of migration. Who would you say most influenced your interpretive framework?

I'm a fairly pragmatic, down-to-earth person. When I embarked on that early fieldwork, I just wanted to gather the facts, as it were, and counter what I saw as the misconceptions. With that end in mind, I think I owed most to Ralph Piddington, not for any urban theory – he had no experience of work in a city – but for his teaching on fieldwork method. He stressed respecting informants, establishing rapport and knowing who *you* are and how your strengths and weaknesses relate to the people you're talking to, being honest and upfront with them.

The other thing I learned from him was the importance of recognizing that everything in a social field is interconnected, so one of the basic tenets of fieldwork is to write everything down, even if it doesn't *appear* to be relevant at the time. So often he was proved right. Things I didn't deem relevant at the time later often proved to be the key to some puzzle. When I came to write up my PhD thesis in London, I'd mostly finished it when I realized that I really had to have some theory about urban migration in there. I scratched around and imported references to the work of the only urban theorists there were at that time: Louis Wirth, Robert Redfield and Oscar Lewis, Walter Goldschmidt and Sidney Mintz. Remember, this was the 1950s and anthropologists were only just starting to work in urban societies. Mostly I disagreed with the conclusions of the theorists I have just mentioned and argued that the Maori situation was quite different. Looking back now, in the light of what's happened since, perhaps I was overly optimistic, but at the time I was trying to *counter* the unduly negative representations that were around. I was aware that the receiving community (predominantly *Pakeha*) didn't make things easy for urban migrants, so that some of the problems that have arisen since are due to the tension between Maori and *Pakeha*. In my PhD thesis, and in my first book, *A New Maori Migration*, I focused on the positive aspects of the migration, but I did also draw some attention to the tensions that develop between urban migrants and their folk back home and to the tensions between migrants settling in the city and their *Pakeha* neighbours and employers. It was out of that situation that I became aware that you cannot separate Maori from the rest of New Zealand society; they're embedded *in* it. So I began to develop an interest in interaction across cultural boundaries.

One outcome of this was the notion of people 'talking past each other'. I first started to explore this idea when I came back from England, in 1961. My old friend Matiu Te Hau – who was a Maori adult education tutor – asked me to do four lectures on the theme of 'Maori society today' in the Northland town of Kaitaia. Now Kaitaia lies about sixteen kilometres from Kotare, the rural community where I'd done my research on the rural end of urban migration. My talk was held at the college there and a large number of Maori from Kotare came to listen. As he walked past me, one of them said – intentionally so that I would hear – 'just coming to hear what she's saying about us'. Now my main aim was to share with the *Pakeha* present in the room the knowledge that I'd gained in that community and to *generalize* from it, without identifying the specific place. The thing about university extension classes is, people come because they want to learn. So I had very receptive audiences for those lectures and I saw that there was a need and a thirst among the *Pakeha* for just *this sort* of knowledge.

The audience turned out to be pretty evenly split between Maori and *Pakeha*, pretty much fifty-fifty. So when I finished, I thought, with all these Maori heavyweights from Kotare present, I've done enough showing off [laughs]. When it came to discussion time, I said, 'Well look, we've got all these experts here. I'm going to toss the questions over to them'. Then I sat back and listened. I discovered that the *Pakeha* all asked really basic questions. These were people who had been to school with Maori, who'd worked with them, who'd employed them and had played rugby with them and were on first name terms. I sat there and listened while the Maori elders did *not* answer their questions, or at least, answered them at such a high level that they made no sense whatsoever to the questioners.

The Maori elders assumed that the *Pakeha* knew a lot more about Maori culture than they actually did. They'd been interacting at Maori gatherings – like weddings and at *tangi* (wakes) – so the Maori assumed that the *Pakeha* knew what a *hapu* (ambilineal descent group) was, what an *iwi* (tribe) was, and what a *mihi* (ceremonial speech of greeting) was about. But the *Pakeha* had seen these things through their own eyes and assumed that what they saw was the same as what they knew in their own experience. So when they asked what a *hapu* was and what it did, they really wanted to know. But the answer they got didn't enlighten them one little bit. One of the questions a *Pakeha* asked was, 'In the past, we heard a lot about the great Maori leaders like Sir Apirana Ngata, Princess Te Puea and Peter Buck. Where are the great Maori leaders today?' The implication was that there don't seem to be any. One of the Ngati Kahu elders stood up and he said, 'In the past, a kauri forest, in the present, a pine forest'. That was all he said. Then he sat down. Now that's a very extended metaphor that needs a great deal of unpacking. The way I've unpacked it is that a kauri forest is a mixed forest, with all sorts of trees. The kauri dominates the forest, overshadowing the other trees, which can't grow as high. In a pine forest, which is tended and periodically *thinned*, the trees all grow to the same height. That's one interpretation. You can interpret it in other ways. The speaker's words shed light on Maori understandings of leadership to those in the know, but they also alerted me to the Maori use of imagery and symbolism. However, they didn't make much sense to the *Pakeha* in the audience. And that's when I coined the term 'talking past each other'. I'm sure someone else must have coined the phrase 'Talking past each other', as it's such an obvious one. But that was the moment when the penny dropped for me.

The four lectures that I gave in Kaitaia grew into the ten lecture courses I gave while I was with University Extension. When Routledge and Kegan Paul approached me to write an introductory textbook for first-year students in their series Peoples of the World, I expanded these lectures further into a book *The Maoris of New Zealand,* which was published in 1967, after I moved to Wellington. But I was never happy with that book. Because it needed some historical background I had included three chapters which were simply a summary of received wisdom to date. And that was really not good enough, as there was no original thinking in them at all. There were also really important aspects of Maori culture that at that stage I wasn't competent to address.

So when it sold well enough for Routledge and Kegan Paul to approach me about a new edition, I suggested a revised edition including a lot of new material. During vacations I did more fieldwork and spent a lot of time with two very important Maori mentors. One was Wiremu Parker, who was Maori adult education tutor at Victoria. He was a Maori expert – one of those people I consider a true scholar – but he'd been stalled in that position for years, because he didn't have a degree. He loved to explain events from both the Maori point of view and the academic point of view and hold these two in tension. He was one of the most completely bicultural people I have known. The other mentor was Tawhao Tioke. He was a Presbyterian minister who had grown up in the Urewera mountain ranges, so he was a member of the Tuhoe *iwi* and had been tutored by his uncle, who was an expert in bush medicines. It was under Wiremu and Tawhao's tutelage that I developed an understanding of basic Maori concepts and values. And that was the time when all the 'talking past each other' stuff really came together. I began to realize how the miscommunication was not only *verbal*, but that it included a whole area of *non*-verbal forms of communication (Metge and Kinloch 1978).

For example: Maori use a quick up-and-down movement of both eyebrows as a way of recognizing someone across the room or across the street. It is a silent 'hello!' *Pakeha* don't 'see' this gesture and so miss the greeting, because we expect greetings to be verbalized. Then there is the difference in the way we use our eyes when talking to somebody. When I was a child my parents and teachers were always telling me 'Look at me when I'm talking to you!' But Maori children were taught it was rude to 'stare' at people, especially superiors. Maori adults – at least back in the seventies – would glance briefly at each other from time to time but let their eyes roam all over the place in-between. Then again, there is the question of how you show respect to your superiors. In those days – though perhaps not anymore – *Pakeha* did it by standing up when someone of status came into the room. Samoans did it – and still do it – by sitting down so that their heads are lower than the person they respect. Generations of Maori and Pacific Island children have got in trouble with *Pakeha* teachers for doing these things differently.

You've highlighted how the penny dropped and you realized that Maori and Pakeha were talking past each other. Were there any other key fieldwork encounters that resulted in similar moments of epiphany? What were your memorable 'aha' moments, or negative experiences that you learned from?

Oh, there were many such moments. You're going to have to stop me! A very memorable one is a story about an engagement party, which happened early in my research in Auckland. A lot my work in Auckland was carried out with women, because the men were all working – and usually working overtime, very long hours and often weekends. I'd been visiting a woman who had quite a big family. Her eldest was a girl in her late teens and the youngest were babies. I found they enjoyed my visits because I brought them a taste of the outside world. One Monday I visited this woman and, she said, 'Oh, we had an engagement party for Lousia on Saturday night'. And my immediate thought was, 'I thought we were good friends. Why wasn't I invited?' Then she started to tell me the whole story. She said, 'On Saturday morning Lousia's boyfriend's uncle rang to say they were coming to visit us at six o'clock that evening. He arrived with the boy's father and various other relatives. They came in and after the *mihi* (formal greetings), they said they'd come to ask for Louisa as a bride for their boy. They knew they'd been going together. My husband responded, we called in Louisa and asked if she was agreeable, she said yes, and so we then started to plan the wedding.'

I saw that this was very different from the 'engagement parties' that I knew about, which usually entailed the couple deciding to marry and then the girl's parents putting on a party at which it was formally announced. What I had uncovered was a *tomo*, the modern transformation of a traditional method of arranging marriages. This opened up a whole new field for me. It was definitely one of those 'aha' moments. But it also exemplified the issue of 'talking past each other' and the assumptions that, because we'd been speaking in English, the words meant the same thing to both of us.

One morning in Kotare I saw a woman standing on the front porch of the house next door, scolding her school-age daughter. It was the girl's attitude that caught my attention. She was standing two steps below her mother, with her head down, her shoulders hunched, a blank look on her face; she was 'not there' at all. Suddenly I realized that this was a case of *whakamaa*, something I had heard described but never seen – or, more probably, not recognized before. Now I know that *whakamaa* is a very complex phenomenon. It involves a combination of a frozen outward appearance with not one, but several inward feelings, ranging from shyness through embarrassment to shame and guilt. This glimpse of its embodiment started me asking questions about it. At first those I questioned said, 'Why do you want to know about that, there's nothing to say', but once they started recalling cases what I learnt was enough to fill a book (see Metge 1986).

As for the negative fieldwork experiences, they're the ones which, in the long run, prove to be particularly productive. In the early stages,

I was trying to work in the city where people lived much more isolated family lives than in the country: there was often no real community. I got a very good introduction to the central city through the good services of a Maori housing officer who introduced me to the Maori Women's Welfare League, which was conducting a housing survey. They made me an honorary Maori welfare officer, and I went round taking notes for the League members and the Welfare Officers working with them. I met and talked to a lot of people and asked if I could come back and see them later. Some welcomed me back and became good friends and very good informants, and some didn't. When I tried to extend the contacts to their neighbours, I struck some attitudes so hostile that I immediately backed off. I accepted that, as a fieldworker, you don't impose on people who don't want to interact. But it also taught me that there are a lot of Maori with very good reasons for being hostile to nosey parker *Pakeha.*

Another occasion I remember was around the time that I'd finished and was tidying up my work on urban migration. I was invited to share my ideas at a meeting of the Maori Section of the National Council of Churches, which was held on the Otiria Marae in Northland. After I'd finished speaking, Maharaia Winiata, who had just returned from doing his PhD on Maori leadership at Edinburgh University, stood up and challenged my right to study – or to come to any conclusions about – things Maori. I was totally knocked back, because we had been very good friends before he went to Edinburgh; sometimes I wonder what happened to him there. But then I felt a hand on my shoulder. It was Horiana Laughton, the wife of John Laughton, head of the Presbyterian Maori Mission. She said to me, and I can't remember whether it was in Maori or in English, 'You just sit there and leave this to me'. And she took up and defended both my right to study Maori issues and my conclusions. That was another 'aha' moment, as I learned that in the Maori world you don't defend yourself. If your cause is good, somebody else will do it. And if they don't do it, you'd better run away! [Laughing]

Unfortunately, that is exactly what subsequently happened to me. During the 1980s, when I had the Cook fellowship, I was interested in Maori methods of learning and teaching. It seemed to me that some of those methods were based on very different presumptions from those underpinning Western systems of education. This was the period when the *kohanga reo* (Maori language–focused early childhood education centres) were being established and the daughter of a very old friend, whom I'd known since her adolescence, was supervising a *kohanga reo* in Auckland. I was waiting for her to finish work and was going to drive her home, when a woman walked in. She was a well-known Maori activist in the 1970s at the forefront of the campaign to revitalize the Maori language. She saw me there and *immediately* ploughed into me, accusing me of building a career on the backs of Maori and making money out of them. In reality, the royalties from my books amount to peanuts and go into a special trust fund anyway [laughing]. But looking back now, I know where she was coming from. It was a phase many Maori went through and, quite honestly, one that they probably *had* to go through. But at the time it was very hurtful. What hurt most was when my friend, whom I'd been waiting for, didn't defend me [shakes her head]. That was a very low point. I took her home and then went to visit some old Maori friends and asked them, 'Do you feel that I've been exploiting you?' And their response was to put their arms around me and cuddle me. There's a wonderful Maori word, '*awhi*', which means 'to embrace' physically, but it also means to 'build up', to 'nurture' and 'care for'. So out of what was a devastating experience came one of the most reassuring experiences of my fieldwork.

But I also knew that all that I had written and produced had been done with the approval of the elders. In fact, many people, including Pei Te Hurinui, Matiu Te Hau, Wiremu Parker and Tawhao Tioke have said to me, '*You* can say things *to* Pakeha that we can't say – if we say them we'll be dismissed as self-serving'. So I've always seen part of my job as making *Pakeha* aware of how Maori feel and to act as a bridge between them.

Looking back over the course of your long career, how has your thinking about anthropology changed?

I was fortunate in that I didn't enter this profession with any great illusions. From the outset, I knew that this area was a minefield of misunderstanding, of totally different viewpoints and different judgements about what was *important*. I learned *in* the field that it *is* possible to establish good communication across cultural boundaries; that boundaries are in fact permeable and you can pass through them. I also learnt that people are people, and while I might have had some romantic ideas, I quickly discovered that there were Maori that didn't like me, and I learnt that there were Maori I didn't like either. There were also Maori whom I liked and learnt to love, and with whom I've kept up a rewarding exchange for over fifty years. For me, the essence of anthropology is that it's people to people, or as Maori put it, *kanohi ki kanohi* – face to face. There are aspects of anthropology where those face-to-face relationships are less central, as the discipline has always covered a very wide field. Even in my time there were people who were abstract thinkers, philosophers and theoreticians. I mean, I struggled with Meyer Fortes's (1945) *The Dynamics of Clanship*, and yet behind the theory there was always a personal interaction. One of the things about those early anthropologists was their endeavour to be as scientific as possible, so they tended to produce books out of which the personalities had been leached. They wrote books in which there were no personal names, for instance. Even women like Audrey Richards did it. I don't think there's a personal name anywhere in her books. I enjoyed her work for other reasons, but that really got under my skin. One reason why I was attracted to Raymond Firth was because he'd always introduce you to the people. He described the people in their setting, gave them names, talked about how they were related to each other, how they interacted and how their interactions changed over time.

Anthropology needs both its theoreticians and those more inclined towards personalized accounts. I noticed at the joint 2008 British, Australian and New Zealand ASA conference, in Auckland, that there are still people who live up there in the stratosphere, but there were also people primarily focused on personal interactions in the field. I really appreciated presentations by young anthropologists who went even further than I ever did. I went to a session where two young women talked about working as apprentice craftswomen, with Slovakian lace makers and Mongolian felt workers respectively. I'm glad to see that kind of very personal and close interaction is still happening in anthropology today.

So what for you are the most exciting developments within the discipline and what are your thoughts about the trajectory of anthropology in New Zealand?

I've been working outside the mainstream of anthropology for too long to be able to comment usefully on these issues. I must say I was mightily relieved to leave the university before post-modernism became such a dominant ideology, and I am relieved to hear that it is less popular now, because I had serious issues with its basic assumptions. When I attended the combined conference in 2008 I was heartened to find that anthropologists are still coming up with new theories and revised versions of some old ones. Kuhn dismissed the social sciences as pre-scientific because they had so many competing paradigms, but I have always thought that diversity of approach was one of anthropology's greatest strengths.

One development which rejoices my heart is the improvement in relations between anthropologists and historians. At least some of us are talking to each other, sharing subjects and methods. I think, for example, of anthropologist Anne Salmond's work on the early encounters between Maori and *Pakeha* and the award of the Elsdon Best Memorial Medal to historian Judith Binney for her work with the Tuhoe people of the Urewera's.

One of the most exciting developments of all is the increasing number of indigenous anthropologists, anthropologists from indigenous groups, who have acquired academic training and use it to look with fresh eyes at their own society. Some of them have realized that before they can do that, they have to look at a society other than their own to put their own into context. For me, *comparison* has always been at the root of anthropology, because we can't really know our own society until we have stepped right outside of it and into another. As Malinowski put it, we need to learn to look though the native's eyes, and then we bring that insight *back* to look at our own society. I am delighted to see some of the young Maori anthropologists like Marama Muru-Lanning and Margaret Kawharu who are doing just that.

I do, however, regret that there are so few *Pakeha* anthropologists working in the Maori field today. Looking back, it's interesting that those *Pakeha* who were already working on Maori issues were well entrenched and were able to continue researching through the 1980s thanks to the long-standing relationships we'd developed. The real problem was a spell of time during the early eighties when Maori were saying 'this is *our* field and only *we* can fully understand it, so keep out'. Young *Pakeha* anthropologists took that to heart, because it was expressed in pretty strong terms and most moved into other fields. But it's a pity that they didn't realize that this was just a necessary phase that Maori had to pass through. A hundred years of being on the receiving end, of being studied, of being *told* what was wrong (and what was right) with them understandably produced that kind of reaction from Maori. I know there are Maori scholars who have now moved way beyond that position, but the old tensions and divisions that occurred in the eighties do tend to linger on.

There is an even older problem that is still with us – that of employment. When I first started studying anthropology Professor Piddington warned me that he couldn't promise me a job in anthropology, and it took me fifteen years to achieve one. Today the vast majority of anthropology students end up in jobs for which anthropology is not a requirement. I don't get too upset about that, because they take the awareness awakened by anthropology out there into the wider world. I constantly run into people in all sorts of situations who tell me that 'anthropology changed my life, because it changed the way I see the world' and 'anthropology opened my eyes to other possibilities'. Anthropology is an excellent basis for doing almost anything, or at least any job that involves dealing with people. I am impressed by the number of anthropology graduates who are currently working as public servants, in local government and education, often in multidisciplinary teams and with responsibility for policy making. But I do worry about how easy it is for them to lose touch with other anthropologists and anthropological ways of thinking. I am proud of the Association of Social Anthropologists of Aotearoa/New Zealand, which has always opened its membership and conferences to nonuniversity anthropologists – but too often and too soon they stop coming. I think we could and should be more proactive in keeping in touch with people.

One of the pleasures of my (working) retirement has been enjoying social as well as academic interaction with young up-and-coming anthropologists. I am reassured that the future is in good hands.

References

Arensberg, C. M. and S. T. Kimball. 1940. *Family and Community in Ireland.* Cambridge, Mass: Harvard University Press.
Binney, J. 2009. *Encircled Lands: Te Urewera, 1820–1921.* Wellington, Bridget Williams Books.
Best, E. 1924. *The Maori* (2 vols.). Wellington: Polynesian Society Memoir Series no. 5.
Campbell, J. L. 1952 [1881]. *Poenamo: Sketches of the Early Days in New Zealand.* Christchurch: Whitcombe and Tombs Ltd.
Firth, R. 1929. *Primitive Economics of the New Zealand Maori.* London: George Routledge and Sons.
———. 1936. *We the Tikopia: A Sociological Study of Kinship in Primitive Polynesia.* London: Allen and Unwin.
Fortes, M. 1945. *The Dynamics of Clanship.* London/New York: Oxford University Press.
Kernot, C. B. J. 1964. *People of the Four Winds.* Wellington: Hicks Smith.
Lynd, R. S., and H. M. Lynd. 1929. *Middletown: A Study in Contemporary American Culture.* New York: Harcourt, Brace and Company.
Metge, J. 1964. *A New Maori Migration: Rural and Urban Relations in Northern New Zealand.* London: Athlone Press.
———. 1984. *Learning and Teaching: He Tikanga Maori.* Wellington: New Zealand Department of Education.

---. 1986. *In and Out of Touch: Whakamaa in Cross Cultural Context*. Wellington: Victoria University Press.
---. 1995. *New Growth from Old: The Whanau in the Modern World*. Wellington: Victoria University Press.
---. 2001. *Korero Tahi: Talking Together*. Auckland: Auckland University Press.
---. 2010. *Tuamaka: The Challenge of Difference in Aotearoa New Zealand*. Auckland: Auckland University Press.
Metge, J., and P. Kinloch. 1978. *Talking Past Each Other: Problems of Cross Cultural Communication*. Wellington: Victoria University Press.
Piddington, R. 1950. *An Introduction to Social Anthropology*, vol. 1. Lothian: Oliver and Boyd.
Salmond, Anne 1997. *Between Worlds: Early Exchanges between Maori and Europeans, 1773–1815*. Auckland: Viking.
Te Rangi Hiroa. 1950. *The Coming of the Maori*, second edition. Wellington: Maori Purposes Fund Board.
Tregear, Edward. 1904. *The Maori Race*. Wanganui: Archibald Dudingston Willis.
Warner, W. L. 1952. *Structure of American Life*. Edinburgh: Edinburgh University Press.

Notes

1. *Pakeha:* non-Maori New Zealanders, especially those of British ancestry. 'The *Pakeha* in power' is a phrase coined by Maori leader Sir Apirana Ngata.
2. Te Rangi Hiroa is also known as Peter Buck. He was for many years director of the Bernice P. Bishop Museum in Honolulu.
3. Jan Pouwer was an anthropologist for the Netherlands government in West Papua, from 1952 to 1962, and professor of anthropology at Victoria University of Wellington, from 1966 to 1976.
4. The Waitangi Tribunal is a commission of inquiry set up by an act of Parliament to hear claims by Maori against Crown action, past (since the Treaty of Waitangi, 1840), present or future.
5. *Mana* in this context can be defined as a quality that has a spiritual source and combines dignity, power and authority.
6. Ralph Piddington was professor of anthropology at the University of Auckland from 1950 to 1972.

Gillian Cowlishaw

Date of Birth: 19 December 1934

Place of Birth: Otakiri, Whakatane, New Zealand

PhD: 'Women's Realm: Socialisation, Sexuality and Reproduction in Aboriginal Society', University of Sydney, 1980.

Fieldwork: Australia: Northern Territory, Bourke, NSW and western Sydney.

Current affiliation: Professor of Anthropology, University of Sydney

Positions held: Gillian Cowlishaw received a Norman Haire Scholarship, 1976–78, from the University of Sydney. She subsequently lectured at Charles Sturt University, the Australian National University and the University of Sydney, between 1980 and 2000. She held an ARC Australian Professorial Fellowship at the University of Technology in Sydney, later transferring to the University of Sydney in 2009.

Major works
- 2009. *The City's Outback.* Sydney: UNSW Press. Shortlisted for Victoria Premier's Award, 2009.
- 2004. *Blackfellas, Whitefellas and the Hidden Injuries of Race.* Oxford: Blackwell Publishing. Winner of NSW Premier's Award, the Gleebook Prize for Critical Writing, 2005.
- 2000. *Love Against the Law: The Autobiographies of Tex and Nelly Camfoo.* Canberra: Aboriginal Studies Press.
- 1999. *Rednecks, Eggheads and Blackfellas: Racial Power and Intimacy in North Australia.* Sydney and Ann Arbor, Allen and Unwin with Michigan University Press.
- 1997, co-editor with B. Morris. *Race Matters: Indigenous Australians and 'Our' Society.* Canberra: Aboriginal Studies Press.
- 1988. *Black, White or Brindle: Race in Rural Australia.* Sydney/Cambridge: Cambridge University Press.

Chapter 4

'CULTURE', 'RACE' AND 'ME'
Living the Anthropology of Indigenous Australians
Gillian Cowlishaw

As an anthropologist you have worked extensively in the areas of Australian race relations and state definitions of what constitutes 'indigenous culture'. Tell us more about your interest in these areas.

I recently wrote a paper entitled 'Culture as Therapy', which examines the appropriation, or deployment, of indigenous culture by schools in New South Wales. It explores how current liberal and multicultural attempts to recognize and engage with indigenous people and 'their' cultures have played out in conditions where those cultures are virtually lost. This means that schools are attempting to recreate and reinvigorate cultural practices with which the children have a very questionable relationship. The relationship of their families to what is supposedly 'their' culture is also very *thin*, to say the least.

What has led me to examining this process of 'teaching the children their culture' is first the oddity of that notion. If it is 'their' culture, how come it has to be taught to them, and who can teach it, and what is 'it'? This concept of culture is clearly far from what anthropologists mean by a 'whole way of life', yet this is the popular concept used by Aborigines and others. Within state-produced discourses of improvement, 'culture' is frequently appealed to for its therapeutic value.

Second, sadly, there is a lot of tension around the question of who has authority over this culture. In western Sydney, where most people acknowledge that the Darug were the traditional owners, there is conflict about whether they 'have' culture. Further, some assert, 'We don't need culture, we need skills in the modern world'.

My paper touches on many elements of these conditions – cultural revival, symbolic recognition, state-sponsored culture, cultural brokers, all of which need to be understood as part of a governance that has emerged in a specific historical period dominated by liberal and neoliberal moral and political convictions.

Tell us more about your personal and intellectual biography and how you discovered anthropology

I grew up in a little dairy-farming area in Otakiri, New Zealand. It was very monocultural, except for the Maori communities that were located in specific places, at Te Teko and Matata. When I went to high school, there was a contingent of Maori boys on the long bus ride to Whakatane who were active and noisy, sitting in the back of the bus; they seemed quite daunting and 'other' to us – to use the contemporary terminology. But in those days they were considered subversive: they were great singers, played guitars, and were always in trouble with the authorities, and I found them very interesting. They liked to pronounce the name of the town, emphasizing the '*wh*' as '*f*' – "Fukatane". So that was my first brush with a cultural domain that was quite different from the rather restrained or repressed – and boring – cultural arena of dairy farming in New Zealand, where nobody sang songs, life was very nuclear family based, and there was very little sociality. I cannot recall anyone coming to our house for dinner, ever. My great intellectual excitement came from reading, and I read a great deal, mostly novels plus a little socialist literature. As soon as I was old enough, at seventeen, I left Otakiri to come to Auckland and go to the teachers' college in Mount Eden, just down the road from here. I subsequently went overseas, trying to discover where the real world was, believing it to be far away from my home.

By the time I went back to serious university study, I'd travelled widely, including through Russia and China, been married to an academic (a biochemist), had two children and lived in Singapore for three years. I'd always been a keen observer of the varieties of human ways of existing in this world, excited by 'otherness' and contrasts in assumptions about how the world works and differing ideologies and everyday practices. So when my children were in primary school I came back to university and studied psychology and anthropology, as well as linguistics. I found all of these subjects extremely interesting and complementary. But in-depth psychology and the philosophy of psychology were only a minor part of the psychology discipline, and the scientism in experimental psychology turned me right off. In contrast, anthropology stood out as the discipline that promised all kinds of understandings of the dramatically contrasting ways human beings conceive of and experience human existence, and how they arrange their affairs.

As a girl growing up in a small country town, were there any particular books or events that opened up your eyes to this sense of 'otherness' and other cultural worlds?

It was not a country town, but the country. Otakiri had one general grocery shop, a four-room primary school, and a hall. The farms were small, though, so I could ride my bike along the gravel roads to visit neighbouring kids.

I remember reading Dickens, Thackeray and others in my mother's rows of classics in the bookshelves, as well as some contemporary novelists. From my father I discovered the 'theory of surplus value' and was warned against 'the great man theory of history' in my mid-teens. Later, at Teachers College I think, I discovered Jean-Paul Sartre and the Russian novelists, which was very thrilling, and still later, some philosophers. I thought otherness was everywhere, *except Otakiri*. I wanted to be open to *other* people, more interesting ones, who led more exciting lives in worlds of ideas like those that my favourite novelists were dealing with.

This was the fifties, you know. One advantage of getting old, Cris, is, that one has one's own history to consider as a source of difference, too [smiling]. The different world I grew up in is *still* a source of contemplation and inspiration for me. When I say 'it was boring', in one sense it wasn't boring for a small child, because growing up on a farm is full of interest; we had a river, we had wild places we could go to. But as a *teenager* I had this sense of being in a very tight, closed and conventional world which I and other members of my family felt was like a prison, a prison of others' opinions and narrow moralism expressed in gossip. I was very conscious of the possibility of exploring the wide, varied and sophisticated world out there, but at that point, anthropology as an avenue for doing that wasn't yet known to me. It's not a subject that is well known in the public arena. Further, while my older brother went to university, I don't think I was expected to, and I had the romantic idea that I would 'learn from the world' rather than from academic books. That seems a bit childish now.

When I did get to university, my initial anthropological excitement came from intellectual and philosophical questions, grand ideas about how language works, how reason relates to emotion, what is human nature, how is individual will shaped by particular social circumstances, how are human hierarchies reproduced, and so on. Over time I became more of an ethnographer and more interested in the empirical detail that informs broader theory – or doesn't. I tend to resist or question theoretical abstractions, because they often seem to conveniently do away with the *complexity* and the *difficulty* of the actual empirical social situations that one studies.

As I progressed in my studies in anthropology, I realized that I couldn't go off and do extended fieldwork in exotic places, because I had young children. At that time I also had a kind of opposition to doing ethnographic fieldwork, because I felt either you would fall in love with the place and the people and want to stay there forever and become one of them, or else you'd dislike them and want to leave. The idea of living among people and studying them seemed very problematic to me. And it *is* problematic; maybe feeling a sense of discomfort is an important part of the practice of anthropology.

That is one theme of my latest book, *The City's Outback*, that follows my research project in the western suburbs of Sydney among suburban Aboriginal people. It was discomforting work, not because there were no 'exotic others', but because the conditions for reproducing any distinctive identity was absent and because these were poor suburban people who were at loggerheads with each other concerning their identity and authenticity. I've become interested in the role of the state in funding cultural activities and how that relates to reproducing 'a people'. But the main source of discomfort is one's research role. Some 'informants' want to join and enhance one's insights and others are suspicious or hostile, but also, one's loyalties are challenged in conditions where the people read and challenge one's writing. I found this difficult, but also very rewarding.

Tell us about your research interests, the way these have developed over the years and the general trajectory of your thinking?

As was typical in 1970s anthropology, my initial fieldwork focused on the radical alterity of indigenous people. With the help of my supervisor, Lester Hiatt, and following the advice of others, I went to a town called Katherine in the Northern Territory of Australia, and then 250 kilometres eastwards, to a remote community in southern Arnhem Land. My interest then was in gender relations in traditional Aboriginal society. The particular questions were about how women controlled fertility, and I was interested in childhood and the contrast between how children were raised in different social conditions. But when I arrived in the Northern Territory, what really hit me right in the face was the *dramatic* difference between the conditions of Aboriginals and white people. A little country town like Katherine was full of whites – the descendents of settlers of course – who owned the town in every sense. The Aboriginal people in the town, by contrast, didn't have the same relationship with the town; they weren't the owners, but somewhat unwelcome visitors in their own country. They seemed like shadow people, hanging around on the edges of white social life. They were always present but ignored, except as the subject of chronic complaints. When I went out to live in the bush with Aboriginal people, they expressed more of a sense of ownership; the sense of being at home in their own county was very evident. That was at Goinjimbi, otherwise known as Bulman. Even their embodied way of being in the landscape was dramatically different from when they were in the town; at home people were confident and in charge of their movements; in town they always seemed a little afraid, nervous, as if aware of a hidden hostility to their presence.

There were so many contrasts in their respective histories – or rather, in the ways indigenous people and white people understood the past, yet there was no popular or academic interest in this dramatic contrast. I was struck by the *racism*, and by that I mean the assumptions that all the white people in Katherine made about Aboriginal people. This was evident in relation to my research. For instance, the one question that I and other anthropologists were repeatedly asked by white people when they heard we worked among Aboriginal people was, 'what's the answer?' The assumption was always that Aboriginal people are *the* problem that is in need of *the* solution. That's what they were really asking – what is *the solution* [smiles]. Which meant, I think, how can we entice them to become more like us and stop disrupting our sense of normalcy. The way Aborigines were being 'othered' in public discourses made them out to be this terrible problem for the nation. I found that shocking, and while it didn't distract my focus away from my PhD research topic, it stayed with me as a puzzle that needed more from anthropology than merely distancing or disapproval.

So later on, after I had completed another research project in New South Wales, I went back to the Northern Territory and recorded more memories and read files in the archives and wrote a history of the culture clash in that Bulman community, one that focused on the Rembarrnga people in relation to white settlers, the pastoral industry, the government processes and the changing policies over the eighty odd years since whitefellas had appeared in their country and overrun it. That book was, *Rednecks, Eggheads and Blackfellas* (Cowlishaw 1999).

What influences at that time prompted you to choose that particular field site?

It came out of my interests in gender and Aboriginal traditions. Much of my education at Sydney University had been very traditionalist. My supervisor, Les Hiatt, was primarily concerned with the question of 'how do we understand these specifically indigenous traditions and the lives of individual human beings in these circumstances?' There had been other courses on race relations and on how indigenous people had engaged with the state, but that wasn't the focus of my PhD research. Also, there was definitely a hierarchy of field sites in Australia: the more traditional and the more remote, the higher the status of the work carried out there. Perhaps I accepted that hierarchy to some extent, but mostly I was intrigued by how gender relations differed so much in different kinds of society. My imagination was caught particularly by the girls and women I got to know in Arnhem Land.

It was only later that I decided to concentrate on the engagement of indigenous people with the state and their experiences with whitefellas over the years of settlement.

Most anthropologists, when they recount their experience, can point to one or two revelatory moments during fieldwork. Where there any such moments for you?

There are an immense number [laughs]. It's hard to put my finger on any *one*. However, here is one outstanding occasion from 1975. I was sitting with a group of Aboriginal people – black-skinned people on the grassy green median strip in the centre of Katherine. I was wearing an Indian-patterned cotton dress and a group of very white English tourists came up to me and asked me, 'Is that material of your dress made by these native people?' They were speaking to me as if the Aborigines weren't even there. And that was a very common experience for Aboriginal people; they were under the radar of white consciousness, or rather, they were *objects* of white consciousness, there, but not as companions or friends or even equal human beings.

Another moment in 1975 was rather more painful. I had been living with people in what had been an old mining encampment composed of a couple of tin shacks and a few huts with canvas shades to extend them. I was living in one of these little huts and one of the men there – a senior man in the community – was of mixed race; he had a Chinese father and an Aboriginal mother and had therefore been classified as non-Aboriginal for years. Because he wasn't fully

Aboriginal, he had been classified as 'European', even though he had *no* European heritage. Now, he liked drink and had been allowed to drink in the period when it was prohibited for Aboriginal people, because he was not classified as Aboriginal. One night he got drunk soon after I arrived. He had already decided some years before, that anthropologists were the enemy of the Aborigines, and he began to pace around outside my hut saying, 'What's this white woman doing here? She's an anthropologist – she'll steal your knowledge'. I can't remember his exact words, but the message was 'She'll do bad things by you'. He was swearing and shouting and of course I was extremely upset. I hadn't been there more than three weeks and had just begun to feel comfortable and welcome. Then his wife, Nelly, who was one of the senior women in the community, said to me, 'Come on *bunji*, grab your swag and get in your truck'. She came with me and directed me and we drove off out of the community and camped in the bush. She was supporting me against her husband – who was having one of his raves. She said, 'Oh it's all right, Tex gets drunk. He always does things like that.' But what that revealed to me was the depth of his own painful history of having been identified as European and yet his loyalty was to the Aboriginal community with whom he'd always identified and lived among. That was one of the *many* moments that illustrated the disrupted and complicated history of engagement between Aboriginal people and the European world. There is a major disjuncture between the two worlds, and yet Aboriginal life became entwined and enmeshed with the practices of the state and white society's hierarchical social arrangements.

I should add that Tex Camfoo subsequently became a good friend, and I recorded and published the story of him and his wife in a book called *Love Against the Law* (Cowlishaw 2000).

Were there any notable mistakes or blunders in your fieldwork which imparted important lessons to you?

We all make thousands of mistakes. It wasn't exactly a *mistake*, but I wished I had stayed longer at Bulman. I couldn't, because of my children. There are things in your personal life that can make it difficult to follow the course one might otherwise have chosen. I could have gone back there and followed the trajectory of the community further, but I became caught up in a different kind of research in New South Wales.

After writing my PhD thesis, I went to teach in a small regional college, later Charles Sturt University, in New South Wales. I realized that I knew nothing about the indigenous people in my own state. The country students I was teaching, though, knew a lot about the different kinds of Aborigines with a very different history from Arnhem Land people.

It is clear that anthropology's major mistake has been to think – like the nation itself – that 'real' Aborigines live in the north of the continent. That is an old myth that anthropologists have been trying to live down, but nonetheless most ethnography of Aboriginal Australia is still done in the north, among people who have a distinctive language and ceremonial life and are not what is known as 'mixed race'. Although no one uses that language of race now, skin colour remains a hidden marker of authenticity. As a result, those Aboriginal people in New South Wales, for instance, in country towns – who have been known as Aboriginal for as long as anyone can remember – get left out of anthropological research.

Now, when I went to teach in a country university in 1980, I decided that I needed to do research in New South Wales, and that's how I came to do this other body of work, which is concerned with the conditions and identities and relationships in communities that do not have 'traditional' knowledge, language or ceremonial life. Their land was lost early, around the 1850s in Bourke, and everyone is 'mixed race', and virtually no one speaks a traditional language. The reasons anthropologists don't take any serious interest in such people says a lot about where Australian anthropology sees 'culture' and about Australian anthropologists' rejection of history. Perhaps my big mistake was not going to New South Wales first [laughs] instead of doing a classical ethnography in the Northern Territory. Today, my real interest is in *changing* conditions of Aboriginal peoples and the nature of Aboriginal engagement with civil society, co-option by state structure and incorporation in the nation's imaginative self-image.

What for you are the most exciting areas, or cutting edges, of the discipline or the most interesting interfaces between anthropology and other disciplines?

I'll speak about Australia, because I know the situation here best. I know there are echoes of these themes elsewhere, but in Australia, one striking phenomenon is the way public interest in the indigenous people operates differently from interest in other minority groups. Other possible anthropological questions, such as how other cultural minorities fare in a liberal and self-proclaimed multicultural society, tend to be seen as sociological and seldom attract ethnographers or antrhopological analysis.

There's a lot of media attention paid to Aboriginality, to indigeneity and to the problems of remote indigenous communities. Resources are made available to support – or we might say 'reinvent' – Aboriginal cultural knowledge. Academics who take an interest in Aborigines since the post-1970s era of self-determination include historians, cultural-studies students and lawyers. All these disciplines now have branches devoted to studies of indigenous issues. Anthropology has almost retreated into focusing on the classical traditions of Aboriginality, whereas cultural studies took up a critique of anthropology and ethnography, and, more recently, takes an interest in the nation's relationship to Aboriginality; mostly such work analyzes discourses, texts and representations rather than getting close to any actual people. Historians' interest in the past means they see themselves as the major player in Aboriginal studies. There are, of course, far more historians than anthropologists, but also because there has been a passionate interest in Australia's past in the 1980s and '90s, and in rewriting our history to include indigenous peoples within the story of the Australian nation, which is always the story of primary interest, indeed the master narrative. There is some rivalry between these three disciplines. If only anthropology was more engaged with relevant contemporary social theory, it would be a stronger player in illuminating indigenous issues – for instance theories of governance, of state structures and of relationships in a hierarchical nation. Anthropology's strength is its being wedded to *fieldwork*, which enables direct engagement with the conditions among indigenous people and how these are experienced and interpreted by those who live these conditions. That is, rather than looking at the past through texts – as historians do – or analyzing contemporary texts – as cultural-studies academics do, the anthropologists can, potentially at least, achieve a more complex understanding from a position outside that of the liberal good citizen.

This sounds as though you're lamenting the fact that anthropology doesn't enjoy a higher profile in Australia. What is the status of the discipline there?

It's rather complex now, because it's a small discipline, but it is now best known through the anthropological knowledge being called upon in the courts for native title claims. These tend to reemphasize anthropology's anchorage in traditional cultural forms, or what I call 'classical culture', which eclipses significant contemporary studies of conditions among the more numerous Aboriginal groups in city environments. Classical forms of Aboriginal culture are continually called upon to demonstrate Aboriginal peoples' enduring connections with the land in support of native title and other land claims. In doing this, anthropology is reinforcing the old perception that indigenous people are only connected to the past, that their authentic claims to Aboriginality rely on those connections. And that perception is still expressed, by implication at least, in the work of many anthropologists.

Now, we don't do that in studies, for instance, of Italian migrants in Australia. We don't assume that their authenticity comes from Italy [smiling]. They're allowed to be modern and allowed to be part of the contemporary Australian nation. Whereas with Aborigines, there is this tendency to grant them the right to be Aboriginal only insofar as they can demonstrate an authenticity that relates them to traditional culture. And Aboriginal people in urban Australia are taking that up to some extent themselves. Although some are battling against 'culturalism', it's an area of *hot* dispute. But for many Aboriginal people, claims to be the 'traditional owners' under state's legislation or to practice native title are problematic, particularly in an urban area where there is very, very *sparse* knowledge of the history of a particular community and often very, very broken, disrupted community and family histories.

Why is that? Is this the fault of anthropologists or does it relate to the land-claim process?

Aboriginal people's double bind in relation to becoming modern citizens and retaining Aboriginal identity is an old and well-recognized one, but it is exacerbated by the land-claim process. But anthropologists have done little to undermine the popular understandings of 'culture' that exacerbates the condition. It's popularly thought that Aboriginal people who 'have culture' have something ancient and unchanging, related to iconic symbols such as boomerangs, dot painting, or performing kangaroo dances with body paint on. So I have suburban schoolteachers in western Sydney *telling* me, 'These people have forgotten what their totems are so we have to rediscover them and revive their language'. There are now programmes that try and help urban Aboriginal people to revive old languages, and this can be thrilling for many people. But some indigenous people find the iconic symbols of Aboriginal culture irrelevant to their lives. Some say, 'We don't want that "culture", we want to be modern urban people like everybody else' [smiles]. But it's a very contentious issue among indigenous people. Also contentious is the question of who has authority over elements of culture in areas where social destruction was extensive (see Cowlishaw 2010).

So are anthropologists in Australia being cast in a role as custodians of traditional Aboriginal culture?

In many cases they appear to accept that role. There is a conventional view among anthropologists that we must take account of history and we must deal with people as they are today. The anthropological idea of culture as a whole way of life does not rely on connections to iconic forms that may have been important to a particular group in the past. Culture is as people live it in the everyday, although the surface manifestations are clues to enduring values and social forms. But anthropology struggles with the Aboriginal present, because the expertise in a particular language, traditional rituals, or art forms – as Howard Morphy's work shows us – represents valuable, unique and endangered forms of knowledge. My question would be, do people like the Yolngu want to *always* be identified *only* with that knowledge? Are young people given space to be something else? And further, what role do white fantasies of ancient traditions play in the attempts to preserve or revive specific forms we call 'cultural', while we make other practices impossible to continue. I think everybody would admit that even the most remote and traditional people *also* want to be identified with other things in the contemporary world. How we, as anthropologists, deal with that is a difficult question and one on which anthropologists hold different views in the face of the national panic about Aboriginal community conditions. Anthropologists have seemed complicit in the common assumption that Aboriginal culture is to blame for destructiveness and violence that has sometimes emerged in remote communities.

You mentioned that anthropological research in Australia is often politically contentious. What contribution has your own work made to wider public debates?

My first book, which was about a country town in New South Wales, was specifically a study of race relations (Cowlishaw 1988). I did the research in Bourke, a town that had a reputation for racial tension. There had been public disorder, riots and fights with police that had hit the newspaper headlines. The Aboriginal people in that area were known to be 'troublesome' and a terrible threat to public order, at least in the public eye [smiles]. Popular views were divided between condemnation or sympathy. They were poor and therefore relatively powerless, so why, I wondered, were they seen to constitute such a threat to the local white population? That was the question that the public panic about the situations in these towns on the Darling River raised for me.

Thus I was interested in the whole relationship between Aboriginal and white people in country towns where the Aboriginals were a substantial minority, a quarter of the population in Bourke. In my work I tried to show the history of the intense emotion vested in racial identities and how the progressive policies in the 1970s, aimed at assisting Aborigines with education and housing, had disturbed the old pattern of race relations as it had developed over the previous hundred years. In the past, most of the indigenous people had been employed on pastoral stations, and a stable relationship with the white people had developed. But then all that work disappeared, and new government policies to assist Aboriginal people with things like housing, health and education had created a great deal of resentment. They had also shifted the ambitions and aspirations of indigenous people. There was a lot more anger expressed over past injustices as a result of recognizing Aboriginal rights and providing forums for Aboriginal expression.

How was work on this received? What, for example, has been the public or government response to your 2004 book, Blackfellas, Whitefellas and the Hidden Injuries of Race?

I don't think the government reads anthropological texts, actually [laughing]. *Blackfellas, Whitefellas* sold well and is used in university courses, but I'd be doubtful that it has directly influenced any policy makers. That is not the way things work. Although I've always tried to write for a wider public, my books are not popular works, though they do reach the so-called 'educated public' to some extent.

The responses to my two books on Bourke from social-science readers has mostly been great, except for a number of anthropologists who disapprove. This is because I am attempting to analyze and thus legitimize – and even celebrate – a social realm that is generally treated with disapproval or distaste. I mean the more disruptive, resistant and challenging aspects of Aboriginal social life. The notion of resistance became overused and devalued, so nothing like resistance is analyzed by anthropologists. This leaves ideas of dysfunction or social pathology in place as the broad context within which Aborigines are conceptualized. My fieldwork showed me an active, often angry, quite destructive – but also a thinking – population who were responding to specific forms of governance. I was surprised how challenging some of my colleagues find these ideas. The term 'oppositional culture' that I used in my first book on Bourke was even said to be dangerous! I think we need to look further than the public stereotypes that function to delegitimize Aboriginal activities.

I hope I live long enough to write two further books, one of which would be about childhood. Core values and habits that make for embedded cultural differences are learned in childhood through different ways of raising children and different parental practices. The ways that children experience other people and the world are crucial, and parental practices also provide insights into social relations between dominant and subordinate social groups. Disapproval of Aboriginal child-rearing is commonly expressed in Australia, even by some anthropologists. Then I've got ideas for another work about the nation's obsessive anxiety about Aboriginal people and the response of indigenous intellectuals to the current political conditions, especially artists who make some of the most incisive comments.

A final question: what do you see as the future of anthropology?

If anthropologists widened our horizons, there might be more hope. There are many forms of anthropological research that do not attract attention in Australia, such as how corporate cultures operate or how Australia's cultural hierarchy is reproduced over time. 'Class' seems to have lost its analytic appeal. 'Popular culture' does not attract in-depth ethnographers but is left to the speculations of cultural-studies scholars. The same is true of youth cultures; for instance, body imaging and anorexia and such like that are sources of anxiety for many, would merit some grounded in-depth research. And violence is eschewed, as if 'not very nice'; I sometimes feel I never left Otakiri!

I think anthropology's going to come into its own. That is wishful thinking, of course, but it seems to me that there is a greater recognition throughout the *world* that we need some different values to sustain this world. Perhaps anthropology could be a part of a resurgence of intellectual appreciation of the *value* of different understandings of the human condition – the old romance of less materialistic cultural traditions! It is certainly being recognized that diversity is a value that the world should appreciate and foster. Yet this 'diversity' has become fashionable, and certain kinds of anthropological work may simply give succour to the forces of capitalism and neoliberalism that want to capitalize on difference. I am thinking of the cosmetic companies and others that employ anthropologists to assist them in producing and marketing suitable products for countries with resurgent economies. Rather than crushing and eliminating 'cultural' differences, they are being colonized, domesticated, neutralized as sources of insight into some other, better, ways of living socially in this world.

Ideally, a more robust anthropology could produce insights into some of the worst conflicts in the world, to understand, for instance, why people are willing to die for their beliefs. And how forms of power are connived in our everyday lives in the comfortable and complacent West – as Povinelli (2006: 10) said, 'when we seem to be doing nothing more than kissing our lovers goodbye as we leave for the day'. I've often thought we need anthropological analysis of the West, of 'us' in relation to the others we usually focus on.

I'd like to see some analytic work on the more pressing or violent engagements, for instance, in the Middle East or with Islamic peoples who are widely *seen* as problematic in ways that are quite mythic and exaggerated. The vulnerability of audiences to the forms of knowledge produced by news broadcasts also intrigues me; the framing of public knowledge, the things we all know to know, could do with some anthropological analysis.

I think I am becoming somewhat fanciful here. And verbose. And I'll finish by observing that there is wonderful intellectual work conducted in other disciplines. Anthropology does seem to me, potentially, especially profound. But like all human endeavours, it seldom reaches its full potential.

References

Cowlishaw, G. 1988. *Black, White or Brindle: Race in Rural Australia*. Sydney/Cambridge: Cambridge University Press.
———. 1999. *Rednecks, Eggheads and Blackfellas: Racial Power and Intimacy in North Australia*. Sydney and Ann Arbor, Allen and Unwin with Michigan University Press.
———. 2000. *Love Against the Law: The Autobiographies of Tex and Nellie Camfoo*. Canberra: Aboriginal Studies Press.
———. 2004. *Blackfellas, Whitefellas and the Hidden Injuries of Race*. Oxford: Blackwell Publishing.
———. 2009. *The City's Outback*. Sydney: UNSW Press.
———. 2010. 'Mythologizing Culture 1: Desiring Aboriginality in the Suburbs'. *The Australian Journal of Anthropology* 21(2): 208–27.
Povinelli, E. 2006. *The Empire of Love: Toward a Theory of Intimacy, Genealogy and Carnality*. Durham/London: Duke University Press.

Nicolas Peterson

Date of Birth: 1941
Place of Birth: London, England
PhD: 'The Structure of Two Aboriginal Ecosystems',1972, University of Sydney

Fieldwork: Australia

Current affiliation: Professor of Anthropology, School of Archaeology and Anthropology at the Australian National University.

Positions held: Peterson's first academic post was as a research fellow in the Department of Anthropology at the Research School of Pacific Studies, the Australian National University (1971–75). Since 1976 he has worked in the School of Archaeology and Anthropology at the Australian National University.

Major works
- 2008, co-editor with L. Allen and L. Hamby. *The Makers and Making of Indigenous Australian Museum Collections.* Melbourne: Melbourne University Press.
- 2003, co-editor with C. Pinney. *Photography's Other Histories.* Durham/ London: Duke University Press.
- 2003, co-author with J. Taylor. 'The Modernising of the Indigenous Domestic Moral Economy: Kinship, Accumulation and Household Composition'. *The Asia Pacific Journal of Anthropology* 4(1 and 2): 105–22.
- 1998, co-editor with B. Rigsby. *Customary Marine Tenure in Australia.* Sydney: The University of Sydney, Oceania Monograph No. 48.
- 1998, co-editor with W. Sanders. *Citizenship and Indigenous Australians: Changing Conceptions and Possibilities.* Cambridge: Cambridge University Press.
- 1993. 'Demand Sharing: Reciprocity and the Pressure for Generosity among Foragers'. *American Anthropologist* 95(4): 860–874.
- 1991, co-editor with T. Matsuyama. *Cash, Commoditisation and Changing Foragers.* Osaka: National Museum of Ethnology, Senri Ethnological Studies No. 30.
- 1986, in collaboration with J. Long. *Aboriginal Territorial Organization: A Band Perspective.* Sydney: The University of Sydney, Oceania Monograph No. 30.
- 1983, co-editor with M. Langton. *Aborigines, Land and Land Rights.* Canberra: Australian Institute of Aboriginal Studies.

Chapter 5

FINDING ONE'S WAY IN ARNHEM LAND
Nicolas Peterson

You are particularly well known for your studies of Aboriginal peoples in Arnhem Land, in northern Australia. Tell us more about your fieldwork and research in this area.

I spent nine months living and hunting with Aboriginal people in Arnhem Land, in the late 1960s, at a time when most Aboriginal people had left the bush. I was privileged to have that experience of living in the bush with Aboriginal people: it fuelled my interest in how people relate to land. Of course, the issue of people's relationships to land has long been an issue of major theoretical significance in Australia. However, in the land-rights era it also raises wider questions of people's economic and religious rights and in what sense hunter-gatherers can be said to own land. I became very involved in all of that initially at the theoretical level, but then more pragmatically in 1973, when I was invited to be the research officer to the Royal Commission into Aboriginal Land Rights. With Mr Justice Woodward, the commissioner, I went round the Northern Territory, interviewing Aboriginal people in communities about how their rights in land might be recognized under Australian law. It wasn't a question of *whether* they should be recognized, but *how*, given that the government had already taken the policy decision to recognize them. As a result, I've done a great deal of work on Aboriginal land and native title claims. I should emphasize that land claims are recognized under *statutory* legislation and are therefore very different from the common-law rights of native title that arrived with the 1992 *Mabo v. Queensland* court ruling.[1]

Statutory rights can be much better than common-law rights if the Parliament is in a generous mood, as they were in passing the Aboriginal Land Rights (Northern Territory) Act 1976, based on the work of the Royal Commission (Peterson 2010a). I subsequently worked on preparing a number of land claims under that legislation. It was an absolutely wonderful experience for all of us who were lucky enough to be involved, as it entailed detailed mapping of remote areas in which the people had lived when they were young. Later on, with Dr Devitt, I prepared the anthropological evidence for the test case for whether Aboriginal people had native title rights in the sea that could be recognized by Australian law. This is known as the *Yarmirr* case, or more popularly as the Croker Island case, which occurred in the late 1990s. Aboriginal sea tenure had barely been investigated before this (Peterson and Rigsby 1998; Peterson 2005a). Nonexclusive rights were recognized.

Take us back to the beginning of your career. Few people study anthropology at school, because it's not usually offered in the school curriculum. How did you discover anthropology?

I grew up as an outsider, in a settlement in the East End of London. During the nineteenth century the middle classes in Britain became increasingly concerned about the conditions of the working class, and as a result the greater public schools and universities established social and philanthropic settlements throughout London's East End. There were quite a few of these, including the Eton Mission, Cambridge House, Oxford House and Toynbee Hall – which became quite famous as a result of Christine Keeler and the Profumo affair. My father was warden of one of such settlement. It was a large institution divided into three parts. The central part, which was the house I grew up in, was also used by him to teach medical students about the social implications of medical practice. He was doing this very early on, right back in the 1950s, so that middle class students at St Bartholomew's Hospital all took a course that combined a seminar with internships with East End medical practitioners to alert them to how their decisions as general practitioners could affect the everyday lives of working class families. Our settlement also ran clubs for young working-class people to come to after work. They had to spend at least two hours doing something 'self-improving', like art, craft, boxing and all the rest of it, and then they could spend a couple of hours socializing and dancing. The third component was the Institute of Community Studies, which became very well known in Great Britain. It was run by British sociologists Michael Young and Peter Willmott. As a boy, every day that I was at home I'd have lunch with them and a number of other sociologists and intellectuals from across the British Commonwealth. These people, and many others, would be floating through our house, because of my father's work for the British Council. So from a very young age I was fascinated by what I learned from them about other people's ways of life.

Another factor, I guess, was that I've always liked the outdoors. I went to a boarding school that was in the country, and it gave me a lot of freedom to ride horses and explore the countryside at the weekends. Anthropology appealed to me as an 'outdoor activity' [laughs]. It sounded like a job in which you would take off to exciting places, get involved in other people's lives and learn about how they made out. Before I went to university I spent time in what was then Rhodesia, working as an African farm labourer on St Faith's Mission farm, leading buffalo around the field by a nose ring, ploughing a field for hours on end. What I learnt was how tough rural work is and why everybody flees to the city at the very first opportunity. I also spent time living with the Sami in Finnish Lapland, as a guest of the director of social services for the Sami.

When did you actually stumble upon anthropology as a subject to study or as a profession you thought of pursuing?

I think I only confronted it as a profession after university. I did it just out of interest at university, but I never actually intended to *be* an anthropologist. I wanted to go into something much more 'applied'. For various reasons, I took a year off after graduating and I travelled overland to Australia. Just as I was about to leave Australia, I saw an advertisement: 'Anthropologist wanted by the Australian Institute of Aboriginal Studies to make films recording men's sacred ceremonies in the Northern Territory'. Well that sounded like good fun. I was probably the only person who applied for the job. I thought it would be an adventure – and it was. With Roger Sandall, the institute's film director, I worked on ten films, gaining instant access to the most esoteric aspects of Aboriginal religious life. Hardly anybody has seen the films in the last thirty years, because since they deal with restricted ceremonies they are locked away, but one day they will be rediscovered as great treasures of Aboriginal cultural heritage. However, it was as a result of working on these films that I ended up doing a PhD. The institute knew very little about filmmaking, and did not realize that after two months of filming, Roger had enough material to edit and to keep him busy for the rest of the year. They didn't know what to do with me, so I said I would like to do a PhD, which was agreed to, provided I would be available to work on films when needed.

Reflecting back to the time when you first saw this job advert, how has your thinking about anthropology changed?

It's changed a great deal. I probably started out with what would today be seen as a less acceptable attitude: I gave no second thoughts to just rolling up and asking people if they would let me into their lives, and I was unconcerned that my pure research interests had no obvious spin-off for the people. Of course, I always accepted that people had the right to say no. Today, students are very concerned with the issue of, 'by what right am I carrying out this research?' And 'what right have I got to intrude into their lives?' I've always felt strongly about the agency of the people on the other end. One doesn't have a *right* to intrude, but one shouldn't be worried about turning up and asking people if you can get involved in their lives, because nine times out of ten they're very welcoming, and they can say no or ignore you if they want to. People in smaller-scale societies are much more 'people oriented'. In our own society we grow up in a nuclear household, in our own separate house with separate bedrooms, and often spend a lot of time alone. But most of the people that anthropologists work with live in situations of much denser sociality and are therefore much more tolerant of having people around.

Tell us about your main research areas and how these have developed?

My training at Cambridge was very 'structural-functionalist', despite having Edmund Leach as my tutor, and we were given no practical training in fieldwork. That was the British system of 'sink or swim'. I hadn't actually intended to *be* an anthropologist, but I became increasingly taken both by the bush and by the idea that there were still a number of Aboriginal people in northern Australia who, although in contact with Europeans, were largely self-sufficient. During my first fieldwork I took up residence with sixty or so people living in two bands on the southeastern fringe of the huge Arafura Swamp in Arnhem Land. There were no roads, but once every three weeks the Reverend Shepherdson would fly in to a small airstrip the people had cleared and stay for an hour, holding a short service, bringing with him some flour, sugar, tea, jam and tobacco, and take anybody who was sick back to the Galiwinku mission for treatment. Apart from that, the people were basically self-supporting for eighteen days out of every twenty-one. This appealed not only to my love of the outdoors but also to my fascination with how people get by. I spent nine months hunting, gathering and fishing with these people. That forced me to get interested in ecology. I was largely self-taught, but my interests coincided with the rise of cultural ecology and Roy Rappaport's work in New Guinea. Subsequently I became even more grounded through the influence of neo-Marxists. But I've never been addicted to ideologies or to particular 'schools' of anthropology. I am fairly grounded, and my thinking has been shaped by structural functionalism, cultural ecology, neo-Marxism and now a healthy eclecticism – which I think typifies anthropology more generally.

Were there any books or authors that had a particularly important influence on you?

At that stage it was *Pigs for the Ancestors* (Rappaport 1968). Having been trained in the school of structural functionalism, which really didn't provide any causal explanations or effective accounts of *why* people had the kinds of institutions they did, *Pigs for the Ancestors* had a 'wow' factor. It brought in the environment as a cause, not in an environmentally deterministic way, but nor, as we came to see, in a particularly sophisticated way either, but it was a liberating leap forward at that time. *Stone Age Economics* (Sahlins 1972) was another influential work at that time and helped consolidate a theoretical move to the mid-Atlantic, something that was going on generally in Australia as links with Britain weakened and as a number of Americans took up jobs here, including Roger Keesing and Jim Fox.

Going back to your fieldwork experience, you said that the methods training you received was virtually zero. What sort of fieldwork training did you receive at Cambridge? Can you be more precise?

None. Absolutely nothing. But in their defence, I should say that doing an undergraduate degree, even in anthropology, was really part of a liberal arts education as much as a vocational training. In fact, I remember embarrassing Meyer Fortes quite considerably. Rather unexpectedly, he came to my rooms in King's with a visitor – I don't even know who the visitor was, but it was some famous international anthropologist – and they asked me a few questions. I think they chose me just because I was available and Fortes knew where my rooms were – and he knew I'd been to Rhodesia and Lapland, so he thought I'd be able to satisfy him on various accounts. He asked me, had I taken any genealogies? I said, 'No.' And he said, 'Oh, well, weren't you trained to take any?' And I said, 'No.' And that caused considerable embarrassment, and at that point the visit was terminated and he left [smiling].

Were there any turning points, key experiences or moments of epiphany for you during your fieldwork?

I had a small one recently while looking through some of Donald Thomson's Arnhem Land photographs taken in the 1930s, when people were living without clothing and independently. Students reading about Aboriginal conception beliefs often ask why Arnhem Land women say that they conceive through the soles of their feet. I have had no real answer to that except to say that it fits with denial of the male role in procreation by implicating the part of the body as far away from the vagina as possible. But I suddenly realized how wrong I was: here was an image of an unclothed woman weaving a bag, sitting with the sole of her right foot against her vulva, as modesty requires. So soles of the feet add a further twist to the whole controversy.

There were some moments of epiphany in the desert. I remember having one which gave me insight into one of the puzzles of ceremonial organization, which underlines a common experience we all have as lecturers. It took anthropologists, collectively, something like forty years, or even longer, to fully understand the nature of the 'ritual manager' role in Central Australian ceremonial life. We now have a pretty good understanding, which I can impart to a student in ten or fifteen minutes, so it is very difficult for students to see the huge intellectual struggle that Fred Myers, Mervyn Meggitt, Howard and Frances Morphy, myself and a host of other anthropologists had to reach what now seems like something pretty obvious.

My epiphany in relationship to this managerial relationship was this. I'd been to see an elderly man, Mick, who'd taken me to see his 'ritual manager' – that is, a person from the opposite patrilineal moiety, whose presence was essential for him when he was holding ceremonies. Mick said, 'Very important this man, he knows everything' and 'He makes sure I do everything correctly'. That was no different from what I expected and was well known. But when I came back two years later, I asked Mick how his ritual manager was, and he said, 'We don't have any'. This was very strange, as every desert ceremony is dependent on ritual managers. 'What happened to the old man who you told me was your ritual manager?' I asked. Mick replied, 'Oh, there aren't any ritual managers.' It was then that I realized what was going on and that there were *two* quite different kinds of managers – those who were '*labourers*' and who were obliged to do the work of getting a ceremonial ground ready, decorating the performers and organizing the ceremony, who were usually kin of the ZS, ZH/WB, or FZS category, and then there could be another category of people who were the, the *keepers* of the knowledge and might not be close relatives at all. With the death of the elderly keeper of the knowledge, Mick was claiming that nobody knew more than him; it was a measure of his absolute ceremonial dominance.

Of course, he was still dependent on junior ritual managers for staging his ceremonies, but he himself was, unusually, the ultimate unchallengeable authority. All this ties in with the large age difference at marriage, which often skews the transmission of knowledge down the patriline, as fathers are so much older than their children that they are not infrequently dead before they have passed on everything to their sons.

People often say that we learn more from our mistakes than our successes. What were the fieldwork mistakes that have taught you most?

Oh, there were multiple mistakes. The first one was getting lost in the bush. Actually, it involved going to the lavatory. Aboriginal people generally go off in pairs or larger groups, men as well as women. Because I am white – and because of my own sensibilities – I went off on my own when we were already some distance from the camp, and I got lost. It took me three-quarters of an hour to find my way back to the others. They were sitting there worried, desperately worried, about where I was, but not daring to come and look for me. That was the very first thing – getting lost and learning how incompetent I was. I discovered that nobody goes off alone, but they also didn't let on to me any of these things [laughs]. From then on I was treated very carefully and watched over to make sure I didn't get lost again.

But there were also many linguistic errors that I made. I wasn't very good on retroflex and rolled 'r's. Aboriginal languages have a lot of 'rs', the differences in the pronunciation of which it is hard for Europeans to pick up initially, but they're crucial in distinguishing meaning. I muddled these when, early in my fieldwork, I thought I was being clever by saying to an older Aboriginal woman, the mother of my main collaborator, that I was going off 'into the bush'. The word

I wanted to use was for the area of bush where men hold their ceremonies and which you couldn't see into. But I muddled it up with the word for 'intercourse'. What I ended up saying was, 'I'm going off to have intercourse.' This caused enormous humour. When these kinds of things happen, you realize just how important it is to work on your ear and on your linguistic controls. They also tone you down a bit and hone your sensitivities, because one thing we all discover about anthropology and fieldwork is that you have to make yourself more submissive to other people's desires and interests and be more passive in your reactions to things than you would ever be in your own society. You put yourself in the position of a pupil, initially always fearful of offending people. In fact, it's a good sign when you can actually lose your temper with people and they are not too offended. You become a lot more 'real' when you start showing a bit more emotion. That's a sort of fieldwork milestone – when you feel confident enough to be yourself and express your everyday feelings – and [it] is the beginning of real friendship.

Fieldwork often takes us outside of our comfort zones. How do you feel about that?

The most difficult part is setting out, but once you're there, it's a hell of a lot easier, even though you may face many difficult situations. In

Illustration 2. Ritharrngu-speaking brothers, wives, children and affines gathered together to sing in memory of a deceased relative. Central Arnhem Land, 1965. (Photo courtesy of the author)

all the places I've worked people have nearly always been very accommodating. Aboriginal people have a high tolerance of human frailty.

They are hugely knowledgeable about people as human beings and are generally more able to read everyday human behaviour than most whites give them credit for. Of course one does often face tricky ethical issues in the field, but many of these can be dealt with by making it very obvious one is doing research. I always walk around clutching a small notebook and I never attempt to conceal it. People who don't want to talk to you don't need to, or withdraw. While this obviously influences what you learn, it does mean that people who *don't* like you or resent your presence generally avoid you, especially as in most areas I have worked, confronting people directly is not an appropriate way to behave.

The best anthropologists are ones who like mixing with other people, the ones who'll throw themselves into other people's lives and have a high tolerance for hanging in there, even when it becomes very boring or just because they're curious about how people manage their lives. I think Sinclair Lewis said it very well – the big puzzle is how other people put in twenty-four hours a day. How does the barrister, the longshoreman, the bushman or the sex worker put in twenty-four hours a day? How do they manage their lives? What are the things that influence the way that they think and do things? You need to bring theory to work on the things that emerge as problems in your understanding of other people's ways of life, but I don't think it's of huge interest going out there with too clearly a honed theoretical orientation; one always goes with some kind of theoretical orientation, of course, but a clearly honed orientation would be just like seeking to tick the boxes. That's what I find disappointing about a lot of evolutionary biology and sociobiology studies. They generate a lot of interesting data – well, some of it's interesting – but lack subtlety and ambiguity, and the categories and explanations are too pre-formed.

What do you see as the most important or cutting-edge issues within anthropology today?

Applied anthropology is certainly one. It has always been seen as the 'poor cousin' in the discipline, partly because others have often defined the research questions, but I actually think this is where some exciting intellectual challenges are happening. Applied anthropology – especially for those of us who live in the same country as the people we work with – forces one to confront not just theoretical and practical issues, but also moral and existential concerns that, in a place like

Australia, involve one as a citizen. This doesn't affect you to the same degree if you're working abroad. Here one needs to grasp the nettle as an anthropologist and face some of these moral and existential issues. The best of this kind of work makes one really get to grips with the nature of the state and bureaucracies and the values that underwrite one's own society. It can, however, get too tied up with advocacy. Not that there is anything wrong with advocacy, but it should be kept separate, particularly from academic writing.

Another topic is the reemergence of an old concern with the relationship between culture and economy, particularly as it relates to change. This is a contentious issue in Australia, where the gap in statistical indicators between Aboriginal people and other Australians is a major humanitarian and political concern. It is summed up in the seventeen-years-lower life expectancy for Aboriginal males. I don't think there is much doubt about the tension between a commitment to life embedded in dense sociality and a strong egalitarian ethic on the one hand, and requirements for improving health and material circumstances on the other. Some disembedding of people from the dense sociality – and the levelling impact of demand sharing so that more economically independent households can emerge – seems essential and inevitable. So far the impacts of cash and commoditization have largely been subverted in remote Australia, but I am interested in the turning point. I have approached this through a model of the indigenous domestic moral economy, which links kinship, economy and sense of self, showing how they have implications for each other. Interestingly, Christianity does not seem to play a central role in the disembedding among most Aboriginal people, but rather the high rate of intermarriage with non-Aboriginal people is, perhaps, the most highly significant in moving the Aboriginal partner into a new more independent social and psychological space (Peterson and Taylor 2003).

Speaking of applied anthropology, anthropologists are sometimes accused of not connecting with the wider public beyond the academy. How would you respond to that, and how does your work address issues of deeper and wider public concern?

In Australia, anthropologists have been very lucky. Since the 1970s several major pieces of legislation to do with land rights and cultural heritage have basically required anthropologists to be engaged. This has led to a huge growth in anthropology in Australia. Aboriginal people wanting recognition of their rights have to prepare a case and make a claim. So they need maps, they need genealogies, they need descriptions of their laws and customs in relationship to land and of their practices. They need outsiders such as anthropologists to help compile this information, not least because, as potential beneficiaries, they are seen as having too great an interest in the outcome to look good in an adversarial situation. This, however, raises another issue, because unsurprisingly, anthropologists are seen as biased in favour of Aboriginal people, a view that is reinforced by the difficulty those opposing Aboriginal claims have in finding anthropologists to work for them. Of course, most people doing applied-anthropology work are sympathetic to the plight of the people they're working with, and the desire to see a fairer world is one of the things that attract many to anthropology.

What people in the resource-extraction industries and others often overlook is that the requirement for informed consent in almost all research makes field research to oppose claims highly unlikely. What Aboriginal group, informed that one is working for interests opposing their claim, is going to collaborate with you? Nevertheless, I do think that it is important for the standing of anthropology that anthropologists work for other interests: normally in Australia this is for government and takes the form of reviewing claim reports. This involves issues of scholarship, argumentation and evidence, which it is then up to the courts to rule on. As an expert witness, the legal situation is that one is 'working for the court', not for the party that pays you, and your most valuable asset is your 'street cred' as a fair-minded and dispassionate researcher. You are a lot more helpful to Aboriginal people if you are seen in that way than if you are perceived as biased.

Another issue that comes up in applied anthropology and which causes conflict is the design of new institutions. In proposing new institutions should one seek to mirror existing social arrangements as closely as possible, maximizing cultural match, or should one propose new institutions that are flexible and forward looking but possibly less comfortable? This is often a choice between reproducing existing relationships or facilitating new ones. The royal commission I worked for was faced with this problem. We recommended forward-looking structures and were accused of imposing inappropriate structures, of cultural insensitivity, and of being arrogant and assuming we knew best, which we did in this case. We proposed two elected land councils to cover the Northern Territory as bodies to represent traditional landowner interests, help them manage their land and mediate negotiations with outsiders. It was pointed out that there was no tradition of representation among Aboriginal people, that representation did not sit easily with egalitarian polities in which individual autonomy is highly valued, and that there is an almost complete absence of indigenous decision-making structures. The main authority structures were based on kinship. The critics wanted codification of these existing Aboriginal arrangements, with the surveying of the territory of each land-owning group, land title issued to the group, and no central bodies to help Aboriginal people administer and manage their land. Under this proposed alternative, the head of each land-owning group – there would have been several hundreds of these – was to negotiate with the government separately. Although not the intention of the proponents of this view, such an arrangement would easily have lead to a divide-and-rule strategy in any conflicts with the government or resource-extraction industries.

Such accusations conveniently obscure a key issue: any recognition of indigenous rights by the state is bound to be an intervention in indigenous social arrangements. Why entrench arrangements based in a hunting-and-gathering economy rather than empower people becoming involved in a market-based economy? Because there were no indigenous structures on which to build the articulation with Australian society, and because of Aboriginal people's deep commitment to personal autonomy and close kin, it would have been extremely difficult for them to develop this kind of institution themselves. With the benefit of hindsight one can say that the two main land councils, the Northern and Central Land Councils, have been among the most successful and empowering Aboriginal organizations in the country, even though the stresses and strains of localism surface from time to time.

Where development is concerned, anthropologists are famous for listing a hundred don'ts to ten do's, which is one of the reasons they are not as influential in this field as they might be. This reflects another version of the kind of dilemma I have just been talking about. One of the aspirations of indigenous people and minority groups across the world is to maintain and preserve their culture. One of the questions this raises concerns the relative autonomy of cultural practices and cultural reproduction. A lot of people doing applied anthropology are sympathetic to these aspirations. Yet even a basic knowledge of the sociological theories of Marx, Durkheim, Weber, Simmel and others informs us that if the conditions of production, consumption and exchange are radically altered – if, for example, you move from the country to the city, or from hunter-gathering to being settled – you cannot expect the cultural and ideational systems to remain unaffected. While some Aboriginal people and other small ethnic groups may use the language of cultural preservation in a politically strategic way, many others are often extremely naïve and believe it possible and are often supported by anthropologists in this view, who see only loss and destructions of the things they've spent time coming to understand and value. As a result of that, anthropologists often find it very difficult to give positive *advice* to policy makers who are trying to eliminate political and social problems such as poverty, illness and educational disparities, all of which require intrusions into people's lives and modifications of the very practices and beliefs which they have built such a long time coming to respect. It's a major problem in Australia. Anyone who goes for the first time to an Aboriginal settlement in Central Australia would think that an atom bomb had hit it. There's rubbish everywhere, mangy dogs roaming around, decrepit and derelict houses and so on; it all looks very uncared for. People often say to anthropologists, 'how can you accept all this?' But you work very hard to see beyond it. Once you're involved in Aboriginal people's lives, it's not very difficult to see beyond all the rubbish, the broken houses and the snotty noses to the very warm people with a rich social system and life. So that to suddenly be asked to turn around and participate in programs that will lead to negatively transforming these very positive things seems to be imposing yet another blow on people who've suffered a lot of blows already. Being involved in development can place one in a very difficult and ambiguous moral and social space (Peterson 2010b).

How do you see the future of anthropology over the next decade or more?

I'm very optimistic. What's one of the fundamental things that anthropologists do? They look at the difference between what people *say* and what people *do,* and that's a core issue that will always be there and in need of understanding. Anthropology has an enormous amount to contribute. I notice that every day when I drive home in Canberra, because the signage at one of the intersections is *completely* wrong. It is correct according to the rules, but everybody's behaviour is confused. One's natural behaviour at that intersection conflicts with the signage, and as a result there are more crashes there than there would otherwise be. Just sitting there for a couple of days and actually watching people would have very quickly informed policy makers about how to manage it a whole lot better. Of course, it is not just a matter of watching people, but, more importantly, [of] talking to them too and then actually hearing what people say. Intel employs half a dozen or so anthropologists who spend time mainly with housewives, watching and talking to them about their everyday activities around the house to see where they might insert chips in order to automate that activity. But I don't see the future just as applied anthropology, although it is probably an interest in development that will keep undergraduate anthropology classes flourishing and provide income from postgraduate course that help people already in this field develop an anthropological sensibility. Anthropology is also an ideal basis for a modern liberal arts education, with its concern for culture, cross-cultural understanding, globalization and development. At its core, however, will always be just sheer intellectual interest in understanding other people's ways of life – not changing them – and there is no reason to suppose that there will not always be people interested in pursuing this.

References

Peterson, N. 1993. 'Demand Sharing: Reciprocity and the Pressure for Generosity among Foragers'. *American Anthropologist* 95(4): 860–874.

———. 2005a. 'On the Visibility of Indigenous Australian Systems of Marine Tenure'. In *Indigenous Use and Management of Marine Resources*, eds. N. Kishigami and J. Savelle, 427–44. Osaka: National Museum of Ethnology, Senri Ethnological Studies 67.

———. 2005b. 'What Can the Pre-colonial and Frontier Economies Tell Us about Engagement with the Real Economy? Indigenous Life Projects and the Conditions for Development'. In *Culture, Economy and Governance in Aboriginal Australia*, eds. D. Austin-Broos and G. Macdonald, 7–18. Sydney: Sydney University Press.

———. 2010a. 'Common Law, Statutory Law, and the Political Economy of the Recognition of Indigenous Australian Rights in Land'. In *Aboriginal Title and Indigenous Peoples*, eds. L. Knafla and H. Westra, 171–84. Vancouver: UBC Press.

———. 2010b. 'Other People's Lives: Secular Assimilation, Culture and Ungovernability'. In *The Crisis of Culture: Anthropology and the Politics of Engagement in Remote Aboriginal Australia*, eds. J. Altman and M. Hinkson, 227–33. Sydney: UNSW Press.

Peterson, N., and T. Matsuyama, eds. 1991. *Cash, Commoditisation and Changing Foragers*. Osaka: National Museum of Ethnology, Senri Ethnological Studies No 30.

Peterson, N., and B. Rigsby, eds. 1998. *Customary Marine Tenure in Australia*. Sydney: The University of Sydney, Oceania Monograph No 48.

Peterson, N., and J. Taylor. 2003. 'The Modernising of the Indigenous Domestic Moral Economy: Kinship, Accumulation and Household Composition'. *The Asia Pacific Journal of Anthropology* 4(1 and 2): 105–22.

Rappaport, R. A. 1968. *Pigs for the Ancestors.* New Haven: Yale University Press.

Sahlins, M. 1972. *Stone Age Economics.* Chicago: Aldine-Atherton.

Notes

1. The 1992 *Mabo* court ruling was a landmark decision in Australia that recognized native title and discredited the so-called *terra nullius* argument that land supposedly 'belonging to no one' could be taken by the government. –Ed.

Howard Morphy

Date of Birth: 1947

Place of Birth: Hampton, Middlesex (UK)

PhD: 'Too Many Meanings: An Analysis of the Artistic System of the Yolngu People of Northeast Arnhem Land', 1978, The Australian National University.

Fieldwork: Australia

Current affiliation: Director of the Research School of Humanities and the Arts, The Australian National University.

Positions held: Morphy began his career as a research assistant at the British Museum (1971–73). He subsequently lectured at the Australian National University (1978–86), before taking the position of curator of anthropology at the Pitt Rivers Museum, Oxford University (1986–96) and junior proctor (1991–92). Morphy was also professor of anthropology at University College London (1996–99) and an ARC Senior Research Fellow at the Australian National University (1997–2003). He became director of the Centre for Cross-cultural Research in 1999, before taking up his present position in 2007.

Major works
- 2008, co-director with P. Deveson. *In Gentle Hands*, film available from the Research School of Humanities and the Arts, Canberra: Australian National University.
- 2006, with Frances Morphy. 'Tasting the Waters: Discriminating Identities in the Waters of Blue Mud Bay'. *Journal of Material Culture* 11(2): 67–85.
- 2007. *Becoming Art: Exploring Cross-cultural Categories.* Oxford: Berg.
- 1998. *Aboriginal Art.* London: Phaidon.
- 1997, co-editor with M. Banks, *Rethinking Visual. Anthropology*, New Haven and London: Yale University Press.
- 1991. *Ancestral Connections: Art and an Aboriginal System of Knowledge.* Chicago: University of Chicago Press.

Chapter 6

ART AS ACTION
The Yolngu
Howard Morphy

In Australia and New Zealand you are known for your work in the anthropology of art and for your work on the Yolngu people of northeastern Australia. You have recently completed a film about the Yolngu. Tell us more about this work.

My film is entitled *In Gentle Hands* (Morphy and Deveson 2008), and it focuses on a Yolngu circumcision ceremony, at Yilpara, on Blue Mud Bay. I filmed the ceremony myself and edited the footage with Pip Deveson, who has had long experience working with Yolngu and editing films with Ian Dunlop. The film centres on the participants' experience of the ritual action, and I try to capture the positive emotions that are created. The title refers to the essentially nurturing dimension of the ritual and counters the initial likely audience preconceptions of circumcision as a violent act.

Much of my work with the Yolngu people of northeast Arnhem Land explores how they engage with the wider world through their art. My argument is that artwork has always been a form of action in Yolngu society, undertaken in order to demonstrate rights of ownership. Particularly in the Yolngu case, painting and other aspects of ritual performance are all connected to land and the rights that people have to land (Morphy 1991, 2006a). My research has also been concerned with how the Yolngu *problematize* the concept of appropriation, because in many respects they are actually quite outgoing in the world; that is, they want to convert other people to a sense of understanding the values that their culture and their aesthetic performances hold for them. They are oriented toward sharing aspects of their culture. So although outsiders may perceive the incorporation of Yolngu art and performance into Australia's self-representation and self-promotion to the wider world as an appropriation of an indigenous culture on behalf of the nation-state, that is not how the Yolngu see it.

You mention the importance of land and appropriation for people in northeast Arnhem Land. How important are concepts of 'ownership' and 'appropriation' for anthropology in general today?

They are incredibly relevant subjects. At a very general level, the discourses of ownership and appropriation are part of the history of anthropology and its relationship to the cultural production of other societies. But in this day and age, they are particularly salient in the context of Australia, New Zealand and other settler colonial societies, where anthropological work on ownership has often resulted in great improvements in the lives of indigenous people and has been useful in their struggles for their rights. It's also an important topic for anthropology more generally, as ownership is a concept that is embedded in a particular way in the history of Western cultures. Even though anthropology had part of its origin in that context, by looking at that concept cross-culturally, anthropology challenges the presuppositions that Western societies and Western legal discourses may have, showing alternative ways in which you can look at things like property rights and so forth.

Let us go back to your own encounter with different ways of looking at things. How did you first discover anthropology?

Well, I had originally applied to university to study law, but having got a place to study law I decided that I didn't really want to be a lawyer. Not that there is anything wrong with being a lawyer, I hasten to add, rather I wanted to learn more about the world before deciding on what my profession would eventually be. At the time I was working as a volunteer for the charity Oxfam. I was also helping to run a folk club, in the Mitre Hotel in Oxford, called Fennario Folk – which was named after a line from a song sung by Bob Dylan on his first album. We managed this folk club on behalf of Oxfam, and I got very interested in Oxfam's agenda. I thought it would be rather important to be able to study and get an idea of what societies in Africa or *wherever* really needed in terms of non-government organizations and aid. I thought that if one was going to help those societies, one ought to know a great deal about them and how they saw themselves in the world. I went to see my geography schoolmaster and I said, 'I've decided that I would like to do human geography in order to better understand the needs of developing societies'. He looked at me and replied, 'For that purpose, human geography is the poor man's anthropology'. And I said, 'Oh really? What's anthropology?' [laughs]. He outlined what anthropology was to me, and so I quickly whipped in an application to go to university to study anthropology, in order to work as an applied anthropologist in the third world.

I got offered a place at University College London, which was absolutely the right place for me. At that particular time it was a tremendous privilege to go to university; that was when universities were just beginning to open up – there was government funding, there were no fees, and there were student grants. Without those benefits I would never have gone to university. But the places were very limited, and not knowing anything about the subject, I applied to six or seven different universities where you could study anthropology. But UCL [University College London] was the one that, after the interviews, I eventually chose. The anthropology programme at UCL was distinctive in Britain, as it was one of the few places that were based on the American 'four-field' model, even though it only had the three fields of social anthropology, biological anthropology and material culture, and did not include linguistics. I learnt a very different anthropology from what was being taught elsewhere in Britain. The head of department at UCL, Darryl Forde, was basically trained in American anthropology – so the core courses we did included a theory paper called 'The Analysis of Culture', which focused on the work of figures such as Talcott Parsons, Clyde Kluckhohn and others. I received a very broad education in American anthropology, but our teachers also included Phyllis Kaberry, Mary Douglas and I. M. Lewis, so I was taught by a really *diverse* set of anthropologists who had very different theoretical frameworks and who introduced us to the full breadth of anthropology.

A key figure for me was Peter Ucko, who had developed courses in material culture. Peter was a magnificent, charismatic teacher. He was also very analytical in his approach to topics, and I think that theoretical perspective was something that attracted me very strongly. We also had excellent lecturers in biological anthropology, so I acquired a very broad set of perspectives on anthropology. Being in London, we were close to the Royal Anthropological Institute, which at that point was pioneering areas that had been neglected in anthropology. There was an RAI [The Royal Anthropological Institute] 'art panel' and an RAI 'film panel'. I went to all their meetings and really became a visual anthropologist through being in London and having that kind of access and being interested in that approach to material culture. In some ways, material culture has always been the continuing thread of my anthropological interests. It's the thing that brings everything in my life back into focus, because I do have a tendency to look very broadly. But then, one of the great things about anthropology is its breadth and its natural interdisciplinarity.

So I did a master's degree, an MPhil at University College, and I studied the '*toas*', which are direction signs of the Lake Eyre tribes in Central Australia (Morphy 1978a). I came across that interest because I actually wrote a theoretical master's thesis. I handed it in to Peter Ucko when it was more or less completed, and he looked at it and said, 'Well, this is all very interesting and very good, but where's the data?' So I had to go back and find some data. I thought at that point, 'well, I may as well give up'. I'd written this theoretical discourse which I thought was really quite good – and after all, it was only a master's thesis, but so be it. So I went to the Royal Anthropological Institute to look for some data [smiles], and I came across a wonderful publication from 1919, I think, on the *toas* of the Lake Eyre region of Central Australia, written by Sterling and Waite. It illustrated some 460 of these objects with all of their meanings but very little about the context, very little about what they were used for. It was a fantastic body of data which lent itself really well to a formal analysis of the structure of its representational system. That was great.

At that stage you could only get one ESRC scholarship, and anthropologists, unlike sociologists, required people to do the MA degree: you couldn't go straight on to do a doctorate. But once you'd used the scholarship for the MA, then you didn't have enough money, or the opportunity, to do a doctorate. So after finishing my MA, I got a job in the British Museum, on something called the 'no number' project. 'No number' reflected the fact that a large number of objects in the ethnographic collection didn't have any numbers, i.e. they hadn't been registered. My job was to register these objects, and I spent something like two and a half years working there as a research assistant, wondering what my future career would be. I really wanted to do a doctorate. Then suddenly I saw an advertisement in a newspaper for scholarships at The Australian National University (ANU). I wrote to the anthropology department at the ANU saying that I wanted to apply linguistic models to the analysis of the art in Vanuatu. I got a letter back from a completely different and recently created department, Prehistory and Anthropology, in the School of General Studies, saying, 'We would be interested in giving you a scholarship as long as you follow up the research you've already done in Australia and carry on working on Australian Aboriginal art' [smiling and clapping hands together]. And so I said 'yes'. My wife, Frances, had *just* finished her master's thesis, so the timing was very good. That was how I came to Australia to study Aboriginal art.

That was 1973. Peter Ucko had been appointed the Principal of the Institute of Aboriginal Studies. He had just received an application from a very famous person, or one who ought to be very famous in Australian history, the Reverend Edgar Wells, who had been the missionary at Yirrkala at the time of the Bark Petition. This was a petition from the people at Yirrkala asking for recognition of their rights (Morphy 2007). Reverend Wells wanted to go back in order to document the collection of bark paintings made by the founding missionary at Yirrkala, the Reverend Wilbur Chaseling. Hearing that I was coming out, Peter Ucko encouraged Wells to undertake the task and suggested that it might be helpful to him if he was accompanied by a newly arrived anthropology graduate student who was looking for a field situation. So I was introduced to eastern Arnhem Land, to Yirrkala, Milingimbi and Maningrida, under the auspices of a returning missionary hero. Because the Yolngu really welcomed him back as someone who had led their struggle for land rights, this was a really good way for me to enter the field. It also helped me with my goal to apply anthropology in order to further the rights and development of indigenous and third world communities.

I could've done fieldwork in any of those communities, but Edgar Wells introduced me to a man called Narritjin Maymuru (Morphy and Deveson 2005). The minute I met him I thought, 'this is one of the most extraordinary intellectuals I have ever met in my life'. He spoke his own kind of English, but it was quite clear that this was a man of incredible knowledge, reason and judgement. I felt that I could learn an enormous amount from him. I decided that I would go to Yirrkala, as opposed to one of the other communities, in the hope that I would be able to work with him.

What would you specify as your main research interests, and how do they relate to your work among the Yolngu?

Obviously I'm an anthropologist of art. Initially I was looking at art as a system of communication. I was interested in formal analysis as an analytical method. I was very interested in creating wider bodies of data that might be used to analyze objects in a context of social change. Part of my methodology before going into the field was to get hold of all the photographs that I could of the collections from northeast Arnhem Land, so that I would have a body of material to work with. Using these, I could begin to work out what were the structures of the systems of communication. Of course, in Yolngu society, I had to look at art in its different contexts, because art was something that was all around me; art was something that would be found painted on the chest of a child in a circumcision ceremony or hanging on display and for sale in the mission art centre. Very quickly, I got the idea both that art was something that people *used* in context and in a variety of different frames. They used it in the frame of their own local institutions, but they were also using it to communicate to outsiders. That then revealed to me the much wider world in which Yolngu lived and operated.

I was very lucky in that, as an anthropologist, I was able to bring a perspective that really brought together historical sources of information with the appreciation that societies and their institutions are all connected to wider worlds. Because the Yolngu are an indigenous Australian society, you cannot work with them without engaging with issues of social organization and kinship. Yolngu were originally known in the anthropological world as the 'Murngin', and there was the renowned 'Murngin problem'. The phrase the 'Murngin problem' was, I believed, formalized by John Barnes (1967) in his monograph *Inquest on the Murngin*. Murngin was the name Lloyd Warner used to refer to the people now more commonly referred to as Yolngu. Warner (1958 [1937]) wrote a brilliant book on Yolngu society, appropriately named *A Black Civilization*. The book centred on the inter-relationship between religion and social organization. The Murngin became a key case study in Lévi-Strauss's *The Elementary Structures of Kinship* (1969). As a result of Warner's, Lévi Strauss's and others' writings, a number of loose ends emerged in the discourse over Yolngu kinship that eventually became referred to as the Murngin problem – it should have been problems! It would take me several hours or perhaps days to unpack them for you. Yolngu kinship is extremely complex, partly because unlike most other Australian kinship systems, an essential asymmetry lies at its heart and the core conceptual problems are involved in coming to terms with that asymmetry. One of the things that was necessary for my understanding of their artistic system was to try to work out the solution to that 'Murngin problem'. Because of the work of Frances Morphy and I, together with our fellow anthropologist Ian Keen, who conducted research at the same time at another Yolngu community, we now have a much better understanding of Yolngu kinship (Morphy 1978b; see also Keen 1982). The main thing I was able to demonstrate was that Yolngu marriage required a minimal cycle of 'exchange', involving six groups. No one can hope to understand any aspect of Yolngu society unless they have a basic understanding of Yolngu kinship and group organization. Hence studying Yolngu art and material culture made it essential for me to contribute to ongoing debates over the structure and meaning of the Yolngu kinship system, which in turn was embedded in broader debates on theory in anthropology.

Given that art, in that form, is an integral part of visual culture, it is no wonder that those issues engaged your interest.

Much of that developed out of my interest in photography. When I was working in the British Museum in London I was a passionate amateur photographer. In those days one couldn't afford a decent camera *at all.* Japanese and German cameras were incredibly expensive. But there was a shop in London that sold Soviet goods very cheaply. So I bought a very good, very cheap Russian 35 mm single-lens reflex camera and did all my own developing and so on. I started using photography as a fieldwork method, and then, in the same mission house where Frances and I were staying, we met Ian Dunlop and his film crew. Ian was at the early stages of his Yirrkala project, filming the impact of the mining town on the Yolngu population there (Morphy 2006b). He watched as Frances and I went out every day, struggling out in the heat, trying to find people to talk to, while carrying our big heavy tape recorders and camera. I think he spent a lot of time laughing at us. But we soon realized that many of the people that we were working with as anthropologists were the same people that he was working with as a filmmaker, so we developed a working partnership. Ian then asked me if I would stay on with him and work as an anthropologist on a film that he was making of a Djungguwan ceremony at one of the homeland centres (Dunlop 1990; Graham 2006). I had a terrible battle with my supervisor, Anthony Forge, who felt I should be focusing on getting my thesis written. But I more or less just didn't take any notice of him. Fortunately, he was forgiving and supportive. We became involved as the anthropologist and linguist working on those films. Frances was an anthropologist who had converted during fieldwork to being a linguist, and she wrote grammars of the Yolngu language. So I – or rather we – had this *incredible* advantage in actually being part of a team that brought together different kinds of skills. It doubled the amount of work that we were able to do.

I gradually got more involved in the editing process and in the wider process of filmmaking. Australia at that moment was a fantastic place for ethnographic filmmaking. The Institute of Aboriginal Studies organized a huge conference, where people came from all over the world. Around that time, David and Judith MacDougall were employed at the Institute of Aboriginal and Torres Strait Islander Studies, and when I eventually finished my doctorate and became a lecturer at the ANU, I co-taught a class in ethnographic film with David MacDougall, Nic Peterson and Judith MacDougall. The opportunities in that area were fantastic.

Canberra is a 'mecca' for visual anthropology and ethnographic film, so you found yourself in the right spot.

Yes, I did. But it's amazing how long it's taken us to get everything together properly. We're only now in the position of producing doctoral students who have films as part of their assessment, and we've got a fantastic master's programme going in 'visual cultural research', of which visual anthropology is a central component.

Many anthropologists talk about specific events or experiences that led to major fieldwork discoveries. Were there any such revelatory or 'eureka' moments during your fieldwork?

Yes, one of the most memorable was whilst working on my master's thesis at University College London. As I said earlier, I'd been analyzing a system of representation, and I got stuck trying to work out how on earth these objects ('*toas*') were used to communicate, when they often seemed to convey insufficient information. Then, one night, I suddenly got an idea which I'm sure is part of what linguists call 'pragmatics', which is that, in many cases there is only a limited range of possible locations that these objects could actually refer to in each case. I called these factors 'PL' – possible locations. This is how people interact with the objects in an interpretative context. I was able to bring that context to the interpretation of this system, and so suddenly I'd solved the problem. I remember feeling a sort of 'Eureka! I've worked this out! Now I'll be able to finish my master's thesis', and I finished it very quickly.

Another moment occurred much later when I was undertaking my research into Yolngu art. There was a wonderful man called Welwe Wanambi, a *great* artist and ritual leader, who hadn't really worked with any other anthropologist. There are very few of his paintings in existence, and he did this fantastic figurative painting where you could see a hunter chasing a kangaroo through the forest, with trees falling down left, right and centre. And then he came up to me and said, 'I've done exactly the same painting again'. I was disappointed, because I had little money as a graduate student and I was buying these paintings. But I hid my disappointment, because he was such an engaging and generous person, and so I went along to see the painting he was doing. But whereas the first one had been figurative, this one was *entirely* geometric; it sparkled! It was *wonderful*, but clearly different. And then it later struck me, 'if I can understand what he means when he says "these are the same paintings", then I'm really getting somewhere.'

There was a third important moment. Frances and I have worked with the Yolngu for about thirty-five years, but I am still uncertain at times about what exactly is my relationship with people. We feel as if we're treated as relatives, and we do have enormous obligations. However there are still moments of uncertainty. When I was filming at a funeral I was too inhibited to film the body being put into the grave, because I felt that would be too much of an intrusion. But even the Yolngu afterwards said that I was completely mad; it was a *funeral*, so what on earth was I doing *not* filming the body being put into the grave. But I had that kind of restraint. On another occasion very recently a large number of Yolngu came down to Melbourne, and there was a very distinguished gathering of people there to see some objects that had been donated to Melbourne University by Justice Woodward – who played an important role in the development of the land-rights legislation in Australia. There are all these distinguished lawyers and other dignitaries going around looking at these objects, but the Yolngu weren't sure how dangerous these objects might be. So the Yolngu said, 'Right, all of you Europeans – *balanda* – we're going to have to rub sweat on you.' We all lined up, and they rubbed their sweat on everybody. When they got to me they said, 'Oh no, no, you're one of us!' [laughs]. That was something! Although anthropologists *always* have to retain their objectivity – their capacity to step aside – at the same time you begin to strongly identify with the society you're working with as if it's your own. And then it really becomes your own. You recognize that of course, cross-culturally, many people are operating in very different kinds of frames and have strong senses of belonging in multiple contexts. Belonging isn't something that is associated with just one structured space in the world. It can be for some people, but in many cases that is not so.

These are all quite positive moments. Do you remember any negative encounters or events? Things that went utterly wrong in the field or moments you found embarrassing, but which you nevertheless learned from?

It was a struggle at the early stages of fieldwork, but in a way I *knew* it would be a struggle, because people like Phyllis Kabbery and Nancy Williams had forewarned me. You are working in a society you don't know initially, with people speaking a language you don't initially understand, and you have to intrude into people's lives. That takes a lot of courage. There are all of these people living in their own worlds, and you go up and say, 'I want to sit down and just watch you for the next few months'. That establishment of relationships is really, really hard. Interestingly, one thing that I recognized is that it's good to go away after about five or six months and then come back again, because it's only *then* that you realize how much you've actually learnt. Also, when you come back again, people have a completely different attitude to you. 'Ah, here you are, coming back, how nice to see you. Welcome.' You get that kind of change. I always try to build that process into my own doctoral students' work, getting them used to the idea of going away and coming back, if that's at all possible.

The other thing that I remember is the total physical exhaustion that you have to fight your way through. Nancy Williams told me that she'd been taught before going into the field that anything written down the following day was 'hearsay', so you had to write it down the day it happened. Frances and I would arrive back home *completely* exhausted, but one of us would always volunteer to write up our general diary for the day, and then we'd wake the other one up so that he or she could write her part of it. We forced ourselves to do that. Those diary entries are just invaluable, because journals that you've written as fully as possible become something which, in retrospect, contains all this information that at the time you didn't even know was relevant.

What would you describe as among the most exciting or relevant areas of anthropology today?

Coming from University College London and being married to a linguistic anthropologist [smiles], I have a tremendously broad interest in anthropology. I really wouldn't like to narrow it down. Our intellectual eclecticism is an important asset, and anthropologists have to be able to *handle* interdisciplinarity while at the same time creating coherent disciplinary themes. I actually think that anthropology is in a very good position now. We got over the necessary corrective of reflexive anthropology. A lot of things to do with reflexive anthropology and the critique of anthropology were actually already part of the discipline but were not widely acknowledged. It was very good that there was a critical discourse that enabled anthropology to make our methodologies and epistemology more transparent. Having worked through that, anthropology has been able to return to its main concern, which is driving knowledge through cross-cultural comparative research and applying that knowledge to the betterment of people's lives. A lot of the challenge for anthropology arises from the fact that much of the world is reluctant to acknowledge the complexity of the social and cultural worlds people inhabit. Anthropology reminds us that problems are complex and solutions are therefore going to be complex as well, but that is what people often don't want to hear. Deep ethnography is an important component of anthropology, but I don't think all anthropologists have to be ethnographers. Anthropology as a discipline is much wider than ethnographic research. But it does worry me that fewer people are able to spend the time doing deep, long-term ethnography.

I think that we are at the moment when visual anthropology is really coming into its own, in part because of the digital revolution. The generations coming along have great facility with visual media, and unless we follow that direction, we will fail. At the same time I think anthropologists have gained a much more sophisticated understanding of the nature of visual media as a means of communication and as part of wider social and cultural processes. In a sense we're able to use that technology precisely because we can stand outside ourselves and see its potential. Of course digital media mean that the whole archive of anthropologists' past work can be brought into the present in potentially researchable ways.

Tell us about the relevance of your work in the wider public sphere.

The 'Blue Mud Bay' native title and land claim I worked on with Frances, Nic Peterson, Marcus Barber and two archaeologists, Annie Clarke and Patrick Fawlkner, resulted in a court case that recognized Aboriginal ownership of 80 per cent of the inter-tidal zones of the Northern Territory. It was the last bit missing from the Australian land-rights legislation and it is going to have enormous long-term impact on those societies (see Morphy and Morphy 2006; F. Morphy 2007). It's not going to provide immediate solutions to all the problems, but it's recognition of long-term rights will be terribly important.

I've also played a significant role in widening people's appreciation of Aboriginal art. I've done that almost as a kind of emissary from the Yolngu, *who, themselves*, felt that they were producing the equivalent in value to what are considered works of art in the West. Working with *them*, I was able to increase people's access to, and appreciation of, indigenous art. I've also played a small part in reconnecting anthropology with museums and museum collections. That is something that the diaspora of anthropologists trained at University College London have carried with them by spreading interest in material culture. I have contributed a little to that by training a lot of doctoral students who then go out into the world and spread these concerns even further.

In Australia, unlike, say, Central Europe, anthropologists get to work on issues of major public concern, such as indigenous land rights. Is anthropology more relevant to public debates in countries like Australia?

No, it's *not*. The consciousness of people in Central Europe, Africa, America and so on – as far as the nature of cultural diversity and how it fits within a globalizing world – is just as important, and anthropology is just as relevant in that context as it is in Australia. In applying anthropology to indigenous Australians we're applying anthropology to our contemporaries. We can do that just as easily with our contemporaries in Europe, America, India or China. Indeed, that's another important change that's happening in anthropology. The idea that anthropology is the study of small-scale pre-modern societies has by now absolutely disappeared. And that's great. On the other hand, anthropology must continue to make minority cultures and local cultures visible on a global stage.

References

Barnes, J. A. 1967. *Inquest on the Murngin*. London: Royal Anthropological Institute of Great Britain and Ireland, Occasional Paper No. 26

Dunlop, I. (director), 1990. *Djungguwan at Gurka'wuy*, Film Australia.

Graham, T. 2006. Ceremony – The Djungguwan of Northeast Arnhem Land, CD-Rom. Sydney: Film Australia.

Keen, I. 1982. 'How Some Murngin Men Marry Ten Wives: The Marital Implications of Matrilateral Cross-cousin Structures'. *Man* (n.s.) 17:620–42.

Levi-Strauss, C. 1969. *The Elementary Structures of Kinship.* rev. ed., tr. from the French by J. H. Bell, eds. J. R. von Sturmer and R. Needham. London: Eyre & Spottiswoode.

Morphy, F. 2007. 'Performing Law: The Yolngu of Blue Mud Bay Meet the Native Title Process'. In *The Social Effects of Native Title: Recognition, Translation and Coexistence Canberra,* eds. B. Smith and F. Morphy. Canberra: ANU ePress.

Morphy, H. 1978a. 'Schematisation, Meaning and Communication in Toas'. In *Form in Indigenous Art,* ed. P. J. Ucko, 77–89. London: Duckworth.

———. 1978b. 'Rights in Paintings and Rights in Women: A Consideration of Some of the Basic Problems Posed by the Asymmetry of the "Murngin" System'. *Mankind* 11:208–19.

———. 1991. *Ancestral Connections: Art and an Aboriginal System of Knowledge.* Chicago: University of Chicago Press.

———. 2006a. 'Sites of Persuasion: Yingapungapu at National Museum of Australia'. In *Museum Frictions: Public Cultures/Global Transformations,* eds. I. Karp, C. Kratz, L. Swatja and T. Ybarra-Frausto, 461–96. Durham, NC: Duke University Press.

———. 2006b. 'The Aesthetics of Communication and the Communication of Cultural Aesthetics: A Perspective on Ian Dunlop's Films of Aboriginal Australia'. *Visual Anthropology Review* 21 (1 and 2): 63–79.

———. 2007. *Becoming Art: Exploring Cross-cultural Categories.* Oxford: Berg.

Morphy, H., and P. Deveson. 2008. *In Gentle Hands.* Film available from the Research School of Humanities and the Arts. Canberra: Australian National University.

Morphy, H., T. Graham and P. Deveson. 2006. *Ceremony – The Djungguwan of Northeast Arnhem Land.* CD-Rom. Sydney: Film Australia in association with Denise Haslem Productions.

Morphy, H., and F. Morphy. 2006. 'Tasting the Waters: Discriminating Identity in the Waters of Blue Mud Bay'. *Journal of Material Culture* 11: 67–85.

Warner, W. L. 1958 (1937). *A Black Civilization: A Social Study of an Australian Tribe.* New York: Harper.

David Trigger

Date of Birth: 1953
Place of Birth: Brisbane, Australia
PhD: 'Doomadgee: A Study of Power Relations and Social Action in a North Australian Aboriginal Settlement', 1985, The University of Queensland.

Fieldwork: Australia

Current affiliation: Professor of Anthropology and Head of School of Social Science at the University of Queensland.

Positions held: David Trigger worked as a site recorder (University of Queensland, 1978–83) before taking up a lectureship at Griffith University in the School of Australian Environmental Studies (1985). Between 1986 and 2007 he held a range of academic positions at the University of Western Australia, including professor of anthropology. In 2000 he established an applied-anthropology research centre at the University of Western Australia.

Major works
- 2008. 'Indigeneity, Ferality and What "Belongs" in the Australian Bush: Aboriginal Responses to "Introduced" Animals and Plants in a Settler-descendant Society'. *Journal of the Royal Anthropological Institute (NS)* 14(4): 628–46.
- 1997. 'Mining, Landscape and the Culture of Development Ideology in Australia'. *Ecumene: A Journal of Environment, Culture, Meaning* 4(2): 161–80.
- 1992. *Whitefella Comin': Aboriginal Responses to Colonialism in Northern Australia.* Cambridge: Cambridge University Press.
- 1986. 'Blackfellas and Whitefellas: The Concepts of Domain and Social Closure in the Analysis of Race Relations'. *Mankind* 16(2): 99–117.

Chapter 7

RETHINKING NATURE AND NATIVENESS
David Trigger

Your work has focused on examining concepts of 'nature' and 'nativeness' in Australia, but you have recently expanded this to explore other contexts. Tell us about your current research interests and why they are important.

Along with some other colleagues, I have a history of working with Australian Aboriginal issues in which drawing comparisons to countries like New Zealand and Canada in particular have been important. But in the past decade, my interest in understandings of indigeneity both in society and nature has led me to become interested in countries that have a different history from first-world, white, post-settler societies. This includes countries like Malaysia and Indonesia, which have very different cultural histories. It also includes South American countries where you have non-British histories of colonial involvement, which I think are not looked at enough. Then there are countries like South Africa, where you have the idea of 'nativeness' negotiated in a different way again, with a small indigenous minority known as San people – that is, unless the whole of the black African population of South Africa were to be defined as indigenous. Alongside that you have a white minority, which seeks to assert its own sense of autochthony and *placed* identity. These are some of the issues addressed by this kind of work, and those are just three examples of the countries that comparisons would be good for.

In my ongoing work among Aboriginal groups I've been looking at the perception and responses to introduced plants and animals among 'traditional' Aboriginal communities (Trigger 2008a). This academic work has an applied aspect, because 'native title' cases are in part about Australian law trying to recognize forms of cultural change within the context of continuing indigenous traditions. But my projects over the last ten years have gone beyond Aboriginal studies to ask questions about other sectors of a population like Australia, i.e. questions of emplaced identities, of in what sense the citizens of a country like Australia might come to think of themselves as *native* to the country, to the place, to the streetscapes and to the landscapes. This has included my reflections on my own personal senses of place and home, and in something of a departure from my usual academic research, I wrote a piece in part discussing where I grew up and the house in Brisbane my father himself built when I was a baby (Trigger 2008b). My parents lived in the house for fifty-five years before my father passed away in 2009, and the property continues to hold memories and meanings in every nook and cranny.

My most recent large-scale project, carried out with postdoctoral fellow Dr Jane Mulcock, is a study of a city in Western Australia – Perth – which looks at people's attitudes to what kinds of city environments they prefer. This also entails issues of 'nativeness', as we are examining whether people are particularly concerned about native plants as against introduced flora, their attitudes to pets and how all this relates to people's often *idealized* thoughts about what constitutes 'pure nature'. Our work in Australia explores how a post-settler society with a fairly distinctive ecology is coming to grips with ecological *and* cultural changes in the context of a history of many immigrant groups, who bring their own preferences for different sorts of species, plants, animals, gardens and backyards, as well as different views of what national parks are for. We know that migrant communities often don't embrace the sort of wilderness ideal that professional ecologists like to promote in Australia. So together with postgraduate, postdoctoral and other colleagues I've been interviewing and doing participant observation with citizens to explore these issues (Trigger et al. 2008; Trigger and Head 2010).

Is this what you mean by 'negotiating nativeness'?

Yes, indeed. What I'm trying to look at is the negotiation of nativeness in society with all of the complexities of different histories of migration, of peoples with different cultural traditions engaging with the formation of a new nation state and a new society. Writer David Malouf, I think, in his Boyer Lectures on ABC Radio, in 1998 (Malouf 1998), asked from a literary and historical perspective about ways

Australians might come to inwardly possess places they inhabit and visit. He spoke of investigating the ordinariness of everyday lives to think our way into such meanings attributed to land and place. For some time I've thought of my own work as seeking to do something similar from an anthropological perspective focused on the idea of cultural assumptions.

But I am also trying to link the negotiation of native and other kinds of identities in society with what people think of as 'natural' or 'native' or 'appropriate' in nature and in the world of environment. This does not necessarily mean out in remote areas of bush, but also in streetscapes and cityscapes. There's an interesting international literature which looks at cultural logics underlying issues like ecological restoration. One of the questions we're asking is, 'What are we restoring nature *to?*' What's the baseline (Mulcock and Trigger 2008)? The answer to that question varies depending on which country and which region of the world we're talking about. Posing that question for Europe or East Asia is very different from posing it for North America, South Africa, New Zealand or Australia. For example, there are some very interesting comparisons arising from settings such as Borneo, the Indonesian archipelago and the Malaysian archipelago, particularly in terms of the historical flows of people and species through those islands. There's a history of mixing, of 'hybrid ecologies' that sharply contrasts with an island-ecology continent like that of Australia, where the idea of some sort of pure 'native nature' has much more resonance.

What were the main intellectual influences in the development of your ideas?

That's always a difficult question [smiles]. Going back to my earlier work, I wrote a book about black-white interaction in an Aboriginal town called Doomadgee, in northern Australia, and the administrative authoritarianism of a local mission there. When I first went to Doomadgee in the late 1970s no anthropologists had ever conducted substantial fieldwork there. I was interested in hegemony and in the work of scholars like Gerry Sider in the US, who were trying to operationalize Gramscian concepts like hegemony by looking at what might lead people to embrace beliefs and ways of thinking that seemed to work against their own interests. I became focused on the complexities of power and race relations, and the significance of benevolent paternalism, through the work of Jeremy Beckett at Sydney University. Beckett was looking at Australian Torres Strait Islanders and their accommodation to colonialism, in part through the embrace of Christianity, and I found instructive his use of Eugene Genovese's work on the history of North American slavery. I have since revised my own work on Aboriginal Christianity to pose some questions about how syncretic beliefs about traditional rights to land might play out in legal claims and negotiations with the wider Australian society (Trigger and Asche 2010).

In my recent research on 'nativeness' in nature and society, I think there's some excellent scholarship in cultural geography, including work by my colleague and co-author Lesley Head, who seeks to apply cultural analysis to the world of ecological science as well as to the everyday fashioning of environments in the city and the bush. I have found particularly useful Michele Dominy's research on multiple forms of 'indigeneity' in the New Zealand context. And I have appreciated the intellectual courage of two Aboriginal writers in Australia, Marcia Langton and Noel Pearson, who write challengingly about difficult issues in the politics of Aboriginal affairs. Peter Sutton's work on what he terms 'the politics of suffering' similarly grapples with important questions as to how the future of indigenous culture may fit with finding a way out of the social and economic crises that bedevil too many Aboriginal communities. And my colleague David Martin's long contributions to applied anthropological studies of the circumstances and conditions in Aboriginal communities has, in my view, been a major contribution. In general, my position is that to look at issues of the negotiation of 'nativeness' in a relatively young post-settler society like Australia and the wide range of analytical and practical matters connected with this issue, we need as anthropologists to read across disciplines as diverse as history, geography and development studies. My previous collaboration with a colleague in post-colonial literature studies has also been rewarding (Trigger and Griffiths 2003). There's a whole wealth of scholarship there.

Let's go back to what started your interest in this field. How did you become interested in anthropology?

I would say a *little* by accident. I did my undergraduate studies at the University of Queensland in the first half of the 1970s, having first tried out a short career in the building industry, which kind of didn't work, so I surprised people by doing something very different from my peers at the time [smiles]. Why on earth would I go to university to do an arts degree, asked my boss at the construction firm where my first job had been [as] a cadet building estimator for a year, in 1971? At that stage I had no answer as to why I wanted to study sociology, philosophy and anthropology other than that the course descriptions took my interest. Like a lot of young students I was attracted to the study of cultural difference. During my undergraduate years I had a couple of lecturers who introduced me to issues in Pacific and Australian Aboriginal anthropology. Through John von Sturmer and Athol Chase I met some Aboriginal people from remote north Queensland communities, when they visited Brisbane. To some extent, anthropology's apparent alliance with the romance of tribal societies provided an alternative means of critiquing the establishment. With hindsight, I think I found the possibility of an egalitarian hunter-gatherer culture more engaging than the Marxist ideals swirling around Australian university student politics in the first half of the 1970s. Looking back, I can see that the risk, of course, was that my left-wing Moral Philosophy lecturer at the time may have been right in asking whether this was a futile attempt to mimic the romance of 'being an Aborigine'.

I do recall, however, that I was never completely convinced that Aboriginal communities represented any fundamental alternative to mainstream capitalism. My questions about outstations then being developed as small-scale residences supportive of traditional culture were not always appreciated by my anthropology teachers. I remember asking John von Sturmer, at the time a lecturer with great influence over several of us studying anthropology honours, how the Wik people would obtain sufficient food at the newly established outstations south of Aurukun. 'That's a Killoran question!', he replied dismissively. Pat Killoran was the then-despised Queensland government public servant associated with crass and insensitive assimilationist thinking, and my question was way out of line in an anthropological perspective that stressed the continuing capacity of Aboriginal culture in places like Cape York Peninsula to sustain people through hunting, fishing and gathering, as well as through the host of customary societal and kinship rules we were learning about in university lectures.

The politics of studying Australian Aboriginal anthropology at that time, the early 1970s, were quite intense, and that led me to temporarily change my focus. Several Aboriginal activists would speak at student rallies with accusatory rhetoric directed at white students, with the implication we were complicit with racist oppression of indigenous people. Largely in response, in my fourth year honours study I decided that I would look at one dimension of 'my own people', so to speak, which meant a small study of young people who'd grown up in the Jewish community in the city of Brisbane. I was hardly centrally involved in Jewish community affairs, but this was a significant aspect of my identity through the family's membership and networks.

This research involving interviewing and self-examination was a highly formative aspect of my education as an anthropologist, as I encountered sensitive and controversial subject matter. Though an insider within the Brisbane Jewish community, my questions about the Jewish Diaspora's relationship to Israel were disapproved of by some. Support for Israel was regarded as a simple function of being Jewish. Though I wished to openly explore this issue among young people, the irony was that I also actually resisted the pretty widespread view among fellow students and lecturers that Israel was an outpost of European colonialism to be condemned. I recall being disappointed, if not traumatized, when one of my anthropology lecturers stated forcefully that he could envisage 'being an Arab', in the sense presumably of empathetic identification with non-European cultural difference and a sense of emplaced identification with the land – but that he could never similarly embrace the prospect of personal identification with those who had taken Palestinians' land away. My understanding of post-Holocaust Jewish suffering and historical rights to the state of Israel sat uncomfortably with anthropology's apparently one-dimensional support for alleged victims of European colonialism.

But if being an anthropologist entailed adopting a particular political position in the university setting, what I simultaneously learned in my first attempts at interviewing on sensitive subjects of identity and ethnicity was that the investigator's questions are not always accommodated. I reported one older Jewish woman's vigorous resistance to anybody writing about Jewish identity at all, when she accused me of 'handing the anti-Semites the information on a platter'. Here was great scepticism, if not resistance, to the value of the research process, and it was not much different from what I was hearing from young Aboriginal activists who, in the words of another of my anthropology lecturers as I remember from that time, 'don't want to be studied'.

A few years after completing my honours degree, I returned to Aboriginal studies, taking up a job as a site recorder funded by the Australian Institute of Aboriginal Studies. Ultimately I went on to do a PhD. I worked recording Aboriginal sites in the northwest of the state of Queensland. That was sort of the trajectory I was on for some years, but I guess I've moved away from there or at least expanded the scope of my intellectual interests.

Most anthropologists have stories about their experiences in the field and particular moments where things 'clicked' or fell into place for them. Do you have any such stories you could recount for us?

I don't know about things 'clicking' into place, but there is perhaps a small story I could tell that relates to that sense of being firmly located in the field, which sometimes comes *after* the initial sense of things 'clicking into place'. It was an incident that wasn't all that pleasant when it happened, but it taught me a great deal. During my fieldwork at Doomadgee in the early 1980s, in essence I was 'ensorcelled' – or had sorcery performed against me. At the time I was a young researcher doing fieldwork in the Gulf Country of northern Australia. An older Aboriginal man took offense, because I wouldn't do what he wanted. He wanted me to transport not just him, but many of his possessions – more than I could carry on my vehicle – to a location some three hundred kilometres away. So his way of dealing with this was – to use the local Aboriginal-English vernacular – to *'chuck a wind'* at me. This was a wind which could potentially damage me or injure me at some time in the future.

The way I learned that this had happened was through the people who were close to me. Some of those people who were travelling with me in the vehicle at the time were my close fictive kin. When they saw this happen, parked outside the old man's dwelling, one woman standing on the back of my utility began to scream. She called to her husband several streets away that the old man 'bin chuck'im wind la this boy, he bin open im arse la this boy'. From the driver's seat, I had seen him in a rage bang the iron wall of his humpy with a big stick and with his back to the vehicle lift one leg and buttock while yelling in his language that I could not understand.[1] The Garawa woman calling to her husband stood to me in fictive-kin terms as 'mother'. She and others quickly assembled off the vehicle to face the old man accused of seeking to harm me with sorcery.

People began to congregate around us. The older people supporting me announced what had happened, that this old man had *chucked a wind* at me. Then there was an argument; a battle of words took place with me as the young fieldworker at the centre. I remember largely remaining silent and waiting to be told what to do next, though I also recall being confused about what was going on. Eventually, the senior people travelling with me got back into the vehicle and said it was safe to drive off. We took a few days to get to the destination town of Borroloola to the west.

When we left Doomadgee, a senior man sat next to me throughout the journey, indicating his role as protector. Another old man on the back of the Ute sat facing towards Doomdagee from where we had come, with his legs looped over the rear tray in order to turn back any sorcery forces that might come from that direction. He explained that he had songs up to the top of his throat, gesturing vigorously with his hand held against his chin, and that he could turn back any sorcery winds that might try to overturn our motor vehicle. Later, when we camped, other people sat up all night to protect me. My 'mother' chided me for suggesting we might have gone back later to placate the old man who had tried to assault me with sorcery; she made it clear you don't make concessions after being attacked in the way it happened. Some months later, when a rear wheel came off my vehicle while driving on a dirt road, the old people commented that this was the sorcery wind eventually catching up with me. My own thoughts were whether I had failed to properly tighten the nuts when changing the wheel earlier that day; however, there was a strong sense in which the account of sorcery made me apprehensive on the nights in the bush immediately following the incident. I recall doing what I was told and sleeping with my .22 rifle next to me! Though obviously without much clarity as to exactly what I might end up shooting at.

There are many things one could say about this story, but to me it was important because it indicated that I had managed to achieve a very genuine degree of incorporation in those early years of research; it indicated to me that I had the capacity to achieve genuine understanding and communicative competence and so on. What it taught me was that as a fieldworker and researcher you're not always on good terms with all people who are your research subjects. In fact, one indication of a degree of acceptance and success in fieldwork could be when people feel sufficiently close to you to *fight* with you. That's why I've always thought of this as an instructive incident.

Did it change how you did fieldwork in the future?

I think it was part of a process which led to a degree of closeness to many of the Aboriginal communities across that region of north Australia. That has continued, and that's perhaps another point that might be made about that kind of fieldwork. Despite the fact that I moved a long way away, living on the western side of the Australian continent for twenty years, I've always gone back, or been called back, often for difficult practical issues like land negotiations, native title claims, or mining-resource development negotiations (e.g. Trigger 1997a, 1997c). On reflection, I guess what it taught me was what is possible through ethnography. And it confirmed for me the value of that kind of qualitative methodology. I have done quantitative work as well, and I think it's important to mix the two, but it's a very different sort of research. I think that we probably need to teach our students to be more competent in quantitative methods as well as producing graduates who are adept using anthropology's signature method of

Illustration 3. David Trigger playing a recording to Garawa men of a deceased Waanyi man singing a dreaming route. Gulf Country, Australia, 2009. Gerald Wollogorang (centre) and Lenin Anderson (left). (Photo courtesy of Richard Martin)

ethnography. In sum, what this experience taught me was what is possible in terms of the methodology of anthropological research.

I've also learned that not everybody appreciates the ethnographic method or the results it achieves. When I turned my analytical attention to the ways mining industry professionals understand nature and the landscapes over which they prospect, my academic colleagues appeared to receive the resulting publication well (Trigger 1997b). However, some of the industry personnel who read it commented that my analysis was merely about language and hence was not really reliable as a research account of the subject. 'That's just how we talk', as one person put it. The idea of language as a window on to assumptions that may not be consciously articulated was foreign to professional geologists and engineers. A senior geologist whose words I quoted fairly extensively commented further that he would have preferred to have been a co-author than just an informant – leading me to reflect on how anthropology as a social science can be viewed as simply an amalgam of common sense, something anybody can do, rather than a specialist discipline resulting from extensive education and practice as an ethnographer.

When working with legal professionals it is clear enough that anthropological expertise is recognized as distinctive in performing a role as translator across cultures. My applied research in Aboriginal land claims and native title cases has demonstrated how working across disciplines can be productive and in fact lead to a strengthening of methods and justifications of results when faced with the task of explaining the research to those unfamiliar with basic concepts. However, I also learned that anthropologists should not assume too much in the context of adversarial proceedings. In findings of the Aboriginal land commissioner in a Northern Territory land claim where I was the senior anthropologist engaged by the claimants I was seen to overstep my role as an expert witness by getting too involved in questioning some of the claimants as they gave evidence. Northern Territory land claims are more relaxed about rules of evidence than are actual court cases, more like inquiries than formal hearings. However, the land commissioner stated in his report the need to separate clearly the role of expert from any function as an advocate who might lead evidence from claimants. The judge pointed out that hearing an Aboriginal land claim is quite different from methods of inquiry in anthropological research, and the barrister with whom I was working needed to explain to me the relevant legal rules and conventions (Aboriginal Land Commissioner 1991).

How has your thinking about the discipline changed over time?

I came to the discipline with what I'd call a degree of political naivety. Like most young students I was attracted by a sense of advocacy. I see this in students today as well, and I think it's a mixed blessing. I then moved through a career where I've now come to a position of believing that anthropological work outside of the academy is much better framed and focused when it is expressed as a pragmatic contribution – such as expert witnessing or the giving of opinions which have pragmatic effects on real-world cases – rather than as a direct form of political advocacy. I'm speaking here about Australian Aboriginal issues, but I think the same applies, for example, to the environmental issues that I've been looking at for the past decade. Indeed, it applies to any anthropologist who is seeking to make contributions outside of the academy.

In the context of Australian Aboriginal studies there has been a particularly vigorous debate about the politics of anthropological research and whether academic critique is somehow more morally righteous than engaging with the messy business of government, industry and legal matters. Some colleagues are sceptical that applied research results are capable of contributing to substantial theoretical developments in anthropology. My own experience is that this concern is unfounded. While it is true that anthropologists can be expected to provide reified versions of cultural continuity in order to support traditional claims to land and waters, I have found it is also necessary to address the challenge of presenting nuanced accounts of cultural change. I have, over the years, taken the results of applied work and integrated them into the sorts of theoretical analyses to which we aspire in academic work.

However, the more condemnatory comments from other anthropologists have been that by participating in legal expert-witness work or contract research commissioned by government, industry or even indigenous community organizations, the anthropologist is somehow selling out the discipline's supposed political role as advocate for the oppressed. Anthropology is said to mainly be a form of 'critique', particularly of powerful interests, and applied research supposedly entails complicity in the domination of indigenous peoples who have survived colonialism. I find that the key argument refuting this condemnation of applied research and consultancy is the ineffectual nature of the criticism. Not only does it miss the intellectual, and indeed, political significance of much applied work, but also, this view remains delusionary as to the beneficial effects of academic critique for the lives of those Aboriginal people at the centre of the issues.

Tell us a bit more about your own role as an expert witness.

Since the late 1970s, a number of anthropologists in Australia have done a lot of work on land rights and legislation involving Aboriginal land claims that requires performing as expert witnesses in courts and inquiries or researching reports required by legislation. For somebody like me, this kind of work has continued for decades. With the 1993 Australian Native Title Act, there has been even greater need for anthropologists to contribute to this kind of research. I think that's an important area of applied anthropology that gets less attention and less support from the professional academy than it *should*. There are a lot of young graduates working in this area and they're positioned somewhat marginally from what's seen as the centre of academic authority in the discipline. That's something we need to deal with.

So what are your thoughts on the future trajectory for anthropology?

We need to ensure that students become less naively enamoured with the romance of 'radical alterity', if I can put it that way [smiles]. My vision for anthropology, which I think comes from a fair way back in my career, is that it's about the study of everybody – our research participants should hardly be confined to the category of 'exotic other'. Right from the time of my PhD and the book I wrote about the town of Doomadgee, I studied whitefellas as much as I did Aboriginal people. That wasn't so common then, and I'm not sure that it is even now, although there are certainly some colleagues who share this view. My vision for anthropology is to turn anthropological method and theory more towards the study of the *powerful* but also to ensure that students understand that it's not solely a matter of empathizing with subaltern groups; i.e. we need to do more than 'critique' when it comes to understanding those with power. We need to focus on the rich and powerful sections of societies with empathy in examining the way they interact with those subaltern groups who, I fear, so many of our undergraduate students primarily come to study.

Having said that [smiles], in a department like the University of Western Australia, where I worked for twenty years before moving to the University of Queensland, we *have* moved students in that way. Probably 70 per cent of the PhD students at UWA are not looking for the exotic 'other'; they're often studying the culture of a wide range of societal groups, including the relationship between subaltern and powerful collectivities. An example of one such project I supervised is the excellent ethnographic study of social life and power relations in an urban secondary school in the city of Perth, carried out by Martin Forsey (2007). A second is a study of environmental contests among farmers, conservationists and scientists, done by my student Yann Toussaint, with whom I have jointly published (Trigger, Toussaint and Mulcock 2010; Toussaint 2005). Contrary to what can be an assumption among colleagues, I don't believe this shift in subject matter is explained solely or even mainly by decreasing availability of the more remote or culturally different settings across the world. Yes, the politics of gaining access for academic ethnographic studies is more difficult in some countries and among indigenous people, such as with Aboriginal Australia or New Zealand Maori. But ethnographic work 'at home' should not be seen as in any way providing less interesting subject matter for an anthropology discipline heading into the next few decades.

Another problem is that those working outside the academy and doing applied work are still somewhat marginalized. It's less of a problem for those, like me, who sit in the academy and who, from time to time, go and do that kind of work. But for our graduates and colleagues who work as policy advisers, or who work in the fields of law and policy on questions of wider societal importance such as immigration, economic development, social-impact studies or indigenous peoples' land claims in countries like New Zealand and Australia, their work is not regarded with sufficient seriousness. As I commented earlier, because such work is often constrained by contracts or defined by targets, many academic colleagues feel that this work is somehow less significant. I think it's a critically central part of anthropology not only because so many young graduates – who consider themselves to be anthropologists – are doing this sort of work, but also because the research has the capacity to contribute to important intellectual questions. I would like to change those negative views and convince more of my colleagues of the importance of applied studies outside the academy.

To go back to my earlier comments, I think the way to handle politically and ethically *difficult* forms of engagement in the great world outside of the academy is not by sitting on the sidelines and refusing to get your hands dirty. It is *not* professionally responsible to say, 'I won't engage with government or industry – or indeed with community organizations – because I can take the higher moral ground within the academy, writing critiques of the Native Title Act or the environmental-impact legislation that I can feel good about, and publish in academic journals read by a small number of my professional colleagues'. We need to be a profession that can make compromises when compromises are needed. We need to focus more effort towards making practical contributions outside the academy, joining those efforts to our intellectual work inside the universities.

You speak about academics' responses to applied anthropology and to using anthropology in the public sphere, but how would you respond to those who portray anthropology as an ivory-tower discipline that has little to contribute to public issues?

In my experience, especially with legal work, many Australian lawyers working on Aboriginal issues feel that anthropology *does* have a lot to offer, although they are at times not sure what exactly that might be. But the point you make is a good one. What do we need to do to change the broad public perception that anthropologists study the past or only exotic things and that that's all that anthropology can be? That's a difficult one. We have to proceed step by step and case by case. With my own PhD students I've supervised people whose work challenges that stereotype – through research on the culture of high schools in urban Australia, the lives of farmers in rural Australia and the nature of 'sea change' communities driven by lifestyle priorities.

We also have to find a way to profile our work better to the broader community. This is a major challenge. In the face of some disinterest from colleagues, I've tried, as have others over the years, to write for the popular media and to do interviews on radio and so on. Book reviews provide a way into more popularly circulating publications with wider readerships (examples from my own work include Trigger 2008c, 2009a, 2009b).

Those opportunities come from time to time, and I think we should use them to better educate the general public about what anthropology is and what it can be. If we look at the history of urban and rural anthropological studies in both the USA and the UK, it is clear that anthropologists have not just been studying remote, exotic locations but that our contribution is the study of culture more broadly and across many types of location. The real challenge, perhaps, is to communicate in a clear and accessible way to the general public – and this includes to politicians, lawyers and everybody else – anthropology's potential. The typical difficultly we all have is that you usually don't have enough space in the widely read media to do that. You've got to write your points in a much more concise fashion than you would for an academic journal. We need more practice doing this, and, if possible, we need to teach our students to do this as well, to be more savvy with the media and with the Internet of course.

Can ethnographic film perhaps play a role in anthropological work of this kind?

Just recently I've been working on ethnographic video recordings from the 1980s which were made for use in my applied land claims work in the Gulf Country. This is what I would call ethnographic '*vision*' material involving people who were Aboriginal land claimants at the time, giving their views about their traditional links to their country. It was created in the context of the material's potential use as evidence in court cases or inquiries, because the representatives of the Australian legal system, judges and whoever else, can't necessarily visit such remote locations. I've been doing this kind of work over several decades, making use of video cameras and, more recently, digital recordings.

A second usage of film and related audio recordings is that Aboriginal people from the Gulf communities are now in a position to be requesting from me records from earlier times. Their older relatives with whom I worked may now be deceased, and cultural materials are no longer known as clearly by younger generations. While it is, in my view, important for the anthropologist to avoid taking on the role of heroic holder or custodian of the cultural records, working with the younger members of these communities is, I believe, potentially productive and rewarding. It is a very practical fashion in which the fruits of academic work can be made available for education of young people and subsequent contribution to their cultural survival. Such a blend of academic and applied efforts is consistent with my vision for an ethically legitimate anthropology.

References

Aboriginal Land Commissioner. 1991. Garawa/Mugularrangu (Robinson River) Land Claim. Canberra: Australian Government Printer, 9, 11.

Forsey, M. 2007. *Challenging the System? A Dramatic Tale of Neoliberal Reform in an Australian High School.* Charlotte, NC: Information Age Publishing.

Malouf, D. 1998. *The Island (Lecture 1).* The Boyer Lectures, presented on Australian Broadcasting Corporation Radio National, Sydney, 15 November 1998.

Mulcock, J., and D. Trigger. 2008. 'Ecology and Identity: A Comparative Perspective on the Negotiation of "Nativeness"'. In *Toxic Belonging? Identity and Ecology in Southern Africa,* ed. D. Wylie, 178–98. Cambridge: Cambridge Scholars Press.

Toussaint, Y. 2005. 'Debating Biodiversity: Threatened Species Conservation and Scientific Values'. *The Australian Journal of Anthropology* 16: 382–93.

Trigger, D. 1997a. 'Land Rights and the Reproduction of Aboriginal Culture in Australia's Gulf Country'. *Social Analysis* 41: 84–106.

———. 1997b. 'Mining, Landscape and the Culture of Development Ideology in Australia'. *Ecumene: A Journal of Environment, Culture, Meaning* 4(2): 161–80.

———. 1997c. 'Reflections on Century Mine: Preliminary Thoughts on the Politics of Indigenous Responses'. In *Fighting Over Country: Anthropological Perspectives,* eds. D. Smith and J. Finlayson, Research Monograph No.12, Centre for Aboriginal Economic Policy Research, The Australian National University, 110–128.

———. 2008a. 'Indigeneity, Ferality and What 'Belongs' in the Australian Bush: Aboriginal Responses to "Introduced" Animals and Plants in a Settler-descendant Society'. *Journal of the Royal Anthropological Institute (NS)* 14 (4): 628–46.

———. 2008b. 'Place, Belonging and Nativeness in Australia' in *Making Sense of Place,* ed. F. Vanclay, M. Higgins and A. Blackshaw, 301–10. Canberra: National Museum of Australia.

———. 2008c. 'Refugees from Wild Time', review of Hooper, C. *The Tall Man* and Waters, J. *Gone for a Song: A Death in Custody on Palm Island. Australian Book Review* No. 304, 9–10 (available: http://espace.library.uq.edu.au/view/UQ:194519)

———. 2009a. 'Sustaining Fictions: Challenging the Politics of Embarrassment', review of *The Politics of Suffering: Indigenous Australia and the End of the Liberal Consensus*, by P. Sutton. *Australian Book Review* No. 316: 42–3, http://espace.library.uq.edu.au/view/UQ:194523.

———. 2009b. 'Whitefellas Hanging on to the Learning Cliff', review of *Seven Seasons in Aurukun: My Unforgettable Time at a Remote Aboriginal School*, by P. Shaw, and *Yuendumu Everyday*, by Y. Musharbash. *Australian Literary Review*, 3 June.

Trigger, D. and Asche, W. 2010. 'Christianity, Cultural Change and the Negotiation of Rights in Land and Sea', *The Australian Journal of Anthropology* 21, 1: 90–109.

Trigger, D. and Griffiths, G. (eds). 2003. *Disputed Territories: Land, Culture and Identity in Settler Societies.* Hong Kong: Hong Kong University Press.

Trigger, D. and Head, L. 2010. 'Restored Nature, Familiar Culture: Contesting Visions for Preferred Environments in Australian Cities,' *Nature and Culture* 5 (3): 231–250.

Trigger, D, Mulcock, J. Gaynor, A. and Toussaint, Y. 2008. 'Ecological Restoration, Cultural Preferences and the Symbolic Politics of 'Nativeness' in Australia,' *Geoforum* 39: 1273–1283.

Trigger, D., Toussaint, Y., and Mulcock, J. 2010 'Ecological Restoration in Australia: Environmental Discourses, Landscape Ideals and the Significance of Human Agency, *Society & Natural Resources* 23(11): 1060–1074.

Yanyuwa families, Bradley, J. and Cameron, N. 2003. *Forget about Flinders: A Yanyuwa Atlas of the South west Gulf of Carpentaria*, Brisbane: Yanyuwa Families, John Bradley and Nona Cameron (publishers), p. 166.

Notes

1. This method of performing a dangerous sorcery attack, established in Dreaming mythology, is described in John Bradley's encyclopaedic account of Yanyuwa culture in the southern Gulf region (see Yanyuwa families, Bradley and Cameron 2003).

Christopher Pinney

Date of Birth: 1959

Place of Birth: Colombo, Sri Lanka. Grew up in Colombo and Birmingham (UK).

PhD: 'Time Work and the Gods: Temporal Strategies and Industrialisation in Central India', 1987, London School of Economics.

Fieldwork: India

Current affiliation: Professor of Anthropology and Visual Culture at University College London. At the time of this interview he was Visiting Crowe Professor of Art History at Northwestern University, Illinois (2007–9).

Positions held: Chris Pinney worked as photographic librarian at the Royal Anthropological Institute (1984–87); held a Smuts postdoctoral fellowship at the Centre of South Asian Studies, Cambridge (1987–89); taught at School of Oriental and African Studies from 1989 to 1997 and has held visiting positions at Australian National University, University of Cape Town, University of Chicago and Jawaharlal Nehru University. He gave the Panizzi Lectures at the British Library, in 2006, and the second Ramakrishna Nataraja Lecture at the University of Hyderabad, in 2010.

Major works
- 2011. Photography and Anthropology. London: Reaktion / New Delhi: Oxford University Press.
- 2008. *The Coming of Photography in India,* London: British Library / New Delhi: Oxford University Press.
- 2004. *'Photos of the Gods': The Printed Image and Political Struggle in India.* London: Reaktion / New Delhi: Oxford University Press.
- 2003, co-editor with N. Peterson. *Photography's Other Histories.* Durham and London: Duke University Press.
- 1997. *Camera Indica: The Social Life of Indian Photographs.* London: Reaktion / Chicago: University of Chicago Press.

Chapter 8

MORE THAN LOCAL, LESS THAN GLOBAL
Anthropology in the Contemporary World
Christopher Pinney

Your recent work has focused, among other things, on contestations over Hinduism and academic authority in the West. Can you tell us more about this issue and its significance?

I addressed this theme in a recent article entitled 'Epistemo-patrimony: Speaking and Owning in the Indian Diaspora' (Pinney 2011a). As you can see, I'm a great admirer of neologisms (Wittgenstein said that a new word is 'like a seed on the ground') and usually feel that I've failed if I haven't come up with a good one. What I'm looking at in the paper are contests over 'enunciative authority' in North America, which also relates to my work in Chicago at the moment.[1] I'm focusing on the activities of various North American resident Hindus of Indian origin who are actively campaigning against a group of scholars – predominantly white Americans – who they feel are projecting an interpretation of Hinduism that contradict and insults their own. The puzzle at the heart of my paper is why there is so little contestation over what we might think of as conventional religious objects or artefacts, i.e. why is all this energetic contestation focused on issues of who can speak and who can interpret rather than the more substantive religious issues and beliefs? My solution to that puzzle is that the reason that conventional objects are disregarded or deemed largely irrelevant to this contest relates to the question of 'iterability'. By this I mean a translational slippage, which tends to occur in every process of enunciation and articulation. What these activists are really seeking is to erase that possibility and create 'the correct' (or pure) interpretation of Hinduism and the Indic tradition. My proposed solution to that theoretical conundrum is that these contests over enunciative authority *exhaust* this question of possession and ownership, because so much practical and logistical energy is spent on targeting what are deemed to be faulty articulators of this tradition. So what is being contested turns out to be not the religious tradition itself, but who has the right to speak or interpret it.

In terms of your own personal biography, what brought you to anthropology and to India?

I would want to separate that into two questions, one of which is my ties to India and the other to anthropology. The India connection has greater coherence, almost a kind of teleology to it. It would start with the fact that I was born in Sri Lanka. My parents were in Sri Lanka for eighteen or twenty years, having met and married there. I left when I was about six, and the boat coming to Europe stopped in Bombay. I have a very clear, almost Kipling-esque memory of being taken around the Bombay docks by my father, who worked in shipping and was based for many years at Colombo Harbour. He wanted to see the harbour in Bombay and I got to see a little bit of the city, and it lodged very powerfully in my memory. There was also a poetic, metaphorical dimension to this – moving from the half-remembered space of Sri Lanka to a cold drizzly Europe and in-between experiencing this space of sunlight, a sunlight so vivid and intense, although there are possibly some false memories mixed in there as well.

The other thing was my maternal grandfather was a working-class engineer who had gone to India and Burma during the Second World War. I was very aware from my encounters with him later in his life that it had had a profound transformative effect on him. So I had the idea that India was a place one ought to go to if one had any sense. It was somewhere very powerful and very remarkable – and that put India firmly on my agenda. Anthropology was really much more accidental, I think. When it came to selecting courses for university, I happened to put 'anthropology at LSE' [London School of Economics] as one of my five or six university choices. I was very politically engaged at that point in my life, and I think I still am, but in different ways. But anthropology was a kind of mysterious concept. I really had no clear idea what it was, but I thought, 'What the hell, I'll mix it in among the other options'. It seemed as though I would probably end up studying politics somewhere, but instead I ended up going to the LSE to do anthropology. I said it was 'accidental', but on further thought, maybe I saw that anthropology could be the 'Fourth International' (i.e. internationalist and radical) version of politics as I might have studied it as an undergraduate. Another explanation which would also erode the accidental dimension would draw attention to the fact that I was interviewed by Peter Loizos (a process I enjoyed), and I distinctly remember on the evening after the interview locating his name in a footnote to Lucy Mair's Penguin Books edition of *Marriage*. That was the first time I had ever seen the name of anyone I had ever met in print (this was before what used to be known as desktop publishing) and there was a kind of magical aura around his name, as though I was suddenly connected to the great world of ideas and publishing. My parents both left school when they were fifteen (during World War II), did not go to university, and this experience is a mark of how 'unconnected' I was.

I think my own experience fits a very common anthropological pattern. Many anthropologists – rather like brutal dictators – have marginal childhoods. They move in from the periphery to the centre, and there's something in that dislocation which then makes them susceptible to anthropology as a practice. But my anthropological trajectory has always entailed a continuity of place. Since the outset, I've worked in the same town in central India, but on a range of different topics. When I first came to India I was driven by an essentially Trotskyite political commitment. I wanted to get close to the Indian working class. I also had a romantic, E. P. Thompson–informed vision of what the Indian working class ought to be like. I was interested in the transition from the rural to the urban, so the town I chose was also the site of Asia's largest viscous rayon factory. I wanted to find my 'dark, satanic mills', and I managed to locate a particular town that fit the picture and did the symbolic work that I wanted perfectly. My original fieldwork explored village resident factory workers and what happens when people move from rural hinterlands to huge factories characterized by continuous twenty-four-hours-a-day production and high levels of pollution. I wanted to find a symbolically monstrous form of industrialism, and I found it. Like Michael Taussig's (1980) work on mining in Colombia, there were lots of interesting discourses around about what was involved in 'selling one's self' to this new lifestyle.

In the early 1980s this factory was extremely polluting – in fact, during my first fieldwork the People's Union for Civil Liberties published a report on this town titled *Gas Chamber on the Chambal*, the Chambal being the river on which the town is situated. Atmospheric pollution and heavy metals in local water sources were all astronomically high, and there was undoubtedly a lot of local illness as a result. I subsequently came to think of this as a 'slow-motion' Bhopal – the Union Carbide Bhopal catastrophe, in which about 15,000 people died, happened a year after I finished the main fieldwork, and Bhopal is only 200 kilometres from the town where I worked. When I first heard about this industrial disaster in Madhya Pradesh, I assumed it was where I had worked. But actually my fieldwork uncovered a whole set of paradoxes and complexities which were very difficult to fit into the E. P. Thompson or Taussig model. For a start, people moving from the agricultural sector into powered industry worked many fewer hours. As bonded agricultural labourers, they were probably required to sleep at their employer's house and be intermittently on call 24 hours a day, and a lot of the work they did would have been physically very arduous. In the factory setting, they worked at most an 8-hour shift (with lunch and tea breaks), with a weekly holiday and several other leave entitlements, and they earned massively more. In fact, most factory workers made more in their annual bonus alone than an agricultural worker made through the whole year. So factory work was undoubtedly incredibly dangerous, because of exposure to various pollutants, but extremely competitively sought after.

There were plenty of 'devilish' discourses about the factory and factory work – especially ones which dangerously associated it with the current degenerate epoch, the *kaliyug*, and also (through a complicated and very widespread 'error') with the goddess Kali, who tramples on her consort, the god Shiva. But significantly, most of these were generated by agricultural employers, i.e. those who were affected by the factory not because they were working in it or were physically or psychically vulnerable to it, but because the factory has stolen their cheap source of labour (Pinney 1999b).

These relatively wealthy villagers turn out to be the rather surprising source of ideas about the dangers of industrial work and the factory system as a moral trope, which they then try and foist on those who are actually working in the factory (some of whom do partially internalize it). So this was a very different mode of ideological causation than conventional social theory leads one to expect – it's perhaps closer to the complexities of abstract expressionism, which I've always thought of as an exemplar for an anthropology of the contemporary world (a bunch of largely alcoholic, Communist and quasi-Communist artists are taken up by the CIA and globally promoted throughout the Cold War as examples of American freedom, i.e. the quintessence of capitalism).

So that was the reason for going to that particular town, and over the last decade I've usually been lucky enough to be able to spend several months there each year. I've often thought about the contingency involved in cementing that fantastically enduring relationship: this town was the first on a list of half a dozen candidates, and on the train from Bombay I got talking with an engineer who visited the factory regularly. He recommended a particular lodging house where I stayed for the first three months, and during the early part of that I met someone who had a cross-caste infatuation with the daughter of someone on the other side of town whom he insisted I meet. He used me as an alibi that would allow him to gaze on the object of his love. I got to know the father really well, and he brokered my subsequently going to live in his natal village. Over almost thirty years I've been back to that village dozens of times. It's become almost literally half of my life and it is all the fruit of those contingencies.

During that original fieldwork, I started to fall in love with what is sometimes referred to as 'calendar art' – the popular, fleshy and vivid, visual culture of Hinduism (Pinney 1997b, 1999a, 2004). That became my chief concern and has remained so throughout my career. So from my initial engagement with industrial sociology I moved to study popular visual culture and developed an interest in small-town photographic practice. The same town that had the very large factory also had many photographic studios, and my research on so-called calendar art – research which started in a village context – also brought into perspective questions regarding the consumers of these images and pan-national networks of artistic production and printing technologies. This has led me into a whole set of *continuing* concerns which mix the ethnographic with the archival, contemporary with the historical. My work has always engaged with genealogies of cultural production as well as questions of locality in relation to national regimes of production. My recent work focuses on early photography and is trying to think about the 'Indian-ness' or otherwise of these photographic practices.

I think there is what sometime seems like a 'hit-and-run' anthropology, which must frown on this strange devotion to one place. I always imagine that it thinks this a very unadventurous practice, insufficiently promiscuous in its choice of locations and questions, but the truth is that I feel I've still merely scratched the surface of this village and its milieu. Plus of course there are endlessly diverting projects. Last year I discovered that the archive of one of the best photographers featured in *Camera Indica* had been largely destroyed by

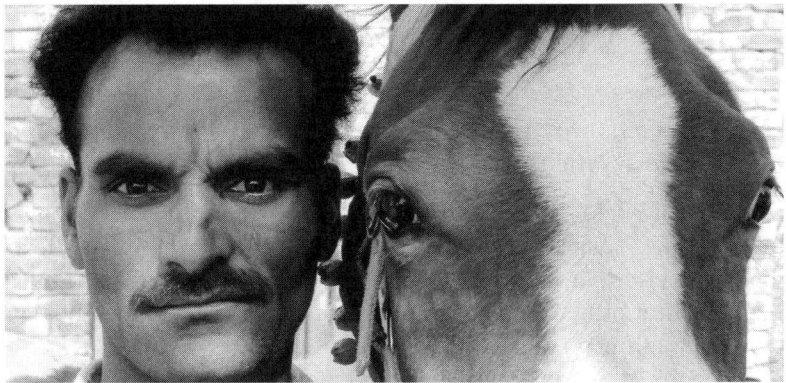

Illustration 4. Raghunath and the horse that cost Rs 70,000. 2010. (Photo courtesy of the author)

monsoon rains that got into his 'godown' or warehouse. Out of tens of thousands of negatives, maybe just a thousand were salvageable. The photographer – Suresh Punjabi – was going to get rid of all these medium-format negatives going back thirty-five years and [the images of] all kinds of aspects of life in this small town. One of the best things about the negatives (which I've started to scan and print, with the help of one of my sons) is that they record a huge amount of the space of the studio. The studio was very small, and because the photographer used a Yashica fixed lens, the negatives record all the surrounding 'profilmic' clutter of the studio (Pinney 2009). The images he printed for his clients were small details from the much greater 'noise' that the negative was forced to record. Walter Benjamin has a great phrase about the photograph being forced to capture 'tiny sparks of contingency' (Benjamin 1999; cf. Pinney 2008), and Suresh's negatives have these in abundance. 'Noise' is a quality I treasure in photography. And then he (Suresh) was (and is) a great photographer – one day I hope he will be celebrated in the same way that Seydou Keita or Malick Sidibé are. So that's an example of the kind of project which forecloses any possibility of foreclosing on this town and this area of the world.

It's also a great privilege to be able to view the transformations in India (after all, one-fifth of the world's total population) not only through diverse urban contexts (I regularly travel all over India as well and have taught and lectured fairly widely), but also through the lodestar of one village. Many eminent Indian academics have little (and surprising often, absolutely *no*) knowledge of Indian villages. I sense something like a fear of the rural on their part, an anxiety about this absence in their experience – and I feel doubly grateful that I'm able to ground myself in this one particular place.

How does your work relate to the discipline of anthropology, and how has that relationship changed since you began?

My sense of where anthropology is as a discipline is that we need it in order to have something to rebel against. In many ways I enjoy feeling peripheral to its major concerns and practices. For a long time I have felt that although what I was doing came out of anthropology and although people in other disciplines want to identify me as an anthropologist, what I actually valued more was operating in what I call a 'post-disciplinary space'. In terms of the conversations I engage in I seem to connect more with people in history, art history, post-colonialism and comparative literature. That's quite a general experience among anthropologists. I'm therefore slightly hesitant about trying to affirm a vision of anthropology as a discrete practice with its own history as though it were somehow an isolated life form. But what's great about it is that it gives you the security and the freedom to go out into other fields. I've recently completed a general (and very short) book about photography and anthropology (Pinney 2011b), which looks at the way anthropologists have used photography – from the beginning right up to the present – but also at photography as a metaphor for the knowledge protocols of anthropology. Writing that involved a crash reimmersion in the history of anthropology, and I kind of fell in love again with that history. I really enjoyed – as I knew I would – rereading people like Julius Lips, who fled Cologne from the Nazis and founded the anthropology department at Howard University (see Lips, J. 1937; also Lips, E. 1938), and wonderful living commentators such as Steve Feld (1992). But I was surprised by how astonishingly compelling Malinowski still remains – I got caught in a bibliophilic whirlwind and had to acquire first editions of his thesis on the family among Australian Aborigines, *Coral Gardens* and other very exciting finds – such as what appears to be W. H. R. Rivers's copy of Codrington's *The Melanesians*. I felt I was rediscovering a tradition – which LSE taught to undergrads with almost Jesuitical zeal – which now seems to me to be heroic. It was wonderful to think of Malinowski travelling en route to Australia (via Ceylon) with Witkiewicz, the modernist photographer. Rivers of course seems remarkable in almost every way, and it was a real pleasure to rediscover what an astonishing text Evans-Pritchard's *Witchcraft, Oracles and Magic* is. Of course the cast of anthropological characters during that period is very limited – there is a sort of nostalgic reassurance to be had from the feeling that you can know that totality. There is none of the bewilderment which one feels now in such a vastly proliferated profession.

But regardless of this recent enthusiasm (doubtless a function of reaching a certain age), the two main things I always got from anthropology which I value the most are a fundamental commitment to empiricism and to falsifiability. That last bit might also be an LSE residue: I always liked Bryan Magees's leftist version of Popper. Anthropology also gives you the freedom to 'do your own thing', perhaps because it was only ever, after all, a method. However, that makes it difficult to try and cast an eye over anthropology as a whole. The great amount of specialization and 'sub-specialization' of anthropology has made it very difficult for anthropologists to engage in coherent conversations.

Where does visual anthropology fit into these sub-disciplinary specializations?

Visual anthropology was for a long time considered a methodological sub-disciplinary zone and very peripheral to central anthropological concerns. It has clearly moved much closer to the centre. I think there are some megalomaniacal discourses about how central it *ought* to be, but I'm not sure that I'm fully signed up to them. But I think unquestionably, the 'pictorial turn', the 'sensory turn' and the 'material turn' mean that what people who call themselves 'visual anthropologists' have been doing for many decades is now of increasing interest to a much broader anthropological audience (MacDougall 1998, 2005; Pinney 2006). The growing importance of material culture is an area of particular interest. One could think about the impact of Bruno Latour or some of Marilyn Strathern's work. What used to be pigeonholed as visual anthropology has now entered a different trajectory which allows it to engage with more central concerns. One way of thinking about that is in terms of the 'final shedding of Durkheimianism', as Latour would put it, so that a new space is emerging in which the visual and the material can be thought of as something other than 'secondary screens' onto which a more primal concerns are projected. I see the visual and material as *originating points* of presentation and contestation that are impacting on anthropology's centre. That would link up with my interest in visual practices and technologies as essentially avant-garde projects which are making worlds in themselves. They're not simply shadows of a set of pre-existing or already-achieved social forces (Pinney 2005).

. . . which is good news for those with research interests in the visual?

It's good news for everyone. But there's still a long way to go. Many anthropology departments, especially many in North America, are completely devoid of visual engagement, and in these places the visual remains very 'exotic'.

What particular fieldwork encounters have been of especial importance in shaping your understanding?

Several spring to mind. One very early experience was when I photographed my immediate neighbour in the village in Malwa, in central India. He was standing under a very ancient mango tree, and I spent a long time composing my photograph. I ought to say that this neighbour, Bherulal, was famously irascible: a very difficult but fascinating and strangely attractive character, someone who projected a powerful personality. I was standing at the well with my camera and I wanted to produce an image that captured some quality of his intransigence, his irascibility. So I took this photograph and I eventually sent off the film to be processed in the UK. I had a twelve-by-eight enlargement made of it, which was then posted back to India. I thought this picture was, by my standards, a masterpiece of portrait photography: half of his face was cast in shadow, which seemed to capture that mysterious, unfathomable quality of Bherulal. Anyway, I proudly presented this image to him, and he was furious. He wanted to know why half his face was in '*chhaya*', in shadow. Couldn't I take a proper photograph? He took it almost as an insult, but he was also clearly disappointed. That was a key moment which made me think about local photographic aesthetics. And that incident triggered much of the focus of my first book, *Camera Indica* (Pinney 1997a). I wanted to figure out what was at stake in these two opposed evaluations and what this revealed about questions of aesthetics, concepts of personhood, self-presentation and so on.

Another incident I vividly recall occurred two days before I left the village at the end of my first long period of fieldwork. I was talking with Biharilal, who had recently become the village *chaukidar* (watchman) about wedding parties. I always rather dreaded accompanying grooms to distant villages for their marriages (there is patrilocal residence and village exogamy) since this often involved hours – usually in the middle of the night – waiting on crowded buses for a priest to determine the auspicious time to depart. Biharilal then said that he didn't like going to other villages, because he 'didn't know where to piss'. It turned out that he was afraid of urinating on various classes of spirits – *jhujhars, sagats, parhis* etc., and of course I frantically scribbled all this down, but I remember thinking with a sinking feeling – after all, I was leaving, and possibly forever, the day after next – 'My God, I don't understand anything about this place'. I'd been there fifteen months and I still hadn't grasped Biharilal's existential dread.

Another key moment, or period, which stands out is much more recent. I've been fortunate to be able to return frequently to the village, and in my current incarnation as a temporary art historian, I've not really been compelled to do serious fieldwork. I do a kind of Geertzian – or was it a Cliffordian – 'deep-hanging out' [smiles]. I'm in the fortunate situation of being in the village where most people there have now grown up alongside my presence and we feel we know each other and there's an *ease* about our relationship. When I don't have my notebook or tape recorder, I'm not being inquisitive and it's a much more pleasant experience for them. As part of that engagement I've become involved with a health centre in the village. This has made me think in new ways about questions of politics, access and entitlement. Provoked by Dalit (formerly Untouchable) and other marginalized social groups' responses to their lack of access to health centre facilities, I've become a kind of 'neo-Habermasian'. The account they give is that this is something radically new in the village context, something to which they have an equal entitlement. I'm interested in quizzing them about their experience of access to the centre.

This is still an ongoing research project of yours, isn't it?

I wouldn't say it's 'research'. When I first went to the village I was impoverished, and now I'm not and am able to return something to the village. I would say it's sort of a citizenly duty, but one that has also produced a moment of theoretical clarification and a certain redirection in my thinking about the political issues at stake. It has hastened my abandonment of the cultural-relativist assumption that hierarchy in this particular situation was more or less immutable and that I shouldn't in any way intervene or take a position on it. My views on that have changed. I see now how fluid and changeable such hierarchies really are. I also get a very strong sense of how different kinds of egalitarian spaces can transform enduring practices, I think for the better. That experience has actually had some knock-on effects in my work. Two of them are worth mentioning. The first would be that it has made me much more sceptical of a very powerful cultural-political position within India, one associated largely with Ashis

Nandy, which looks to the nonmodern as a cultural resource and rejects a valorized Western modernity and all the Habermasian baggage that entails. In the past, in an interview with Nandy, I called him a 'noble essentialist' (Pinney 1995). I now find myself much more sceptical about those positions and arguing for critical rationality as intrinsically more desirable as a mode of political empowerment. I know this is something that can never be perfectly achieved, but I'm interested in striving for it and the subjunctive possibilities it entails. I would say that personal, citizenly experience has made me think very differently about theoretical questions and has had a knock-on effect on one of my current projects, which is a study of a century or more of popular representations of punishments in hell, that genre of fascinating popular images that show punitive inflictions of pain on transgressors of traditional hierarchic social practices. In thinking about that as a cultural historical practice, I've found myself taking a much more critically engaged stance towards it. I now see this as a set of vested interests that are being manifest, promulgated and proselytized through these images. Maybe the correct mode of analysis is to be *critically* opposed to them, rather than adopting the conventional anthropological 'affirmative' stance.

But of course I'm also doing what looks like conventional research in that village. In 2004 I took a video camera with me for the first time in order to film at the Kumbh Mela, a huge fair which is held every twelve years in a nearby town called Ujjain. I'd been to the previous event in 1992 and found it pretty punishing (seven million people flood a city of 400,000). But having the camera (which was quite large) changed all that. It was assumed that I was the conduit to some desirable global mediascape, and I found that the police would force back the crowds for me, gurus would delay their activities until I was comfortably set up, and so on. And in the village the camera had similar kinds of mediating effects. I was 'forced' to film practices of which I had – until then – a hazy awareness. Specifically, various Dalit shamans demanded that I film them 'thrashing' while possessed by various goddesses.

I was valuable as a documenter of what I later came to understand as a different form of radical (we could say 'revolutionary') empiricism. Their argument was that they [Dalits] are closer to the gods (because they 'thrash' with them in a way, and to an extent, that Brahmans don't) than higher castes. And the evidential protocol is empirical observation, which assists them in their campaigns against higher castes who claim that is all fraudulent trickery. They all say 'look around' and decide who is closest to the gods. My camera is a

Illustration 5. Goddess factory, Guna, Madhya Pradesh. 2009. (Photo courtesy of the author)

valuable adjunct to that political project (Pinney 2010b). So that's a very different kind of engagement, but one which also involves taking a position or, rather, allowing oneself to be put in a position.

So your change of perspective is linked to your field experiences and to the fact that you've become a 'citizen' as it were, in that particular village.

Yes, but I'd add to that that I've taught and lectured fairly widely throughout India. I'm delighted that my work is widely read in India – it gets reviewed in mainstream media and I get interviewed in and by that media. So I feel that I'm able to contribute to a broader conversation. I think that there are other points of contact that change one's relationship to forms of discourse and what one feels one can appropriately say.

What do consider to be the most exciting developments within anthropology or where it might go in the next decade?

I think the fundamental issue is the Latourian challenge. I appreciate that that could also be formulated also as the 'Strathernian challenge', but it impresses itself most urgently on me through the work of Bruno Latour. I am thinking here of his slogan, 'Must anthropology be forever condemned to study territories rather than networks?' We might call this the post-Geertzian predicament of anthropology, namely, how does anthropology disentangle itself from its attachment to 'locality' and to 'specificity' – which have become a prison for many forms of anthropological description? One endlessly encounters responses to work that praises rich, nuanced detail, but this is another way of saying that ethnographic study is a closed box from which it's difficult to escape. The Latourian challenge is, how do we conceptualize an anthropology that isn't simply this field of regional specialities or methodological sub-branches? But then, if our approach is not locally specific or based on deep immersion in a place, the problem is, how does one conceptualize the network? There's a danger here of universalism and new kinds of comparativism which we don't' want to return to. My own feeling is that the biggest current threat to the humanities and social sciences in general is neo-Darwinism: or more specifically, 'neo-providentialist', totalizing and universalizing explanations. Cultural and social anthropology need to formulate a strategic response to that. So the question then comes down to the space in-between the local and universal. That's where we have to put our energies into thinking about new categories of analysis (Pinney forthcoming). A slogan I like to utter whenever I have the chance is 'more than local, less than global'. It strikes me that most cultural practice occupies that space. But our analytic language – and this would be a point that Derrida might make – our analytic language gives us dichotomies of the local *or* the universal. It's very difficult to articulate that middle space of a qualified flow. That is where we need to turn our attention to – and I think some of my own visual-culture work has tried to do that in thinking about 'corporeal aesthetics', which, I argue, are not specific to South Asia. South Asia simply becomes a site of investigation in which you can develop a new analytical model that is transportable and which, in practice, turns out to explain quite a lot of behaviour, but certainly not *all* behaviour. One can then explore this 'more than local, less than global' space in general terms. Most social behaviour is not about presence *or* absence, universal *or* local, but about *intensity* and *distribution*. For me, that's where anthropology has to go, but without repeating the errors of comparativism. I'm a great admirer of early Soviet cinema, so I think of the montages of Eisenstein and Vertov. I like the idea of juxtaposition as a montage technique: the bringing together of bleeding edges of film strips, or socio-cultural phenomena, in order to think analytically about the intransigence or fluidity of that encounter. At UCL I've recently been teaching a course with Mike Rowlands on the material culture of South Asia *and* West Africa. We wanted to take an interesting problematic and ask, 'What happens when you try to align or montage these apparently dissimilar, unconnected zones?' and 'What does it do, analytically?' It was also a way of trying to think about a post-comparativism using a 'more-than-local' analytic frame, which would not involve the superimposition of totalities but a different sort of modality of splicing unexpected conjunctions together and seeing what results from that.

In relation to visual culture, I think we need to ask that question in such a way that we problematize the 'culture' bit. Visual culture suffered from what a lot of new areas of enquiry suffer from, what appeared to be a radical opening up of a new territory was undermined by the resurgence of an archaic analytic concept. One can clearly see that with visual culture. Visual culture became this attractive new domain, a seemingly new paradigm of thought. But in reality, all it did was allow the extension of an archaic mode of anthropological thought in which culture was given a new second life – it was exported into the visual and material domain. For visual culture the key problem now – and again we can think of it as a Latourian problem, as a 'more than local, less than global' problem – is how we think about techniques of viewing, the technics of media and of reproduction, in ways that don't then bind them to a locality or into an archaic notion of culture. My most recent work on early photography in India is really trying to grapple with that problem (Pinney 2010a, 2010c). In some ways it's also a counter-argument to my earlier work in *Camera Indica*, which I think was that mode of visual culture as suggested by the very title, which seems to be saying, 'Let's start with the universal notion of a photography, and then we'll Indianize it, we'll particularize it, we'll localize it'. The problem with that mode of analysis is that we always end up producing locality as a kind of a footnote to a modularized global process. The task of anthropology, and specifically of visual culture, is to try and reverse that trajectory, to think about how different techniques produce certain effects which we can then see echoed elsewhere in the space of the 'more than local, less than global'.

What I'm trying to do in the most recent work is to think about the transformations that photographies produce. That means turning away from the idea that a modular technology or technical practice is captured by local cultural practice, to focus on the complex experimental zone in which technical practices of camerawork *define* new subjects and new cultural practices which are genuinely transformative. Once we approach photography in that sense, we are contributing to a general theory of photography as a technical practice which should ideally have applicability in the 'more than local, less than global' and can then be exported beyond India. Strathern's work on the 'dividual person' would be a perfect exemplar of this approach in other fields – the concept moved from India (starting with McKim Marriott) to Melanesia and then became partially globalized, because what ethnography shows us is that a 'more than local, less than global' condition has extra-local applicability and relevance.

References

Benjamin, W. 1999. 'A Little History of Photography' in M. W. Jennings (ed). *Walter Benjamin: Selected Writings Volume 2 Part 2, 1931–1934*, trans. Rodney Livingstone. Cambridge, MA: Belknap Press, pp. 507–30.

Feld, S. 1992. *Sound and Sentiment: Birds, Weeping, Poetics and Song in Kaluli Poetics*. Philadelphia: University of Pennsylvania Press.

Lips, E. 1938. *Savage Symphony*. New York: Random House.

Lips, J. 1937. *The Savage Hits Back*. Cambridge: Harvard University Press.

MacDougall, D. 1998. *Transcultural Cinema*. Princeton, NJ: Princeton University Press.

———. 2005. *The Corporeal Image: Film, Ethnography, and the Senses*. Princeton, NJ: Princeton University Press.

Pinney, C. 1995. 'Hindi Cinema and Half-Forgotten Dialects: An Interview with Ashis Nandy'. *Visual Anthropology Review* 11(2): 7–16.

———. 1997a. *Camera Indica: The Social Life of Indian Photographs*. London: Reaktion Books / Chicago: University of Chicago Press.

———. 1997b. 'The Nation (Un)Pictured: Chromolithography and Popular Politics in India, 1878–1995'. *Critical Inquiry* 23(4): 834–65.

———. 1999a. 'Indian Magical Realism: Notes on Popular Visual Culture' in *Subaltern Studies X*, eds. G. Bhadra, G. Prakash and S. Tharu, 201–33. Delhi: Oxford University Press.

———. 1999b. 'On Living in the Kal(i)yug: Notes from Nagda, Madhya Pradesh'. *Contributions to Indian Sociology* 33(1and 2): 77–106.

———. 2004. *'Photos of the Gods': The Printed Image and Political Struggle in India*. London: Reaktion / New Delhi: Oxford University Press.

———. 2005. 'Things Happen: Or, From Which Moment Does that Object Come?'. In *Materiality*, ed. D. Miller, 256–72. Durham: Duke University Press.

———. 2006. 'Four Types of Visual Culture'. In *Handbook of Material Culture*, eds. C. Tilley et. al, 131–44. London: Sage.

———. 2008. *The Coming of Photography in India.* London: British Library / Delhi: Oxford University Press.

———. 2009. 'Coming Out Better'. In *Where Three Dreams Cross: 150 years of Photography from India, Pakistan and Bangladesh*, ed. K. Ogg. 23–31. London: Whitechapel Art Gallery.

———. 2010a. 'Camerawork as Technical Practice in Colonial India'. In *Material Powers: Cultural Studies, History and the Material Turn*, eds. T. Bennett and P. Joyce, 145–70. London: Routledge.

———. 2010b. '"It Is a Different Nature which Speaks to the Camera": Observations on Screen Culture, Prophecy and Politics'. *BioScope: South Asian Screen Studies* 1(2): 111–18.

———. 2010c. 'Must We Be Forever Condemned to Study Territories Rather than Networks?'. *Trans Asia Photography Review*, http://quod.lib.umich.edu/t/tap/7977573.0001.102/--why-asian-photography?rgn=main;view=fulltext.

———. 2011a. 'Epistemo-patrimony: Speaking and Owning in the Indian Diaspora'. *Journal of the Royal Anthropological Institute (N.S.)*, S192–S206.

———. 2011b. *Photography and Anthropology.* London: Reaktion.

———. in press 'Anthropology in the New Millennium'. In *Sage Handbook of Social Anthropology.* Eds. R. Fardon, O. Harris, T. H. J. Marchand, M. Nuttall, C. Shore, V. Strang, R. A. Wilson. London: Sage.

Taussig, M. 1980. *The Devil and Commodity Fetishism in South America.* Chapel Hill: University of North Carolina Press.

Notes

1. At the time of the interview Pinney was Visiting Crowe Professor in Art History at Northwestern University, Illinois. He subsequently decided to return to UCL.

Nelson Graburn

Date of Birth: 1936

Place of Birth: London

PhD: Taqamiut Eskimo Kinship Terminology', 1963, University of Chicago.

Fieldwork: Canadian Arctic Inuit (and Naskapi), Japan and China

Current affiliation: Professor Emeritus at University of California, Berkeley

Positions held: After a postdoctoral research appointment at Northwestern University, Illinois (1963–64), Graburn taught at the University of California Berkeley. He has held visiting positions in Japan, France, Brazil and China and has served as Senior Professor, International Institute of Culture, Tourism and Development, London Metropolitan University (2007–2010). He was a founding member of the International Academy for the Study of Tourism and is a Fellow of the Arctic Institute of North America.

Major works
- 2010, co-editor with Han Min. *Tourism and Glocalization: Perspectives in East Asian Studies,* Senri Ethnological Studies. Suita: National Museum of Ethnology.
- 2008, co-editor with J. Ertl and R. K. Tierney. *Multiculturalism in the New Japan.* Oxford: Berghahn.
- 1983, editor. *'The Anthropology of Tourism',* special issue of *Annals of Tourism Research.*
- 1976, editor. *Ethnic and Tourist Arts: Cultural Expressions from the Fourth World.* Berkeley: University of California Press.
- 1973, co-author with B. S. Strong. *Circumpolar Peoples.* Pacific Palisades: Goodyear
- 1971, editor. *Readings in Kinship and Social Structure.* New York: Harper and Row.
- 1969. *Eskimos Without Igloos.* Boston: Little, Brown and Co.

Chapter 9

BEYOND SELLING OUT
Art, Tourism and Indigenous Self-representation
Nelson Graburn

You are particularly known for your work on the Canadian Inuit and for your pioneering contribution to the anthropology of tourism. Could you tell us more about these areas?

I've been studying among the Canadian Inuit for fifty years, and although I haven't focused narrowly on tourism there, lately these issues have gained importance as part of a growing sub-field of anthropology, which is looking at indigenous-run tourisms and the problems of making money versus commercializing culture. A key issue here is that in many tourism situations international companies or large outside vendors or neo-colonial government institutions try to control local cultures, the places they live or the nature that belongs to them. Aboriginal and indigenous peoples around the world whose lands have been swallowed up by modern technocratic nations are now trying to take back that control so that they can represent themselves and their culture, control access to their lands and at the same time, make a profit – which is something everybody has to do.

One of the ways this has been talked about is in terms of 'selling out'. That is a phrase used by Alexis Bunten, who was National Science Foundation postdoctoral scholar with me at Berkeley for two years and is now at Humboldt State University. She is a native Alaskan who did her PhD by acting as a tour guide for the Sitka Native Corporation in Alaska. She spent two years leading cruise-ship tourists and others around Sitka, not only the Russian remains of Sitka but particularly the Tlingit native people's homeland, houses, totem poles, etc. She was particularly aware that people who work as tour guides or who have any direct relationship with the public are always in danger of saying or doing things in order to attract increasing numbers of tourists. So there's a danger of unconsciously, or perhaps even consciously, bending the rules, showing secrets that shouldn't be shown, telling stories that are not appropriate for outsiders, etc.

This is part of much larger phenomenon. In my own work in ethnic and tourist arts for the last forty years I often found people making art to sell – whether it be small souvenirs or major pieces – in accordance with what they *think* the outside world wants, rather than what their own aesthetics or traditions would have them do (Graburn 1976). The pressures to 'sell out' to external demand or what you think it is, is always very great. But people are now increasingly reflexive and aware of this, whether they are employed by large tourist companies or running their own tourist businesses. This is one of the first occasions where people from different continents – Maori, Native Americans and others – are getting together to talk about their mutual problems with tourism. We're hoping to raise this to a worldwide level, maybe even with some UNESCO involvement, so that indigenous tourism operators and guides can take control over the interpretation of their own culture and the admission of people to their lands.

Could you tell us something about your intellectual biography? How did you 'discover' anthropology?

There are two stories about how I discovered anthropology. On the one hand, I was, in a sense, probably 'born' into it, and on the other, I discovered it when I was at Cambridge University (see Graburn 2007). I was the child of a couple in England, and my father's side of the family (five siblings) had spent nearly all of their adult lives in Southeast Asia, particularly Singapore and Malaya. The first to go were an uncle and aunt who were in Amoy (now called Xiamen), an island off the Fujian mainland, between 1896 and 1900, when it was under British control as a treaty port for China. Later they moved to Malaya and Singapore. Eventually they all retired and moved back to England. So I was brought up amongst a group of people who spoke foreign languages, talked about 'the natives' and who enjoyed cuisines that were definitely not English. My father's older sister had married a man from Ceylon who had trained in law at the Inner Temple in London at the same time as Gandhi, who soon went to practice law in South Africa. So here, in the middle of our family, was a man from Ceylon who looked nothing like me and who had immense knowledge of other cultures. Then many of *his* family, especially the younger generation, came from Ceylon to live in England. Because I didn't have any brothers and sisters, these cousins were the people I was brought up with and usually spent Christmas, New Year and summer holidays with. I don't think this was such an unusual situation in England, i.e. being raised in a family where faraway places became quite close and those 'pink bits' on the map were real places where you knew people from.

To begin with, I had a very intensive classical education in England. At my prep school (age seven to thirteen) we were forced to learn Latin and Greek and to know how those other societies worked! But, though I was very successful at it, I didn't like that and got away from it as soon as I could. When I went to my public school (the King's School, Canterbury) in England, I got away from the classics and humanities as fast as possible and got interested in the natural sciences, which I loved. I took the 'A levels' (Advanced, university entrance) exams at fifteen, before taking the 'O levels' (ordinary, school graduation), because under the Socialist government nobody was allowed to take 'O levels' before the age of sixteen, to prevent those in elite schools from scoring ahead, but there were no rules about the more advanced 'A levels'. Eventually I took 'S level' (scholarships level) exams in physics, chemistry and biology and won a State Scholarship to university. I also took the Cambridge exams for the Clare College group, including a number of languages and in geology, which I had taught myself as a hobby (and won the school science prize) – a unique exam and a number of test specimens (fossils and rocks) were sent down from Cambridge for me. I won a Cambridge University scholarship to study natural science.

I attended Clare College, and I finished my bachelor of science degree after two years, as required of scholarship students. I was wondering what to do for my third year of required residence, as I was allowed to study whatever I wanted and I happened to be living next door to an undergraduate who was studying social anthropology, which I thought sounded rather interesting. I went over to the department of anthropology and met Edmund Leach. There was a requirement that undergraduate students must spend one summer of their degree *in* Cambridge, doing courses during the long vacation. Leach said to me, 'We're a very small department. We don't have a long vac term, but go and read these books and come back and talk to me about it in the autumn'. He gave me two books; one was Bartlett's *The Study of Society* and the other was Malinowski's *Sexual Life of Savages* (1929), so I thought, well this must be a very interesting discipline! The next term I went back and took anthropology.

My first supervisor was Nur Yalman, an anthropology graduate student from Turkey who later went to Chicago and has been at Harvard ever since. My other supervisor was Edmund Leach. We had wonderful debates and he was an amazing man to know and to study with. But after that, I knew I would be called up to serve in Her Majesty's Army for National Service and to learn how to maintain a rifle and go out and shoot coloured people around the empire, or something like that. I decided that I'd rather study them than shoot them [smiles]. So I ran away, got on a ship and went to Canada, where I had made arrangements to get into the department of anthropology and sociology at McGill University.

The first week I was there I said to Professor Wesley, the chair, that I had come to do a PhD in anthropology. He replied, 'Well we don't give PhDs in anthropology, only sociology.' And I said, 'Oh gosh, I read the catalogue wrong' [laughs]. So I only got an MA, but it was very instrumental in my career, because the two professors of anthropology there, Jack Fried and Toshio Yatsushiro, had both begun to work with the Canadian government doing research in the North, which was *just* beginning to be opened up. The government was beginning to supply services to the Inuit and many of the Indians in the North. Every year the Northern Coordination and Research Centre employed maybe twenty to thirty people to do fieldwork in different communities in the Arctic. Before the Department of Northern Affairs embarked on full-scale implementation of development, they actually asked advice from anthropologists! In the summer of 1959 I travelled on the

Illustration 6. Nelson Graburn, in Kautchakuluk and Ikaujurapik's tent, Kimmirut village, Hudson Strait. 1960. (Photo courtesy of the author)

Eastern Arctic Patrol ship to the village of Sugluk (now called Salluit) on the south coast of the Hudson Strait, where I stayed about five months. I wrote my MA thesis based on that study (Graburn 1960, see also 1969).

The following summer, before I went to the University of Chicago to work on my PhD, I was employed again by the NCRC, this time to work in a small Baffin Island community called Kimmirut (Lake Harbour NWT). The population of the area had declined from over four hundred down to only ninety-three people by that summer, as most of the Inuit had travelled a hundred miles north to get work, welfare and medical services at the much bigger 'town' of Frobisher Bay (now Iqaluit, the capital of Nunavut Territory), which was then an American air base. I wrote suggesting to the government that they should try to revive the village of Kimmirut by putting in services there, because it was an extremely healthy place, both sociologically and in terms of the amount of game available (Graburn 1963). That was my introduction to 'applied anthropology'. The government eventually heeded my advice, and I went back forty years later and found a thriving community of over four hundred Inuit.

While I was at the University of Chicago for my PhD I studied with Fred Eggan, Sol Tax and a whole group of people who had just arrived from the University of California, Berkeley. One was David Schneider, who became my closest mentor and confidant. The others included Clifford Geertz, Lloyd Fallers and Seth Leacock. Chicago's Department

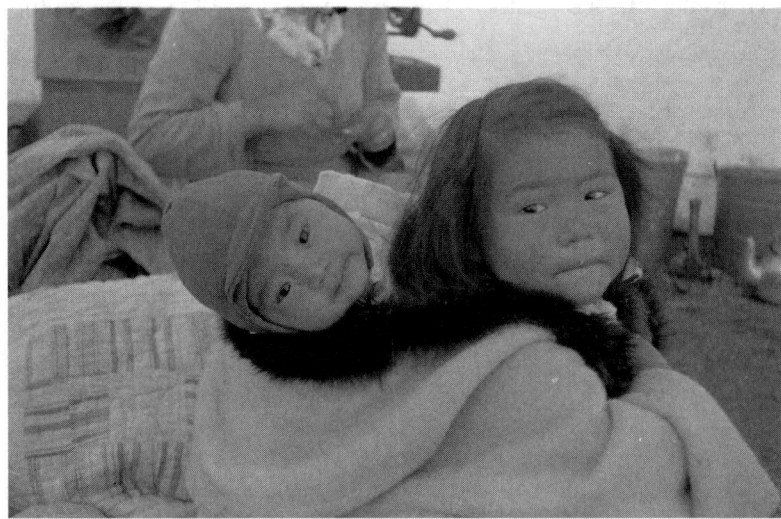

Illustration 7. Nelson Graburn, Ilisapi Kululak girl carrying her brother Jimmy in Kimmirut village, 1960. (Photo courtesy of the author)

of Anthropology was undergoing huge changes. Indianists McKim Marriott and Milton Singer were also there, but Schneider and Geertz really took over the direction of socio-cultural anthropology and attracted a new set of students, such as Sherry Ortner, Paul Rabinow, Harriet Whitehead, Robert Paul and others. There was a big divide there between the newcomers and the old anthropology of kinship and social structure of Fred Eggan and Sol Tax. Another thing happening at Chicago was that Sol Tax had started 'action anthropology'. He brought together a big group of American Indian leaders – they weren't called 'Native Americans' at that time – on projects for education and self-empowerment. It was a very exciting place to be.

Unfortunately, the fieldwork I was supposed to do for my PhD dissertation was stopped, because the Canadian government went into debt and cut its budget and research grants. So I never got back to the field and had to write my PhD using mostly the same data I had gathered for my MA in 1959. I took what was then a somewhat radical approach towards kinship, severing it from genealogy and anchoring it in behavioural norms, following the approach of Leach in his 'Jinghpaw Kinship Terminology' (1945), later taken up by Schneider himself. I finished my PhD in 1963 and immediately went on to do a post-doc, which allowed for another year of research in the Arctic, working for Bob LeVine, in Chicago, and Donald Campbell, in psychology at Northwestern. The Carnegie foundation funded the Co-operative Cross-cultural Study of Ethnocentrism to study the nature of ethnocentrism and relationships across ethnic boundaries all over the world. I returned to the Arctic for a year to study the relationships between the Eastern Canadian Indian and the Naskapi Cree (Graburn 1972). While I was there I got offered a job at UC Berkeley. That was 1964, and I have been teaching there ever since, with stints at the National Museum of Ethnology, in Osaka, and various museums and universities in Canada, France, Brazil and China.

How has your thinking about anthropology changed over the course of your long experience in the discipline?

I thought they taught anthropology very badly at Cambridge, because they never told us *why* they were doing it. They assumed that if we read all these books we'd *know* why we were doing it. But it wasn't at all clear. I was having wonderful conversations with Edmund Leach and Jack Goody about their research, but I never really understood what anthropology was as a whole. Leach was attacking anthropologists for just gathering kinship terminologies as if they were making typologies like butterfly collecting. He was almost debunking anthropology itself. There was a lot of division within the discipline. It was largely about kinship and social structure and ritual and *very little* beyond that. For me, anthropology's fascination remains the opportunity to do ethnography and to understand other peoples. But at Cambridge I didn't get the overall picture at all. They were just *beginning* to study what I would call cultural dynamics. Leach claimed that his book *Political Systems of Highland Burma* (1954) was about long-term change, but it wasn't. It was about oscillating change and long-term stability, because the endless transformation of egalitarian into hierarchical communities and back again had gone on for hundreds of years. It was very functionalist and therefore static.

When I got to McGill in autumn 1958, I was in for a huge shock, because the two professors of anthropology there had been trained in American psychological anthropology in the tradition of Margaret Mead and Ralph Linton. I'd never even heard of psychological anthropology. So when I started as a teaching assistant at McGill, the first thing I wanted to do was to tell the students what anthropology *is* and why we're doing it. And in my view it was more about kinship, social structure, lineages and things like that. This was a *complete* disconnect from culture and personality, child-rearing and projective tests!

It wasn't until I went to Chicago that I began to get a broader view on anthropology and the changes taking place in the discipline. At that time I continued to study kinship, but I was using Edmund Leach's model of kinship (Leach 1945, 1951), which was not nearly so static and functionalist. I also worked with David Schneider on the American Kinship Project. Schneider and Raymond Firth had received a big National Science Foundation grant to do a comparative study of American and British kinship systems. This was to counter all those decades of studying the kinship of obscure peoples around the world and leaving the centre unexamined. Raymond Firth had already started to study British kinship and the family after World War Two – probably because the British government didn't have enough money to send people overseas. And David Schneider, having done his doctoral fieldwork on Yap, decided to do studies of kinship in the United States. So they had this large, well-funded comparative project with a whole team of people working on Schneider's research. I was one of the team's six interviewers; we had our own office, we chatted about anthropology all the time and it was a wonderfully formative environment. Schneider was very knowledgeable, well connected and opinionated. We were ringside witnesses to the vicious battle with Rodney Needham about 'alliance vs. descent'. Homans and Schneider had taken the 'descent' (sentiment) position, countering Lévi-Strauss, which Needham counter-attacked in a defence of Lévi-Strauss's alliance (structure) axiom, which Lévi-Strauss later repudiated. With people like Fred Eggan and Paul Friedrich there too, Chicago was a very exciting place to be.

Are there any particularly important or revelatory fieldwork stories that you would like to share?

[Laughing] Well at my age it is difficult to pick things out from many years of fieldwork in many different places. I had a very strange first fieldwork experience working for the Canadian government in the summer of 1959. I had been sent out on a ship to look at the Inuit community of Salluit, and I was living in a tent amongst the Inuit. The white people in the community amounted to two missionaries and a trader. Anyhow, I asked the anthropologists Vic Valentine and Martin Greenwood, my government employers in Ottawa, 'What do you want me to study?' And they replied, 'Well, you're an MA student at McGill, you study what your professors tell you to study. We're pretty open.' So I asked my professor Yatsushiro, 'What should I study?' And he said, 'I can't tell you, you're working for the government, do what they tell you to do.' So I went there relatively unprepared. I took one or two anthropology books with me and I had a checklist. It was like a vacuum cleaner approach – just write down everything.

When I got to Sugluk I discovered the community at that time was very hungry. They had several weeks of poor hunting. The Arctic Patrol ship *CGS MacLean*, on which I had arrived, was anchored for three days in the nearby fiord, so I took a small boat back and asked in the ship's galley if I could buy some food. I bought maybe 70 or 100 pounds of meat and brought it back to my tent. I told the Inuit that I had some food, and in the first week I had 121 Inuit – which was nearly the whole village – visit my tent to eat with me or take some food back home with them. I didn't understand much Inuktitut language. I had learned the kinship terminology and a few other things, so when people visited I tried to get their names and their genealogy, and I began to construct the shape of the community through its genealogies. These genealogies eventually grew to include more than 10,000 people. The great thing was, after the food was finished, I was then welcome to go into any tent at any time of day or night and take any food of theirs that I wanted. So I was welcomed into every single household. Not just when *they* felt like it and were having tea, but anytime of the day or night. Nobody locked their doors – well they couldn't; they were in tents. So that was quite an eye-opener about Inuit reciprocity (Pryor and Graburn 1980).

The other thing that happened during that summer was that I realized that all the books I had brought were absolutely useless. I saw very little relationship between the work of John Honigmann or Ralph Linton (both cultural-psychological anthropologists) and what I was doing in the field. The genealogies were a useful fieldwork method in that they provided me with a way of interacting with people, getting to know them and having a reason to visit everybody. I wanted to make sure I got everybody right on my kinship charts. And they were interested in making sure that I was accurately describing the big picture of their family, which now I have given to their archives, and this has become a great treasure for them. But it was also a framework for understanding almost anything that came up. How people decide to move to summer camp, who co-owned boats, who were hunting partners, who shared food with whom, in what ways and so on. The genealogies were not biological records but were the *framework* for social action, as I argued in my doctoral dissertation.

There is another interesting story which connects my recent and past fieldwork. I've been going back to my field sites some ten, twenty, thirty or even forty years later (from 1959 to 2005) to give back photographs and other data that I took of people and their villages. In one case I also gave back digitized versions of old sound recordings from the 1950s. The place I went to in 1960, a little village called Kimmirut, on the south coast of Baffin Island, was on the verge of disappearing, although it seemed very healthy in terms of its relationship to the land, to food supplies, and in terms of its social relationships (Graburn 1963). The village is so out of the way and airfares have risen so high that it wasn't until 2000 – exactly forty years later – that I went back again.

I took with me 165 photographs that I'd taken that summer 1960, just black and white, as I could not afford colour film in those days. I put them in slide form, and I also made a set of prints for each of the families I could remember. But I couldn't remember too much about who was in all the photos, who the babies were, etc. So, two things struck me returning forty years later. The first was that I should never have left it for forty years. It was very sad, because people I had known as young teenagers were already old and widowed, some with hardly any teeth, others very sick or deceased. We seemed to have just gone from being too young to being too old and missed so much in between, although we might have been very good friends at the time. It was sad to learn that one of the children that I expected to see as grown-ups had fallen through the ice at the age of twelve and had never grown up. And here I had these wonderful photos of them to bring back to people who'd almost forgotten them. But it was also a thrill for people to see each other as they were forty years ago, when they still lived only in tents and igloos.

One of the extraordinary things was that when I tried to find out who were these people in the photographs, it generated big arguments. People would say, 'Is that Sitjak, no that's Imutjak' or, 'Her mother never made boots like that!' People couldn't recognize each other very well and some people couldn't recognize even *themselves* or their own children. I realized that at that time in 1960 they didn't have mirrors or cameras, so how could they know what they or their kids looked like on, say, July the 4th 1960? People didn't know what their kids looked like on July 4th because they saw them on July 5 and July 6th and every day thereafter for the next forty years. We only have that kind of visual memory because we have photos! They experience the visual world in an entirely different way, and we can't even imagine what it's like never to have looked at our own faces or seen photos of our kids. This kind of discovery demonstrates how the human dimensions of fieldwork can be very revealing.

What other research projects have you engaged with?

I'm somewhat unorthodox, as I generally don't have 'projects', but I work in an unusual way. It's a little bit like that first fieldwork, it just hits you. In 1966 I married a woman I met in Berkeley whose family came from Japan, and she was brought up speaking Japanese. They came from a small village in southern Japan, where people actually didn't even speak Japanese but another language, which she understood but her parents didn't allow her to speak. Anyhow, in 1974 we travelled to Japan with our two kids (aged two and four) and my mother-in-law. We spent a month in the household where my mother-in-law was brought up, in Kamou-cho. The house had just got electricity that year – one bulb – and the kitchen still had a dirt floor; baths were taken in a cauldron (*Gaemon-buro*), in the garden, heated by a wood fire, and water was pulled up from the well in buckets. This was a fascinating, almost pre-modern part of Japan. When we got back to Berkeley we realized that just speaking Japanese is not enough, one should read and write. So we put our kids in a Japanese-language Saturday school at the Oakland Buddhist Church for twelve years. I forced them to go, which they didn't like most of the time, until it all ended – and then they were very glad. I actually went with them for four years myself, because I wanted to learn to read and write Japanese.

So we returned to Japan in 1979, where I worked at the National Museum of Ethnology (Minpaku), which is just outside Osaka. I had met a young Japanese anthropologist, Ishimori Shuzo, at the second conference of the Pacific Art Association in Wellington, New Zealand, in 1978. He was taking up a job at the new National Museum, so I invited myself to Japan, when I had a sabbatical in 1979. Our family lived in Kyoto, and I commuted to Osaka, and that's when I got interested in Japanese domestic tourism. In Kyoto we got to know a retired provincial-art official Kimura Mikio, who volunteered to take us all over Kyoto and to meet important artists. There was practically nothing written on the subject of tourism in any language. Everybody was interested in 'pilgrimage', you know, *serious stuff,* 'spirituality', 'tradition', etc. But it turned out that Japanese domestic tourism was built on this same model of social relationships and travel as Japanese pilgrimage. I wrote a monograph *To Pay, Pray and Play: The Cultural Structure of Japanese Domestic Tourism* (1983), which I couldn't get published anywhere in the United States – possibly because at eighty-three pages, it was too long for an article and too short for a book. It eventually got published in France; sooner or later, scholars found it, and it actually turned out to be very influential. That is one way how I got into the anthropology of tourism, again, by accident.

Ten years later I received an invitation from Professor Ishimori to help Japanese anthropologists initiate the study of tourism, at a time when Japanese tourists found themselves being studied by Western anthropologists. In 1988 Professor Ishimori organized a joint study group, 'Ethnological Study on Travel and Tourism', composed of twenty-six researchers (including non-anthropologists), and he invited me to join them at Minpaku for the year 1989–90. During that year we met with Japanese scholars, including Professor Shinji Yamashita, who was later to become the leading anthropologist at the University of Tokyo, and we invited visiting scholars, including Erik Cohen, who flew in from Thailand, Jafar Jafari, the founding editor of the *Annals of Tourism Research,* and Okpyo Moon, the leading Korean anthropologist who had studied tourism in Japan. Later in 1989, Ishimori and I attended the first full meeting of the International Academy for the Study of Tourism, meeting in Zakopane, Poland. Since then, he and Yamashita have continued to spearhead an internationally important branch of the discipline (Min and Graburn 2010).

I also got into the study of art and tourism through my work with the Inuit, who had been making and exporting soapstone sculptures since the 1950s. This is an example of export folk art, or what some people call 'indirect tourism', because people visiting Canada can 'visit' and 'encounter' the Inuit without ever going north, but instead by buying these little metonyms of Inuit culture. I therefore started to write about this and found it fitted in very well with emergence of ethnic arts around the world. One of the other key people working on this was Professor Stuart Morrison of Auckland University, who told me the same thing about the Maori who were selling Maori art – not just for themselves, but in order to maintain their identity and for political advantage. This inspired me, in 1970, to convene a small conference of people working on similar issues in Africa, Mexico, southwest United States and Southern Asia. I published the volume, *Ethnic and Tourist Arts: Cultural Expressions from the Fourth World* (Graburn 1976), even though I initially had extreme difficulty finding a publisher. Editors and publishers would say, 'But this is not serious stuff! These are kitsch souvenirs, not works of art!' They didn't see that these are actually *key* points of articulation between minority societies and the wider world systems in which they are located. I think it made people realize that ethnic and tourist art *is* one of the main ways that people recreate their identity in a pluralistic world. We ran into the same problem with Valene Smith's pioneer edited book, *Hosts and Guests: The Anthropology of Tourism* (1977), which was also rejected by dozens of publishers on the grounds that 'tourism isn't a serious topic'.

What are your thoughts about the future of anthropology? Where would you like to see anthropology go over the next decade or so?

An interesting thing that is happening now is that a lot of the things that we thought were less important are coming back into fashion again. For instance, I published a major collection on kinship (Graburn 1971), at about the time when Schneider and others were beginning to deny its very existence (Schneider 1984). This was the accumulation of my training at Cambridge and Chicago combined with my field research and teaching experiences. Yet interest in the topic and enrolment in the courses continued to fall for two decades, until revived by the discipline's incorporation of gender and LGBT issues. More recently there has been a surge of work on kinship in terms of diaspora, 'roots' tourism, fictional kinship and so on. Other important new areas of anthropology include the media, advertising, the influence of the Internet and other things that couldn't have been done in the past.

At Berkeley perhaps more than some other places we try to work on what we call 'critical anthropology'; that is, you're looking at phenomena not just from the ethnographic point of view but from the perspective of who are the powers behind it, providing what might be called 'emancipatory knowledge'. This can apply to many areas of study, including tourism and medicine. Organ transplants (Scheper-Hughes 2004) and medical tourism (Bookman and Bookman 2007) have now become well-known subjects, even what has been called 'reproductive tourism' (Inhorn 2003). Anthropology is now studying peoples other than those living in the peripheries of the world, the formerly colonized or hinterland areas; pioneer anthropologists such as Hortense Powdermaker and Laura Nader have advocated and practiced the study of those in power in their own societies, and now it has become commonplace in spite of the extra difficulties of facing closed doors and mobile populations.

The formerly tacit boundaries between anthropology and other disciplines have changed and weakened as anthropology focuses on societies already studied by sociologists and political scientists, except that that anthropologists don't usually rely heavily on quantitative work. And globalization, international development and migration have allowed those disciplines and others to research areas previously known only to anthropologists, missionaries and colonial traders. So we are no longer alone with our own special expertise on that 'island'. We look at the new media just as do cultural studies and comparative literature. And we anthropologists are reading the works of these disciplines, so anthropology has become more interdisciplinary or even nondisciplinary. In the graduate seminar I have taught at Berkeley for almost two decades, 'Tourism Art and Modernity', we rarely stop to consider the background training or disciplinary home of the authors we read, unless they are using quantitative methods. But we still retain the critical edge that comes from our intense participation, our holistic view of socio-cultural systems and comparative perspective. Anthropologists can often be seen as subversive in many societies, because they tend to identify with the marginal, the colonized and the underprivileged instead of towing the official the line of those in power.

Related to this are the changes brought about as increasing numbers of anthropologists originate from and work in places other than the Euro-North American metropoles. Those who used to be 'the studied' are now the anthropologists doing the studying, be they Maori, African, or Turkish anthropologists. Under the Lula regime, anthropology is *extremely* healthy and popular in Brazil and growing *wonder-*

fully in China. Unfortunately, institutional anthropology is receding in some parts of Europe, like France and Germany, although there are many brilliant young Europeans who are doing exciting research, whom I encounter at the biennial meetings of the European Association of Social Anthropology and similar events. Many of these young professionals find few positions in their own countries, but they may work at other professions in order to pursue their anthropological avocations, and/or they move to Northern and Northwestern Europe or to North America, competing head-on with the rising local stars.

Intellectually, anthropology is doing very well. No longer is it confined to the small scale and the esoteric, and it is well suited to tackling the latest things in the world, including instant communications, uses of the media, nationalism, the effects of advertising on the worldviews of children, etc. Anthropologists have got to the point where they can deal with all of these kinds of problems whilst retaining the magic of anthropology – which is to know people as *people*, not just as numbers or representative samples. We don't just generalize, we work though case studies, and that must never disappear. We must always strive to know the local people as individuals and their understandings of the situations in which they live.

What has been your main contribution to public debates beyond the academy?

People have sometimes asked me, 'Why don't you do applied anthropology? You should be out there with the villagers, digging a ditch, or, or putting in a well', or something like that. My reply is that I could do that, but probably my main contribution to 'applied anthropology' is that each year I take the unformed minds of fifteen hundred or so of California's future leaders and I teach them a *totally new view* of the world and humanity, which will affect them for the rest of their lives. That is my main contribution to public concerns.

Many other things happen that one cannot predict. Back in the 1980s, I received a phone call in my Berkeley office from a lawyer who was a negotiator for land claims between the Canadian Inuit and the Canadian government. He said, 'You're the only person that ever wrote that the Inuit traditionally used shrimp. If you can prove this and if you've got evidence, then they will have exclusive rights to all crustaceans in the Arctic for commercial exploitation, from this treaty forwards.' They took my evidence, and based on that the Inuit now can have a $6 million shrimp industry.

Recently I have become involved with tourism-development projects in China. These are not projects I have set out to do, but they have resulted from my Chinese colleagues inviting me to join them in advising on governmental and private projects. These have ranged from the fate of poor minority farmers who maintain rice terraces in the Honghe highlands, which the regional governments are trying to get listed as a Natural and Cultural World Heritage site, to the establishment of an all-China museum of leather puppetry collected by a wealthy enthusiast that might be a candidate for UNESCO Intangible Heritage status. More enduring projects have involved working with the dedicated and much-loved officials, Mme. Yang Shengmin and Professor Zhang Xiaosong, of the Guizhou Province'sbody that deals with rural tourism and poverty alleviation, especially among the minority *minzu* Miao and Buyi people of the hinterlands. This large-scale and multi-decade effort allows development at the pace and direction decided by the villagers, with support for cultural preservation of songs, dances, clothing and cuisines and artisanal commercialization of the crafts, producing local pride and economic results intended to counter the mass emigration of young people to dead-end jobs – or worse – in the big cities.

At the other end of the continuum, I have been working with two other (Chinese) anthropologists in advising a self-made Beijing billionaire who wants to do something remarkable and positive with his fortune. He has taken the fifty-year concession on developing tourism in Jinzhongshan agricultural valley in the karst mountain region of Guanxi autonomous region. The businessman took our advice in keeping all the farmers in the valley and employing some of them, and helping others to open small businesses such as restaurants, against the advice of the regional government who expected them to be completely displaced and had built new shop house residences for them all outside of the valley. Some small hotels and facilities have already been built and two caves developed with pedestrian routes and colourful lighting, but the plum project is his desire to build inside the biggest cave a luxury six- or seven-star hotel, the greatest in China, with nationalistic allusions to Choukoutien (Peking Man) and the development of art and humanity itself in caves – I immediately thought that associations with wine and cheeses might be even more appropriate! At a meeting in August 2009 he persuaded me to give him a copy of my recent book on the anthropology of tourism (Graburn 2009), promising to read every word of it (Graburn 2012). And then he decided to sponsor a Tourism Research Institute/NGO in the provincial capital city Guilin, where, as a member of the board, I attended the opening. None of these things would have happened if I had set out to plan them!

References

Bookman, M. Z., and K. R. Bookman. 2007. *Medical Tourism in Developing Countries.* New York: Palgrave Macmillan.

Graburn, N. 1960. 'The Social Organization of an Eskimo Community: Sugluk, P. Q.', unpublished MA thesis, McGill University.

———. 1963. *Lake Harbour, Baffin Island: The Decline of an Eskimo Community.* Ottawa: Government of Canada NCRC-63-2.

———. 1969. *Eskimos Without Igloos.* Boston: Little, Brown and Co.

———, ed. 1971. *Readings in Kinship and Social Structure.* New York: Harper and Row.

———. 1972. *Eskimos of Northern Canada*, 2 vols. New Haven, CT: Human Relations Area Files.

———, ed. 1976. *Ethnic and Tourist Arts: Cultural Expressions from the Fourth World.* Berkeley: University of California Press.

———, 1983. *To Pray, Pay and Play: The Cultural Structure of Japanese Domestic Tourism.* Aix-en-Provence: Centre des Hautes Etudes Touristiques (Les Cahiers du Tourisme) Serie B, Numero 26

———. 2007. 'Tourism through the Looking Glass'. In *Tourism Study: Anthropological and Sociological Beginnings*, ed. D. Nash, 93–107. London: Pergamon Press.

———. 2009. 人类学与旅游时代 [*Anthropology in the Age of Tourism.*] Guilin: Guanxi Normal University Press.

———. 2012 "*Jinzhongshan*: Experiments in Cave Uses." UNESCO V GeoParks Conference, Unzen, Japan. May.

Inhorn, M. 2003. *Local Babies, Global Science: Gender, Religion and In Vitro Fertilization in Egypt.* New York: Routledge.

Leach, E. R. 1945. 'Jinghpaw Kinship Terminology: an Experiment in Ethnographic Algebra.' *Journal of the Royal Anthropological Institute* 75 (1/2): 59–72.

———. 1951. 'The Structural Implications of Matrilateral Cross-Cousin Marriage.' *Journal of the Royal Anthropological Institute.* 81 (1/2): 23–55.

———. 1954. *Political Systems of Highland Burma: a Study of Kachin Social Structure.* Cambridge: Harvard University Press.

Malinowski, B. 1929. *The Sexual Life of Savages in Northwestern Melanesia.* London: Routledge

Min H. and N. Graburn, eds. 2010. *Tourism and Glocalization: Perspectives in East Asian Studies.* Senri Ethnological Studies. Suita: National Museum of Ethnology.

Pryor, F. and N. Graburn. 1980. "The Myth of Reciprocity". In K. J. Gerjen, M. S. Greenberg and R. H. Willis, eds. *Social Exchange: Advances in Theory and Research.* New York: Plenum Press.

Scheper-Hughes, N. 2004. 'The Last Commodity: Post-human Ethics and the Global Traffic in "Fresh" Organs.' In *Global Assemblages: Technology, Politics and Ethics as Anthropological Problems*, eds. A. Ong and St. Collier, 145–67. London: Basil Blackwell.

Smith, V. ed. 1977. *Hosts and Guests: The Anthropology of Tourism.* Philadelphia: University of Pennsylvania Press.

Schneider, D. M. 1988. *A Critique of the Study of Kinship.* Ann Arbor: University of Michigan Press.

Nigel Rapport

Date of Birth: 1956
Place of Birth: Cardiff, Wales
PhD: 'Are Meanings Shared and Communicated? A Study of the Diversity of World-Views in a Cumbrian Village', 1983, University of Manchester.

Fieldwork: England, Canada, Israel, Scotland

Current affiliation: Professor of Anthropological and Philosophical Studies and Director of the Centre for Cosmopolitan Studies, Department of Social Anthropology, University of St Andrews.

Positions held: Following a year of teaching at Ben-Gurion University of the Negev, Israel (1988–89), Rapport took up the post of lecturer at the University of Manchester, moving to the University of St Andrews in Scotland (1993). He has held a Canada Research Professorship at Concordia University of Montreal and visiting professorships at the Universities of Copenhagen, Trondheim, Melbourne, Newfoundland and Aarhus. In 2003 he was elected Fellow of the Royal Society of Scotland, and in 2012 awarded the Rivers Memorial Medal of the Royal Anthropological Institute.

Major works
- 2012. *Anyone, the Cosmopolitan Subject of Anthropology.* Oxford: Berghahn.
- 2012, co-author with Vered Amit. *Community, Cosmopolitanism and the Problem of Human Commonality.* London: Pluto.
- 2008. *Of Orderlies and Men: Hospital Porters Achieving Wellness at Work.* Durham, NC: Carolina Academic Press.
- 2003. *I Am Dynamite: An Alternative Anthropology of Power.* London: Routledge.
- 2002, co-author with Vered Amit. *The Trouble with Community: Anthropological Reflections on Movement, Identity and Collectivity.* London: Pluto.
- 2000 (2nd edition 2007), co-author with Joanna Overing. *Social and Cultural Anthropology: The Key Concepts.* London: Routledge.
- 1997. *Transcendent Individual: Towards a Literary and Liberal Anthropology.* London: Routledge.
- 1994. *The Prose and the Passion: Anthropology, Literature and the Writing of E. M. Forster.* Manchester: Manchester University Press.
- 1993. *Diverse World-Views in an English Village.* Edinburgh: Edinburgh University Press.
- 1987. *Talking Violence: An Anthropological Interpretation of Conversation in the City.* St. John's, Newfoundland: ISER Press, Memorial University.

Chapter 10

SOVEREIGN INDIVIDUALS AND THE ONTOLOGY OF SELFHOOD
Nigel Rapport

Among the areas of anthropology that you are particularly well known for are discourses of violence, the anthropology of Britain, and the anthropology of the self. Tell us a bit more about your recent work in these areas.

I recently presented a paper on the 'ethics of apology' and apology as a kind of claim to knowledge and responsibility. My argument was that an apology is an ambiguous instrument: when you 'apologize' to someone you claim to know something about which you're sorry (and about which they should be sorry). You also claim a kind of responsibility for something that happened – an apology can be a kind of expression of, or claim to, power. I explored how difficult it might be to receive an apology since it can sometimes be construed as a form of passive aggression: the person apologising presumes to know something about another, something that that other should wish had not occurred, and places themselves in a position to 'correct' that occurrence.

The conference panel on 'Apology' was timely in the light of apology's recent role as a political instrument: a formal act demanded of governments and institutions (the British government vis-à-vis Atlantic slavery or the Australian vis-à-vis Aboriginal suffering, or the Vatican vis-à-vis the Holocaust). The communitarian assumptions here add to the ambiguity. I wondered how I would feel if, say, I were treated as representatively 'Jewish' and expected to receive an apology for the Holocaust. I don't think I'd like that claim on their part to *my* identity, my relationship to a history, my ability to embody or represent others' suffering. To make such apologies 'legitimate' is to collude in category-thinking and in all manner of collectivist classification. I do not mean to derogate an injustice: I mean to claim a right to be free from essentialist classifications of identity. An individual life is the precious possession of its individual owner. It need owe nothing to a past, a community, even a family, that it does not itself choose to identify with. The repression or theft of an individual life is a kind of absolute. That life – a world of its own, as Immanuel Kant described it – is absolutely distinct and when lost, absolutely irretrievable.

This tragedy is not ameliorated by apology to someone else, albeit that one publicly mourns the injustice and condemns the deed. One cannot claim to represent the life of another – even that of one's child of whose life's potentiality a parent is a kind of custodian – unless that representative status has been granted by the other. Culture is, ideally, an affiliation of ongoing, voluntary, individual determination. I am 'Jewish' – and 'Welsh' and 'British', and 'Nietzschean' and 'Forsterian', and 'Arsenal-FC-ian' and 'The Incredible-String-Band-ian' – as and when I say I am. What the rhetoric and ethic of 'real humanity' needs to know of me, as a form of politesse, is that I am 'Nigel Rapport', and in the process of authoring the nature of a precious, finite life – its world-views and life-projects – according to my determination of truth or beauty or pleasure or duty or right – while also according others, as individuals, the right to do likewise.

Is this the theme of your current fieldwork?

Yes, I've been taking up similar issues in my most recent fieldwork, working as a hospital porter or orderly in a large Scottish teaching hospital. I looked at how the porters, individually and as a kind of sub-community, appropriated the space of the hospital and thereby *re*-appropriated the symbolic discourse that locates them at the bottom of this organizational hierarchy. Acting as 'men of the world', they transcended the limits that the institution would seem to impose upon them.

How significant are these themes of 'appropriation', 'reappropriation', and 'personhood' in your work – or in contemporary anthropology more generally?

I was recently on a panel on 'British ethnography' which had Marilyn Strathern as its discussant, and she asked each of us what we thought 'ownership' or 'appropriation' meant anthropologically. For me the only form of ownership worthy of that title is self-ownership, and I don't feel that's something of which I can be disenfranchised or disabused. I am the *owner of myself* as long as I live. Whether I am able to express that self-ownership in public space, whether I find myself reflected in the rhetorics of public culture, is another matter. And self-ownership is the form of ownership from which all others follow. If, in order to express my self-ownership, I feel the need to own this piece of land, this cup, these clothes – those are epiphenomenal issues. That is, they serve to establish the *fundamental* ontological phenomenon of *self-ownership* from which other kinds of possession derive. 'Appropriation' is the possible practice of others telling me who I am and how my life should proceed, and having the structural power to impose those alien and often unjust symbolic or 'cultural' constructions upon me.

How important is this in anthropology? Well, an anthropology that begins from the ontology of selfhood is very important for me (Rapport 1997, 2003). In recent years I have called this 'cosmopolitan anthropology' (Rapport 2012). It recognizes the universality of humanity: that we are all human beings, human actors, and fundamental to our humanness is the capacity to own ourselves as individuals. Every human being owns himself or herself, *is*, intrinsically, himself or herself, and neither is, nor can be, someone or something else. I would like anthropology to begin from the recognition of that universal human self-ownership, which is also a way of asserting the right to *be* oneself, the right *to* one's self. I'd like anthropology to begin from recognition that we intrinsically are who we are before we are anything else. *Before* and *beside* and *beyond* being members of this community, this ethnicity, this church, this nation, this locale, there's a fundamental sense in which we are ourselves and own ourselves. I'd like anthropology to take seriously that kind of ownership and defend the human individual – 'Anyone', as I call him or her – from being appropriated by other people's institutionality, structuration or classification. The right to selfhood, the right not to be an instrument of someone else's power play, entails an individual *taking forward* their own sense of self, their own life-project; I would like to describe the *futurity* of a life—that which it continually becomes—to be seen as an individual's birthright, as opposed to the *traditions* of how others might conventionally presume to know him or her. I appreciate that I may be using such terms in particular ways.

In terms of owning your own personal biography, tell us how you came to discover anthropology? What was your intellectual path?

I found it by accident. I was born in Cardiff, in Wales, and was sent to an English 'public school' – that is, private, fee-paying, boarding – in Bristol, just over the border. From the time that I was born my parents had been saving up. Their families had been Jewish immigrants from Lithuania, Poland and Romania (during late nineteenth-century pogroms), and having established themselves economically (in wholesaling and tailoring) they sought more intellectual and symbolic capital. So I was sent to Clifton College to become more of an English gentleman, with a rounded education. As part of that education, at the age of fifteen I chose as my A-level (Advanced) subjects, German, Latin, English, and Political Science. It was the latter two, English and Political Science, which really fired my intellectual imagination and ambition. I loved English – and I still do. Reading fine literature is one of my major endeavours. But I also loved political theory: learning about moral philosophy, human rights and government. We read books such as John Stuart Mill's *On Liberty*, Marx and Engels's *Communist Manifesto*, and Hamilton, Madison and Jay's *The Federalist Papers*. I found the idea of the politics of society very exciting; *On Liberty* spoke passionately, ontologically and politically to a sense of self that I could immediately relate to. When A-levels finished, these private English schools were focused primarily on getting students into university, preferably 'Oxbridge'. I really wanted to go to Cambridge. I'd visited the university town and found it both beautiful and homely. I was fortunate to do well enough in my A-levels to be accepted without further examination, by Gonville and Caius College. But the problem was that you couldn't study politics at Cambridge except in the second year: I really wanted to concentrate further on political philosophy. So I had to find something to do for a year until I could switch to what was then called at Cambridge 'SPS', or Social and Political Studies. And Anthropology and Archaeology was the first-year option that I chose, because I'd liked archaeology as an amateur pursuit – watching programmes on TV and going on digs. I also liked the thought of again taking on a new discipline. I signed up for archaeology, and this thing called 'anthropology' came along with it. I didn't really have any idea of what anthropology was about, except something concerning primitive tribes. The person who interviewed me at Gonville and Caius was an archaeologist, Eric Higgs, so it didn't really matter between us that anthropology was its accompaniment.

When I began my first-year studies at Cambridge in 'Arch. and Anth.' there were three parts to the subject: archaeology, physical anthropology and social anthropology. The archaeology lectures were rather dry and didn't fire my imagination. Equally, I was not so excited by social anthropology. The first-year course was begun with a course on the history of anthropology, but I wasn't committed to the subject, so I didn't see (then) why its history should concern me. I had some very helpful tutors, including Carol MacCormack, Ray Abrahams and Alan Macfarlane, but in the first year it was physical anthropology – hominid evolution, monkey behaviour, genetics – that stimulated me, and I got on well with my tutor Alan Bilsborough. After the first year, therefore, I decided to focus on physical anthropology for the remainder of my BA degree rather than political science. I was too uncertain, unconfident, I think, to leave this new intellectual home: Arch. and Anth. was a small, friendly discipline. I had also just achieved a First-Class grade in my exams. So I didn't leave for SPS and I kept with the cosiness. Maybe that was an error.

I stayed on in Arch. and Anth., planning to do physical anthropology. However, in the British educational system you specialize early, and I hadn't studied any science since the age of fifteen. Specializing in physical anthropology, I suddenly discovered, would mean me competing with people who had had science right the way through school, since the small Anthropology Tripos now shared its teaching with Natural Science. Coming from an arts background, I didn't want to put myself in a situation of not being able to get the best possible Cambridge degree that I could. So in the end I decided to carry on with *social anthropology* even though it wasn't a subject that I had particularly liked up till then. The Cambridge focus on Africa and New Guinea was not my interest. What I could do, I realized, was supplement the curriculum with my own reading in the Gonville and Caius College Library: I found it had a good collection of ethnographies on American Indians, a subject that had appealed to me romantically since childhood – dressing up as an Indian and siding with their individual and underdog status against the cowboys. Over the next two years of my degree, therefore, I versed myself in the Comanche (my favourites) and the Cheyenne, in old American ethnographers like Hoebel and Wallace, Grinnell, Lowie and Linton. I interested *myself* sufficiently to finish the degree. I was also very taken by Edmund Leach. He had just published *Culture and Commutation,* in 1976, which was my second Cambridge year. He was also lecturing on the 'Unity of Man' – Vico and political philosophy – he'd given the Munro Lecture in Edinburgh on 'Custom, Law and Terrorist Violence', and he was president of the Humanist Society. Edmund Leach was an inspiring figure for showing the relevance of anthropology to contemporary questions: globalism, secularism, modernity. Alan Macfarlane was also important to me for showing how anthropology could focus on the reconstruction of historical communities and also on the UK.

When I finished Cambridge I didn't know what to do next. I'd had a wonderful time volunteering on an Israeli kibbutz between school and university (1974–5), so now I went back there to reflect. I fell in love, again, with the kibbutz balance between pursuing an intellectual mission – its secular, back-to-the-land ethos – and practising a very physical, fit lifestyle. So I thought, 'Why not do an anthropology PhD on kibbutz life'? But where could I do that in a British university? There was really only one place – Manchester, because of Max Gluckman's long historical legacy of sponsoring research projects on Israel. So I came back to Britain, applied to Manchester (also Cambridge and LSE). I was fortunate enough to be offered a PhD place by each of these, but I chose Manchester as the best place for my specialities. It also appeared extremely welcoming and encouraging – in the form of Paul Baxter and David Turton at the interview. I felt that I could be a 'member', with a legitimate individual anthropology project, in a way that would be different from my undergraduate experiences at Cambridge.

For a year I worked on Israel with Dick Werbner. I'm not going to give an account of the micro-politics of the Manchester department – quite an eye-opening experience for a naïve student of twenty-two – but Max Gluckman had died and his successor as Professor, Emrys Peters, had brought a change of ethos to the place. Emrys said to me, 'If you want to make something of yourself in the discipline, then don't do Israel, don't study the kibbutz; it's been done enough.' He said, 'Why don't you work with me and study patronage and small-scale politics in the Mediterranean?' I found myself torn between two powerful figures, my supervisor and the Professor. To cut a long story short, I negotiated a 'compromise' with Emrys and went to work with Anthony Cohen, on England. Emrys found this acceptable: Dick less so, but I continued to benefit from his advice and support – and have done so since. But this was the beginning of a very fruitful relationship for me with Anthony Cohen. I undertook fieldwork in a small English village near the Yorkshire Dales, 'Wanet', and I obtained my PhD in 1983.

What fieldwork experiences have you had in your career?

There've been four. The first was in this rural English village, and the crucial experience of my career. Tony Cohen had warned me that there was no status or license to be 'an anthropologist' doing 'fieldwork' in a British milieu, so I shouldn't advertise that fact unnecessarily. I soon discovered the truth of this. People in Wanet didn't like strangers and didn't like academics. I had to work hard to show myself to be nonthreatening and not a spy. Astrid Proll from the Baader-Meinhof

Sovereign Individuals and the Ontology of Selfhood

Illustration 8. Nigel Rapport in the field, Cumbria. (Photo courtesy of the author)

Gang was said to have passed through Wanet in the past, and people wondered if I was linked to her in some way. Why did I have a beard? What scars was I hiding? In short, I had to prove myself *not* to be a threatening outsider. So I got a job firstly as a waiter in a local restaurant and then as a farm labourer. I explained to people that I was a student of history, that I had taken a year off from college do a project, but that it was extremely boring and I could do all the dusty archival work I needed one day per week at local libraries. The rest of the time I'd really love to be in the village, on the *land* primarily, making up for a 'lost' urban childhood. Most of that fieldwork, therefore, was working as a farm labourer and then as a builder's mate. One particular farm was run by Fred and Doris, and they, their children and their helpers, such as Sid (a builder they employed), created a micro-social milieu which provided the tenor and the flavour of the fieldwork as a whole. I moved into a little caravan on their land, Cedar High Farm, and I became very privy to the details of Fred's, Doris's and Sid's lives as a kind of surrogate family. Next door there was Florence, over the road there was Hattie, and all in all, some half a dozen people became my key informants. In the evenings I'd go to a pub and play darts and dominoes, so it wasn't a narrow social circle in that regard, but I became very close to a small number of people, close enough to hazard interpretations of what I would call their 'world-views' and 'personae'. I came to understand the extent to which individuals were formulating versions of the world that were not necessarily shared or communicated with one another (Rapport 1993).

My PhD became a study of how a cultural community or social milieu as small as a village could throw up such individual diversity whereby people could be unwittingly creating unique versions of the world. I felt I was privy to this in a special way. Being treated as an inexperienced child on the farm, not interacting like an adult in conversation, I was talked *at* for hours of every day by Doris, by Fred and Sid, learning from each of them how they felt the world worked. As a 'child' I wasn't meant to respond, but they gave their full attention to teaching me their individual world-views. I could also watch them interact with one another, observing the only partial and ambiguous ways in which their full world-views were actually enunciated in public. My research became a study of the ways culture might be lived as a *surface* of ambiguous symbolic forms. Beneath and by way of that normative surface, individuals are formulating, maintaining, expressing, developing and fulfilling individual world-views. The collective symbolic form comes to be *animated* – brought to life – in the context of a diversity of individual intentionalities that might never come to coincide or be communicated to others.

Another aspect of this research was that I became interested in the way that individuals can contain multiplicity and contradiction within themselves, even while remaining solely responsible for the meaning and action they determine. Doris could be nine different people, I contended. Sid could be seven different Sids; each of these different Sids was a different construction *by* Sid *of* himself, with a full complement of voices, moods, values and versions of other people. I would watch how Doris and Sid would zigzag chaotically from self to self as they spoke to me. I felt that I was meeting different beings. Diversity *within* the self as well as diversity and noncommunication *between* selves by virtue of the ambiguities of symbolic exchange became the key themes of that fieldwork.

The next fieldwork I undertook was in the city of St. John's, in the Canadian province of Newfoundland. After I finished my PhD I gained a postdoctoral fellowship at Memorial University. The department was headed by Robert Paine, but it also had Jean Briggs and several other prominent anthropologists, including George Park, Elliot Leyton, Adrian Tanner and Raoul Andersen. Indeed, it was a thriving blend of both anthropology and social theory (Victor Zaslavsky, Judy Adler, Volker Meja, Ron Schwartz). My study there developed some of the themes of the Wanet study by focusing on public conversation as a means by which people could integrate themselves into a city. How did strangers to the city attach themselves to that city and to one another? The clichés and the catchwords of public conversations – in hospitals, in the university, pubs and courts of law – served as building blocks of 'talking-relationships', I argued (Rapport 1987). People would use catchwords and clichés to form initial attachments with one another and then develop those into interactional routines with particular 'talking-partners'. Each talking-relationship deployed and complexified the micro-institution of the public cliché in an individual way. In different relations, the same people used the clichés differently.

I was funded by Memorial University to undertake a study of violence in Newfoundland – this was Elliot Leyton's big topic. I translated this into a phenomenological question: 'How does 'violence' as a common public-symbolic form – the 'violence' of drug addicts, of drunkenness, of masculinity, of nuclear weaponry – becomes personalized and domesticated into very different cognitive and relational contexts in the city of St. John's?' In the ubiquity of phrases like, 'Isn't it a shame how violent the world is becoming?', I also interpreted a community-wide sense of a 'violent' North American mainland threatening Newfoundland island society; the latter symbolically proclaimed it didn't feel part of Canada even though it had nominally belonged since 1949. Violence was a *useful* figure, its ambiguity bespeaking a diversity of ranges and levels of identity, of claims to identification and affiliation from self through dyadic talking-relationships right up to the city of St. John's or the province of Newfoundland as such.

I spent four years in Newfoundland, following which, in 1988, I was fortunate to be offered a lectureship at Ben-Gurion University of the Negev, in Israel, at a desert studies centre run by Professor Emanuel Marx. I undertook fieldwork in a development town in the Negev desert called Mitzpe Ramon, focusing on why people were moving to such an extremely remote and 'pioneering' setting. In particular, how did American immigrants to Israel make sense of this in their life-stories? Why retire to Mitzpe when you've spent all your life in Boston or Chicago, I wondered? The move across the globe actually maintained and extended a narrative of self, I discovered, bringing different parts of themselves together. My neighbours had perhaps felt Jewish *and* American, now they wanted to be simply *Jews*. However, now that they were new immigrants, they found themselves on the necessary pioneering mission of bringing American democracy to the Middle East. They discovered that people who'd come to Israel from Yemen, Iraq, Morocco, Russia or Argentina didn't really know how to *do* democracy, or bureaucracy or even government. 'But we Americans – that's our heritage.' The irony, I felt, was that having gone to Israel to escape from a duality, they then become Israeli by reinterpreting and refashioning their Americanness.

I returned from Israel in 1989. I had almost given up hope of a tenured position at a British university; the Thatcherite-era cuts were so swingeing that it was extremely difficult to find anthropological employment. There was talk of a 'lost generation' of 1980s academics – since newer-graduated PhDs were fresher and cheaper to employ. I was very lucky to be offered a lectureship at Manchester. Marilyn Strathern had assumed the Chair, four of the eight members of the department had retired or left, and Marilyn was in a position of rehiring. From 1989 I spent three intense years in Manchester – primarily learning how to lecture and how to cope with a new audit culture – before the opportunity arose, in 1993, to move to a lectureship at St Andrews. Scotland's 'first university' offered a unique mixture of stone architecture, seascapes and research prominence. In 1996 I was appointed Professor of Anthropological and Philosophical Studies.

This is where I still am, although I have spent some periods away – Copenhagen, Melbourne, Trondheim, most recently as Canada Research Chair in Globalization, Citizenship and Justice, at Montreal.

My most recent fieldwork was carried out in a hospital near St Andrews. As part of a project looking at notions of national identity in Britain, particularly 'Scottishness', after the instituting of a new Scottish Parliament, in 1999, I came to examine identity at work in a complex organization (Rapport 2002, 2008). If the movement to create a new Scottish Parliament represented more than just a change of political policy, was a sense of Scottishness visible in people's lives? How did a discourse of nationalism and regionalism manifest itself, if at all, in a hospital whose ethos was universalist – the healthiness of the human body? How, if you will, did 'real humanity' abut against 'real Scotland' as rhetoric of social engagement? In order to fulfil this study I spent a year in the hospital. My letter of application was passed down the managerial line at 'Constance Hospital' until, almost by chance it seems, it fell on the desk of someone junior enough not to be able to pass it to somebody else. This was the so-called Director of Hotel Services, whose brief it was to manage the dining-room assistants, the receptionists – and the porters. He and I met: 'Nigel you should be a porter', he said. 'That would take you anonymously around all parts of the hospital, seeing all walks of life, talking to all kinds of people.' So that's what I did, for ten months (then spending a final two months interviewing the doctors and administrators). And what was initially a project on national identity subsequently became a study of the porters as an occupational community: their place within, and their symbolic contestation of, a hospital's hierarchical institutionalism.

Given this wide range of different fieldwork projects, what would you say are your over-arching areas of anthropological interest?

I've been centrally interested in the relationship between the individual and the cultural, and social or societal. I regard individuality as a fundamental *ontological* human state, quite distinct from cultural conceptions of the person such as individualism or dividualism. As individuals, we universally make our own sense of the world around us; we use symbols, languages and histories that we borrow from our milieux, but we import them into the self and use them to express meanings that come out of our own self and its interpretative mechanisms. My anthropology aims to elucidate the *nature* of our universal, human, embodied individuality (Rapport 1997, 2010).

Consequent upon this is an interest in *aesthetics* as means to do justice to individuality. Anthropology is a science of the human, but it is also a form of writing, hence its relation to other humanities such as literature and philosophy. I have experimented with addressing E.M. Forster's writing and Stanley Spencer's painting (Rapport 1994, 2003), in particular, for insights into conveying the diversity and complexity of experience – the lived individuality that I encounter in the field. There is no disciplinary 'boundary' to anthropology: the researcher's 'allegiance' is to their experience; it is their duty to make sense of this in as complex and full a way as they can. If there is a literary or artistic representation of consciousness or relationality that I can adopt, or a philosophical conceptualization or a psychological insight, then I'm going to be 'dilettantish', methodologically eclectic, and be confident and unapologetic in this. My anthropological duty is to encompass the complexity and authenticity of the data on individuality and inter-individual relations that I encounter in the field (Rapport and Cohen 1995).

A third concern – beside the ontological and representational – is to do justice to the individual *politically* or *morally*. How may one secure the best kind of social condition for self-expression and self-fulfilment? I feel that we are intrinsically who we are, *independent* of, or *irrespective* of, the particular cultural, historical, social or local setting in which we happen to be doing our interpreting. How can I secure the right to expression and fulfilment of this individual human being – wherever he or she happens, coincidentally, to have been born? What kind of society, of state? What kind of regulation of cultural and communitarian institutionalism?

The three issues of ontology, aesthetics and morality come together for me in the current research endeavour which I call a 'cosmopolitan' project of anthropology, whose key conceptual figure is 'Anyone'. As a kind of rationalist translation of the Christian notion of 'Everyman', 'Anyone' is the universal human actor: the individual as manifestation of the human. 'Cosmopolitanism' dwells in the tension between the most general and the most particular aspects of the human condition. On the one hand, then, there is the human species, the global universals of human life, or '*cosmos*'. On the other hand there is the human individual, or Anyone, embodying a life of unique local experience – '*polis*'. To comprehend the human, according to 'cosmo-politanism' is to see these two polar realities always in relation to one another. The human species is only and ever embodied in its individual exemplars: the human individual is to be known always by way of capabilities and liabilities that are species-wide. Between individual and species there may exist a host of *symbolic* classifications and groupings – nations, communities, ethnicities, religions, classes – but these are matters of cultural discourse, of rhetoric, only: they are epiphenomenal upon the concrete realities of individual and species (Rapport 2010, 2012). Only individuals and species possess an abiding reality, an ontology. Cosmopolitanism as a science of the human leads us to search out ways to 'annul' the language of cultural essentialism concerning the exclusivity of collective-symbolic categories, as Michael Jackson phrases it, and so attend to the nature of the capacities of the species as exemplified in individuals. Cosmopolitanism as a moral philosophy enjoins us to see beyond category-thinking to attend to the conditions of the life of the species, and how each of its individual manifestations might best fulfil its potential for expression.

The *ontology* of Anyone, the *representation of* Anyone, the *emancipation* of Anyone: these are three planks of anthropology as a cosmopolitan project. They outline the broad research agenda of the Centre for Cosmopolitan Studies that I have been able to institute at the University of St Andrews. The centre is in its early days, but 'cosmopolitanism' is a convenient conceptual label for outlining an approach to a particular set of questions.

You have defined a very particular path for anthropology. Where do you think the discipline is heading in general at the moment?

My interests have been somewhat heterodox, even heretical, I admit. But if I say my project is as much personal as professional, then this *is* something common to anthropology, at least in Britain, and a reason I am after all happy I stuck with anthropology at Cambridge. British anthropology is an enterprise of personal engagement, even of personality, whose key figure is the individuality of the ethnographer making do in the field and making sense thereafter. Each anthropologist has the right – even the duty – to write his or her anthropological disciplinarity, as it were, guaranteed by an experience and interpretation of otherness that cannot be gainsaid. Where is our discipline heading? My answer is going to be a personal one: How do I wish it to proceed?

I wish for anthropology to take seriously its Enlightenment heritage. We owe to Kant the term 'anthropology' as a modern concept. At the same time, we also owe to Kant the notion of the 'cosmopolitan', which recognizes, as I have said, that Anyone and humanity form a dialectical pair. Kant's vision was for the ethnography of everyday human-individual life – the science of human-individual capabilities and liabilities, fulfilments and sufferings – to feed into a moral arrangement of universal just society (Rapport 2005). How best – rationally and morally – to succour the human-individual? I would wish for anthropology to situate itself, methodologically and politically, amid this Kantian dialectic.

In practical terms, the most important thing we can do is to take forward the notion of human rights as individual entitlements. We are individual members of one human species, I have contended, leading *local lives* but of one *global condition*: we must not let rhetorical devices, political fashions or political expediency obstruct our recognition of this dialectic. Anthropology mustn't allow itself to be waylaid by an essentialist politics of identity. It must affirm the distinction between *real* difference – i.e. the ontological difference of individuality – as opposed to symbolic differences, such as might appear in claims to religious, ethnic, national, regional, occupational or class-based identities.

Let me be clear. Cultural belonging of communitarian kinds should be deemed a right: a form of self-expression freely undertaken by a mature individual at every moment of his or her life. I choose to support Arsenal or Cardiff City football clubs – or none. As human beings, we aspire to meet one another, at least on the surfaces of our individual selves, by way of cultural symbologies – whether concerning football or religion or class or art – that provide us with catchwords and habituses of alignment, even mutual entanglement. The 'trouble with community' (as Vered Amit and I have phrased it, see Rapport and Amit 2002) is that such discourses of collective belonging and exclusivity – 'real Elmdon', 'real Arsenal', 'real Britain', 'real Islam' – translate easily into nefarious practices of essentialization, stereotypification and massification: the 'honour' of 'Muslim lands', of 'pious womanhood'. The cultural is not a thing in itself: the cultural is a symbolic form or clothing, a medium of expression, even a 'vehicle for a conception', after Geertz. But experience, expression and conception exist apart from the cultural and remain responsible for filling the cultural with purpose, meaning and force. It is human usage, individual intentionality, as I have said, which animates the cultural form and brings it to life in particular instances. It is the 'existential power' of Anyone, as I would phrase it, to deploy cultural forms – and other environmental inheritances – as resources in the fashioning of personal contexts and circumstances. We must not confuse the cultural form – 'community', 'religion', 'class' – with personal existence.

Anthropology is the science of the human. Its laboratory is everyday life. It uses the individual experience of the ethnographer to attempt to grasp the individual experiencing of certain others *amid* their lives. We can never know for sure what it is to be another, but we live closely alongside them so that we gain as full a sense as possible – corporeal and intellectual, intuitive and observational – of what those bodily inhabitations *might* be like, and we build up databases of accounts in a multitude of genres, from the novelish to the quantitudinal. From our accounts of the *substance* of other individual lives we can hope to distil an apprehension of the *capacities* of individual human embodiment, the capabilities and liabilities of the human as embodied in Anyone. This, we discern, is what human beings *can* achieve in the way of imaginative, physical, emotional, intellectual endeavour. This, we discern, is what human beings *can* suffer in the way of imaginative, physical, emotional, intellectual repression. To complement our fieldwork accounts of the everyday practice of human lives we adapt the conclusions of other human 'scientists', from novelists to historians, philosophers and psychologists. What emerges is Anyone as a more fully figured phenomenon. This, we assert, is the *truth* about human individuality, construed not on the basis of tradition, of revelation, of symbolic classification, of political expediency, but of the best knowledge scientifically derived.

Anthropology opens up individual lives to global possibilities in terms of morality as well as knowledge. A cosmopolitan anthropology is an emancipatory project that would improve the conditions of human life. To be considered here is not only the 'despotism' of famine and disease, but also the despotism of ignorance, of tyranny, of lives circumscribed by narrow symbolic-classificatory limits. To distinguish between true individual natures, true human capabilities and liabilities, and merely traditional (cultural, communitarian, rhetorical) versions of these is fundamental to our anthropological endeavour to do justice to our informants: to foster their rights as individual human beings to fulfil the precious finiteness of their lives and not to be constrained by straitjackets of the merely customary and conventional.

What do you see as the future of anthropology? Are you optimistic or pessimistic about where anthropology is heading?

I'm committed to an anthropology envisaged as at once natural science, literature and political philosophy. For such an integrated – and, yes, ambitious – human science to go forward is vital.

Whether a future anthropology will actually be one that I recognize or value is another issue. I have described my fearfulness of 'culture' as a pernicious instrument – essentializing, ghettoizing, straitening. This might seem perverse. But cosmopolitanism offers a very different perspective on human nature and identity from a communitarianism that insists we're first and foremost members of particular communities and classes that then provide the constituent units of any social space and also determine their members' essential natures. This is the discourse of the Spanish Inquisition, of Nazism and contemporary Islamic radicalism. Am I *essentially* 'Jewish'? Will my daughter be classed *essentially* as a 'woman'? Is evolution merely another 'creation account'? I'm fearful that anthropology might become a maidservant to identity politics: to fundamentalist culturalist discourses which for all their purported recognition of 'difference' assign the latter an incorrect status. Instead of discovering difference in self-ownership it comes to be located in symbolic discourses concerning religion, class, community and ethnicity.

One of the deliverances of globalism is to sharpen the focus upon questions of sameness and difference. What is the status of human universals concerning our nature, our governance and our identities? I would hope for anthropology to retrieve the words 'civil' and 'societal' from its Enlightenment heritage, to regulate expressions of 'cultural' sovereignty and aspire to a human and humane 'civilization' beyond. 'Cosmopolitan politesse' I would define as that ethos of universal individual recognition, individual succouring and individual fulfilment that envisages human beings as free to explore global social spaces: what he or she is or would become; how he or she would wish to seem to others (the forms of self-expression used, the collectivities and life-worlds joined).

Globalism renders a human sameness more apparent beyond superficial cultural differences, and individual particularities more apparent beneath political discourses of cultural homogeneity. And yet, the politics of cultural identity is a powerful movement. Whether anthropology will be a servant to this movement or be able to offer an intellectual critique of it is the key question for the next decades.

References

Amit, V., and N. Rapport. 2002. *The Trouble with Community: Anthropological Reflections on Movement, Identity and Collectivity.* London: Pluto.
Cohen, A., and N. Rapport, eds. 1995. *Questions of Consciousness.* London: Routledge.
Rapport, N. 1987. *Talking Violence: An Anthropological Interpretation of Conversation in the City.* St John's, Newfoundland: ISER Press, Memorial University.
———. 1993. *Diverse World-Views in an English Village.* Edinburgh: Edinburgh University Press.
———. 1994. *The Prose and the Passion: Anthropology, Literature and the Writing of E. M. Forster.* Manchester: Manchester University Press.
———. 1997. *Transcendent Individual: Towards a Literary and Liberal Anthropology.* London: Routledge.
———, ed. 2002. *British Subjects: An Anthropology of Britain.* Oxford: Berg.
———. 2003. *I Am Dynamite: An Alternative Anthropology of Power.* London: Routledge.
———, ed. 2005. *Democracy, Science and the Open Society: A European Legacy?* Muenster: Lit Verlag / Piscataway, NJ: Transaction.
———. 2008. *Of Orderlies and Men: Hospital Porters Achieving Wellness at Work.* Durham, NC: Carolina Academic Press.
———, ed. 2010. *Human Nature as Capacity: Transcending Discourse and Classification.* Oxford: Berghahn.
———. 2012. *Anyone: The Cosmopolitan Subject of Anthropology.* Oxford: Berghahn.

Susan Wright

Date of Birth: 1951

Place of Birth: Wanstead, England. Wright moved frequently as a child. She was one week in Wanstead in an incubator and then lived in six houses in four counties by the time she was nine, ending up on a smallholding in Essex, until she went to university.

D. Phil.: 'Identities and Influence: Political Organisation in Doshman Ziari, Iran' 1985, Oxford University.

Fieldwork: Political transformation in Iran (1970s and 1990s) and in England (1979–93); university reforms in England (1990s and onwards) and in Denmark (2003 and onwards).

Current affiliation: Professor of Educational Anthropology, Department of Education (DPU), Aarhus University, Denmark.

Positions held: Wright was associate researcher on the project 'Decision Making for Rural Areas' at the Department of Planning, University College London (1978–83), and after holding a fellowship from the British Council for Persian Studies (1983–84), became a rural community worker for the Cleveland Council for Voluntary Service (1984–85). In 1985 she became lecturer in social anthropology, at the University of Sussex. Alongside this, from 1987 to 1991 she was convenor of Anthropology in Action, and in 1995 she set up the Network for Teaching and Learning Social Anthropology. In 1997 she became senior lecturer in cultural studies at Birmingham University and alongside that, from 2000–2003 was founding director of C-SAP, the UK's Higher Education Academy's Centre for Learning and Teaching in Sociology, Anthropology and Politics. In 2003 she moved to Denmark, to her current chair. She has held visiting professorships in Stockholm, Copenhagen, Lund and Auckland. In 1997 she was president of the Anthropology and Archaeology Section, British Association for the Advancement of Science. In 2008 was the First International Visiting Fellow, CoPAA (Consortium of Programmes in Applied Anthropology), Society for Applied Anthropology, USA, and in 2010 she was a visiting fellow at CRASSH (Centre for Research in the Arts, Social Sciences and Humanities), Cambridge University.

Major works
- 2011, co-editor with C. Shore and D. Però. *Policy Worlds: Anthropology and the Anatomy of Contemporary Power*, EASA Series. Oxford: Berghahn.
- 2007, co-editor with D. Epstein, R. Boden, R. Deem, and F. Rizvi. *Geographies of Knowledge, Geometries of Power: Framing the Future of Higher Education, World Yearbook of Education 2008*. New York: Routledge.
- 1997, co-editor with C. Shore. *Anthropology of Policy: Critical Perspectives on Governance and Power*, EASA Series. London: Routledge.
- 1994, editor. *Anthropology of Organizations*. London: Routledge.

Chapter 11

HIDDEN HISTORIES AND POLITICAL TRANSFORMATIONS
Susan Wright

Can we go way back to the beginning of your interest in anthropology? What was it that led you to taking up anthropology as a profession?

As with a lot of people, I think it was by sheer accident. As an undergraduate at Durham University, I had done a history degree for my BA, but I was getting more and more upset with history – especially the way it was taught in Durham – because it was very much the Whig version of history, in which everything marches inevitably forward in a progressive sequence of events towards the present. Not only was history depicted as making the present inevitable, but it was also construed as something all about the great and the good. However there was an undercurrent of such history which was usually about the 'common man' (rather than the 'common *person*'), and there seemed to be no connection between these two strands of history. One of the most interesting things about history for me was what was going on in the daily lives of the ordinary people whilst the great and good were busy trying to change the society they lived in [smiles]. In short, how did these two realms interconnect? By complete accident, I had just applied to Oxford University to do a post-graduate diploma in ethnology, when some of my fellow students, who heard about my interest in ethnology, told me about a lecturer in the Durham anthropology department called David Brooks and suggested that I go and sit in on his lectures to find out what this subject was all about. At that time I didn't know what the connection was between ethnology and anthropology, because dictionary definitions of these terms didn't offer much help. I remember going to the lecture room in the anthropology department when David Brooks was giving one of his lectures on the Bakhtiari in Iran, and it was absolutely packed to the rafters. I ended up sitting on the steps in the middle of the lecture hall and being confronted by the sight of this transfixing guy dressed in a Bakhtiari robe, enacting a lot of dances and talking about Bakhtiari politics. Ninety-nine percent of what he was talking about went over my head, but he analyzed everyday life in relation to political orders and it certainly felt gripping.

Soon afterwards, I had an interview for the diploma in ethnology at Linacre College, Oxford. It was a hilarious interview. There was the college president, four or five other people I didn't know, and Bernard Fagg, the head of the ethnology department. They were talking about everything under the sun *apart* from ethnology – which I still didn't really grasp as a subject. Then Bernard Fagg said to me, 'If you were to be accepted onto this degree programme you would have to specialize. Would you specialize in any one of the areas that you have visited in the world already? And if so, which one would that be?' Well, as an undergrad I'd done the kind of backpacker thing around America and Canada, and I'd been looking particularly at the Native Indian reservations. I'd also been to Iran with a fellow student who was studying Persian language for her degree and wanted somebody to travel with her. So, off the top of my head I said, 'I think I'd go to Iran'. There was also another factor here. After I came back from travelling around Iran with my friend, I decided to specialize in diplomatic history. If I had to study the 'great and the good', I thought I might as well study them in a place like Iran, so I did a course in Iranian diplomatic history from the 1880s to the Second World War. I had also fallen in love with the language. At school I'd been absolutely hopeless at learning languages in a classroom. I scraped through French and I don't know if I can even say whether I scraped through in Latin. But when I was travelling around Iran with this friend who was studying the Iranian language and was therefore a very good person to learn from, I found that language just wonderful. I thought that if I chose an area where I loved the sound of the language, I might stand a chance of learning it.

When I went to Oxford and embarked on the diploma in ethnology, it just felt like I was slipping into a warm bath. You know, it just felt so wonderful. Here were people connecting what was happening in government and what was happening amongst ordinary people. It was a whole different vocabulary and a very different way of thinking about people and events. For me, it felt like coming home. I suddenly realized, this is the discipline that I wanted to be part of. I still haven't quite worked out the difference between ethnology and anthropology at Oxford. I was in the ethnology department in the Pitt Rivers Museum and yet going to some things in the anthropology department. It seemed to me that we were in the same discipline somehow. The questions that it raised, the issues that it engaged with, the way it went about things – it was exactly what I was looking for and it answered my dissatisfaction with history.

As I went on to do a B. Litt. in 1973 (later converted to a D.Phil.), another thing that really shaped where I went for fieldwork and what I studied was the growing crisis in 'community studies' at that time. This wasn't just in anthropology but across other disciplines. There was a particular take on it within anthropology which led people to reflect more on the colonial context in which studies of, say, the Nuer and the Dinka had been written, as if the people's lives were not influenced by government. This echoed my own discomfort with the prevailing perception within academia that the great and the good and ordinary people were somehow not connected. I wanted to study what happened in a society where the government had instituted massive change. The government's forced settlement of nomadic people seemed like a pretty good example of such sweeping changes. Iran at that time was known as one of the main centres in the world where such processes were taking place. So my PhD focused on how nomads – who had been settled in a classically remote mountainous tribal area where, outside the village, you couldn't see anyone else on the horizon

Illustration 9. Susan Wright in her field site in Iran, 1976. (Photo courtesy of the author)

– were interacting with processes of modernization and the creation of the Shah's state.

So I sat on this mountainside watching representatives from the Ministry of Health and other government agencies arrive in Land Rovers. For some of these settled nomads it was their *first* contact with bureaucracy. One of the really central issues in my research was the way in which people were taking over positions within the new bureaucracy. Old tribal leaders who had previously been dismissed and marginalized now found their way back into controlling aspects of the legal system. They also gained positions in the Ministry of Forests and Natural Resources, which controlled people's access to firewood. Through these positions the old tribal leaders were able to reinstitute their control.

Another group in the village had heard early on about a new Ministry of Tribal Education and they became the first teachers in tribal education for the *whole* of Iran. By the time I got there, they had positions in the bureaucracy of that ministry. They were trying to teach literacy in order to empower people to know their rights and know how to deal with the new bureaucracy on their own and not have to go through their tribal leaders. This was just before the start of the Iranian revolution. Although one never knew *when* the revolution was coming, there was clearly a debate going on about what kind of new Iranian society people wanted to create.

Soon after I finished that fieldwork and was back in Oxford trying to write up, the Iranian revolution took off. During the height of the revolution I got a message from some of the people in the tribal area saying that the new regime had placed them under suspicion. One of the grounds for that suspicion was they had hosted me during my research. There is a very old discourse in Iran that Western powers, particularly the British, foment revolutions by inciting the tribes to rebellion. In modern-day Iran this is probably the last thing any Western government would do; i.e. no serious Western government would send in spies via the tribes. However, that discourse remains deeply embedded in Iranian politics so that even though I clearly wasn't a spy, it was easy to exploit such accusations. My hosts asked me not to publish anything from my fieldwork, because it might endanger them. So I didn't and I still haven't. That meant I had to switch to a completely new research area.

When I came back from Iran I realized that I knew more about Iran, Iranian politics and how the Iranian state works than I did about Britain, so I thought I'd better do something that would help me work out what was happening in Britain. At that point the big debate was over how to reform Britain's welfare state. There were discussions on the left about how to sustain the welfare state whilst making its operations less paternalistic and disempowering. Then, in 1979, Mrs Thatcher came to power and she instead wanted to 'roll back' the welfare state. There was a bunch of anthropologists, all of similar age and status to me, who really wanted to play a part in finding ways to sustain yet reform the welfare state, and who were equally interested in similar debates over international development. I got a job as a research assistant on a big project that was looking at the effects of government decision-making processes on people in rural areas in England. This was almost equivalent to what I'd been researching in Iran. But in this case the research was commissioned by the government, as it was worried that many of its policies for rural areas were actually creating, rather than solving, problems. I spent four and a half years working on that project, doing multi-site ethnographies in the House of Commons; in government ministries and regional and local authorities; and in local areas in different parts of England. At the end of it all, I was really very clued up about what was happening in contemporary Britain.

I found that whereas people in government talked about democracy as a joined-up system that connected people to decision making, there was a really big disjuncture between what politicians and bureaucrats thought they were doing or trying to do for a local area and the local people's experiences and concerns. Even if decision makers and local people did talk about the same issues, they did so in such very different language that they talked past each other. Rural community workers were the key people whose job was to mediate between decision makers and local people and translate across that chasm (Wright 1992). For my next project, I decided to focus on their role. Because I couldn't get research funding to study them, I got a job as one of them and worked for just over a year as a community worker in Cleveland, a region in the north of England.

In 1985, I was offered a lectureship at Sussex University which was to develop a focus on the anthropology of contemporary Britain and on people's relations with the modern state. That was absolutely consistent with what I was interested in. So I turned the work I'd been doing in Cleveland into an ethnographic study of the transformation of governance during the Thatcher period and beyond. I continued a multi-sited approach. I followed debates – or rather, conflicts – within the cabinet and Parliament over the contested emergence of Mrs Thatcher's 'enterprising individual'. I was seconded to a local authority for a year to do an organizational ethnography of how they tried to resist the rollback of the state by mobilizing support for 'public' services through 'community action'. In one of the 'community action areas', I participated in the work of a community-arts organization and saw how they operated in terms of yet different concepts of 'community' and 'participatory development' (Nelson and Wright 1995). In this same area, in an ex-mining village, I did two to three months' participant observation each year throughout a seven-year period to explore their own gendered concepts of 'individual' and 'community' and how they (and I) misunderstood, negotiated with, or contested the very different and continually evolving visions of 'individual' and 'community' they encountered from voluntary organizations, local government and central government.

I focused on the contestation over keywords as a way to analyze the transformation to a new form of governance under Thatcher (Wright 1994, 1995, 1998). Keywords did not change meaning on their own, but in association with other words, in what I called semantic clusters. Whereas 'community' used to be associated with collective, public, society, family and individual, gradually 'individual' was prised loose from that cluster and became associated with enterprise, competition, markets and a much more limited concept of family. After the miners' strike, 'collective' became almost unsayable; 'public' seemed to disappear from parlance; and when, in 1987, Mrs Thatcher proclaimed, 'There is no such thing as society', it was difficult to challenge her effectively. By the end of my fieldwork, I had witnessed the conceptual transformation of Britain into a space no longer made up of society and communities, but of 'individuals and their families', each supposed to do the best for themselves in competition with everyone else in numerous markets and pseudo markets. The role of government within this space was also transformed – instead of managing society, it supposedly orchestrated these multifarious markets. Expectations of the individual also changed. The idea was that enterprising individuals would adopt the values of government and freely choose to govern themselves accordingly – what later became known as Foucault's 'conduct of conduct'. At that time it was popular to talk of 'studying up' when you tried to look at the multiple organizations and agents of government from the perspectives of ordinary people, but one of the PhD students at Sussex (Sue Reinhold) coined the idea of 'studying through' to describe what she and several others of us were trying to do. This is a much more accurate depiction of the way I traced processes of contestation over keywords through time and back and forth across the different sites of my fieldwork, so as to analyze how a process of ideological transformation came about and became embedded in new forms of government (Wright and Reinhold 2011).

At some point it dawned on me that I was still adopting a very conventional anthropological approach, i.e. studying people in the former mining village who were poorer and weaker than me, and far removed from the centres of power. I also realized that as a lecturer, I was getting pummelled with a new kind of language and new requirements or requests to introduce 'competencies' and 'transferable skills' in my students. I was encountering a whole new vocabulary and set of bureaucratic demands. I thought, 'What the heck's going on here?' Then, gradually, it struck me that universities are actually a very important site of the government-led transformation of power that I had been researching. Having completed the work in Cleveland, I shifted focus and started studying universities, both as a site where academic labour is being reshaped in ways consistent with the demands of new managerialism, but also with the expectation of producing new kinds of students who will become self-governing individuals and a self-managing, high-skilled labour force in the new knowledge economy (Wright 2004b).

This has been my focus ever since. First in Britain and then, with some sense of déjà vu, in Denmark, I've witnessed and studied the introduction of a raft of technologies which turn academic work into measured and ranked activities – research assessment systems, teaching-quality assessments, and league tables now on a world scale. Universities appoint strategic managers with the aim of improving performance in these terms, and governments increasingly tie funding to performance and ranking too (Wright 2004a). You [Cris Shore] and I have published on the coercive dimensions of such 'audit culture' (Shore and Wright 2000), but I also established a network of anthropologists and then a national centre – C-SAP – to explore how academics and students could find space to reflect on these changes and take more control of the development of their own teaching and learning.

Let us turn to your fieldwork experiences. Were there any key moments of discovery or observations that led you to rethink your previously held conceptions?

One of them occurred while I was doing the study in Cleveland. As I mentioned, I was closely following the debates within the Thatcher cabinet and the conflicts these generated over the *key terms* of this transformation. I was following speech by speech how Mrs Thatcher's conception of 'the individual' rose to prominence as a keyword and how it became closely associated with 'enterprise', 'competition', 'the market' and a string of other terms. The home secretary, Douglas Hurd, tried to soften some of her wilder claims about the importance of individuals and entrepreneurship by bringing some sense of *sociality* back into the debate. Mrs Thatcher responded quickly with another public speech, which, as we used to say at that time, 'handbagged' him, i.e. bludgeoned him, metaphorically speaking. I was intensely caught up in following these conflicts amongst the great and the good of the Conservative Party. But I was struggling to try and work out how this process of contestation in government articulated with what was happening in the local authority, the community arts organization and the former mining village. I had a sense that something was working across these sites, but there were very few connections between actual people and I just couldn't fathom how processes of change were spreading.

I would sit watching television with the person whose house I was staying in. We'd watch Mrs Thatcher and we'd turn to each other at the end and say, 'What on earth is she talking about?' I mean, it was really impossible at that point to fathom what she meant by this new 'individual'. Then it came to me in a flash. One of the things I was trying to follow through all these debates was the 'Local Management of Schools Act', and I bumped into a woman in the village who she said to me, 'I've become one of Mrs Thatcher's individuals' [smiles]. I said, 'Oh, what's happened to you?' She replied, 'I'm now a parent governor for the school, and they've sent me on a course to teach me how to be empowered and they've given me all this documentation about the school. They've told us about the budget, how the budget works, and they've pointed out that it isn't big enough to cover the current staff costs. They've told us that we can either make some cuts by sacking somebody or else we can hold jumble sales to raise more money.' Then, gesturing to this whole area of high unemployment, she added, 'Do you know how many thousands of jumble sales we would need to raise a teacher's salary?' The teacher they were having to sack was her daughter's best friend's mother. And *this*, she said, is what Mrs Thatcher means by the empowered individual.

What struck me was not only her ironic reflection on what it meant to be an 'empowered individual', but also the fact that it was actually policy that was linking these things up and that she was being recruited as an agent of that policy. I'd heard this same policy being discussed in the House of Commons. I'd seen glimpses of it in the local authority. That's what really set me to thinking critically about policy as the articulating concept across these different sites – and which is when you [Cris Shore] and I started writing on the anthropology of policy (Shore and Wright 1997).

We often discover things about our own and other cultures by making blunders. Were there any key mistakes that you made during fieldwork that opened your eyes to new ways of thinking?

I can think of a million of them in Iran, but really the most significant or transformative thing that happened to me in Iran was that it politicized me. When I first turned up in Iran I was struggling to find a way to conceptualize relations between a remote mountain village and the modernizing state. I was in a classic anthropological site – a village which was high up the mountains and felt like it was a world unto its own – so one question was how to not fall into the trap of treating physical remoteness as social and political discreteness. A second issue was that I wanted to have an open and honest discussion with the people there about what role I could play while I was there, living among them, and how I should locate myself in their society. I did not want to just extract information, but to engage in an exchange between their local knowledge and what I hoped would be my anthropological analysis. It was clear to me that some of the teachers in particular wanted me to be there in order to see how they could work to improve people's lives without ending up in conflict with the old tribal leaders and the state. But soon after I got there, a close relative of one of the teachers refused to say hello to me. In the morning when you get up and walk out of the house you usually say '*Salam*' (peace/greetings) to everybody you meet. The only one you wouldn't say *salam* to was the dog. This neighbour treated me like a dog and not a human being. I noticed that there were a few other people who similarly refused to greet me. My host was too embarrassed to explain. It took a long time, but eventually, after about three months, I came to understand that this man and the little group around him had analyzed the problems of Iran in the Second World War and had decided that the real root of the country's problem was British and American exploitation. They had therefore tried to expel every British and American from the country. While this may seem like a very aggressive response, it was actually based on an amazingly well-informed and sophisticated analysis of where they were in the world's political economy.

I discovered all this when he and I eventually reached a point where we could talk frankly about these issues. I was joining in with all the different activities that were going on, and one day I went to harvest wheat with the father of the man whose house I was staying in. The man who would not say *salam* was there too, and when we took a break, we sat together on a hillside, both of us absolutely covered in dust, because the soil there is very dusty, with rivers of sweat pouring down our faces. We must have looked an incredible sight – the classic picture of the dusty peasant. Sitting there next to me he began to tell me why he'd taken this stance during the Second World War. He followed his analysis right through to the present day. He knew all about Western policies towards oil and about OPEC's recent hike in oil prices, which vastly increased the national income of Iran. In this part of Iran there was an oil pipeline that went though the next valley and which you could see from where we were sitting. Yet the village depended on collecting ever-more scarce firewood in the mountains or, in winter, bringing cans of fuel in from the provincial capital – a twelve-hour hazardous journey, with people, sacks of food and cans of fuel perched on the back of a tractor as it lurched along viscous mud tracks and forded rivers. It was evident to him that all that wealth was going to the centre to create a bureaucracy, a military and a new middle class. It was bypassing people like these villagers. I suppose it was a bit of a shock for me to realize that even though I was trying to step outside of the assumptions of the society I'd come from, I was still looking at a dusty peasant as a dusty peasant, and here he was giving me what was probably the best lecture I've ever had on international

Illustration 10. Susan Wright and Iranian villagers collaborating on participatory research, 1996. (Photo courtesy of the author)

politics. That's what really opened my eyes to the level of politicization of maybe not everybody in that village, but an awful lot of them. They had a really sophisticated grasp of the way they were positioned and wanted to position themselves in global political events. It was an extremely fraught time, and people had to work out where they were positioning themselves day by day, not just in local contexts, but with an awareness that these choices were about the kind of political environment they wanted for the future Iran.

All of this *really* educated me and I think that's how I became a very reflexive anthropologist. I didn't learn that reflexivity though reading anthropology; I learnt it through fieldwork.

Looking back, I see now the naivety of someone who had done a degree specializing in diplomatic history yet still didn't have any knowledge of the utterly different way that people on the ground viewed their own diplomatic history. That really shook the understanding I'd had until that moment, both my understanding of where I was coming from and my understanding of my own position within that society and its history. It wasn't just an encounter between me and people in the village as single individuals; we would have these fantastic debates with the men in the village sitting around in a very big circle. They would accuse me of 'being British', and I would say, 'Well yes, you can say that I'm British, but you can't *accuse* me of being British'. You can't make me responsible for what the British have done historically in Iran, just as you can't accuse me of responsibility for what the current British government is doing in the world, much of which I don't agree with. But on the other hand, I had to accept that it was only because of a historical legacy that I was currently doing fieldwork in their village for a D.Phil. at Oxford University, whereas none of them had yet gone to university. My grandparents were working class and my father gradually rose from working class to middle class during my childhood, and I had all the benefits of the post-war welfare state, including free education and, for the first time in my family, access to university. All this came from Britain's accumulated wealth, extracted from round the world, including from Iran. In our discussions I accepted I was obviously a beneficiary of this and was in a more privileged position than any of them could dream of; yet I would not actually take *personal* responsibility for that legacy or what had happened in Iran. We spent a lot of time discussing how to situate each other as members of our wider societies whilst recognizing the nuances of our positions and personal responsibilities. It really was one of the most enlightening things about that whole eighteen months of fieldwork [smiles].

You've highlighted the themes of history, politics and diplomacy. What, for you, are the most exciting developments between anthropology and other disciplines?

I still locate myself between history, anthropology and political science. I suppose one of the interesting things that's happening at the moment is the way in which political scientists are interested in the work that you and I are doing on policy and the invitations we get to engage with them. They are keen to introduce what they think of as 'the anthropological perspective' on critical policy analysis, which they sometimes equate with 'interpretive' approaches that draw on the work of Clifford Geertz. But there is much more scope here for opening up new areas in the interface between anthropology and politics. It is an exciting field that anthropology can contribute a great deal to, as we have tried to point out in some of our writings on the anthropology of policy. One of the key themes that we can glimpse in the current discussions is what will happen next after so-called 'neoliberalism' (Shore and Wright 2011). The contradictions of neoliberalization have become very clear. Even if politicians are likely to continue riding that wave for many more years to come, academics are now seriously asking, what comes after neoliberalism? I think that there is scope for some excellent debates between political scientists and anthropologists on that subject; that's a topic that promises considerable excitement in the future.

Picking up on that theme of 'what comes next', what are you currently working on and what is your next research project?

I have just finished a massive piece of fieldwork with a team of researchers looking at Danish university reform, and I'm immersed in trying to finish a book on that subject (Wright and Ørberg 2009). One of the things we have been exploring is the way in which the Danish government has turned universities into *self-owning* institutions. There is large literature about neoliberal governance and about 'self-owning', 'self-governing' and 'self-managing' that relates to the subject of the individual. But my aim is to connect these themes to the way institutions are created as subjects of power. My work therefore explores what the Danish government means by constituting universities as 'self-owning institutions' and how Danish academics appropriate and contest that discourse. In the current Danish context, 'self-owning' means having a governing board with an external majority and a string of contracts that flow all the way down through the system with the very clear *aim* of making the people at the bottom more directly responsible to those at the top, i.e. in an apparent paradox, the aim of self-ownership is to make the academics respond more clearly to the political aims and agendas of the government (Wright and Ørberg 2008).

One of the general issues I'm currently struggling with in this project is how to connect discourses and politics that are occurring on different scales, i.e. when a government embarks on a reform agenda, how do you analyze the influences of that on everyday life within universities? This is where we need to engage more with political science, because there's still a tendency amongst most academics and policy makers to see laws or reforms as a 'trickle down' process, the idea being that the government passes a law, which then gets enacted through particular technologies, which then change people's subjectivities. We're really exploring other ways of thinking about that process. We've been focusing on the different ways in which the objects and subjects of policy are being imagined not just by policy makers, but by leaders, academics and students, all acting as active creators of the future, and how those imaginings are contested on the ground. That entails a very wide-ranging investigation involving, among other things, the media and popular literature, as well as all the other 'usual suspects' involved in the policy field. An important aspect of this is how people engage with those *imagined* figures both in their everyday lives and in moments of crisis. So the central focus is on the relationship between imagining and enacting in a policy context.[1]

How does your work connect with issues of wider public concern, and how important is it, in your view, that anthropologists do that?

I think it's absolutely crucial. It's been central to most of what I do. When I became a community worker, I saw myself as an anthropologist who was going off to do fieldwork. I was working in a nongovernmental organization but *as* an anthropologist engaged in participant observation. I wanted to generate theoretical ideas from that engagement, ideas which I hoped would both be useful in community work and would feed back into the discipline. One of the dons at Oxford, who I had great respect for and who had been fantastically supportive throughout my career, looked at me and said, 'What a shame that you're no longer going to be an anthropologist!' That was another kind of 'aha' moment for me, because I thought, 'No, that's *completely* wrong. That's just plain wrong!' As soon as I became a community worker and started working in that field, I realized that there were hundreds of us who were 'no longer anthropologists' in his sense of the term. So I got involved in the Group for Anthropology in Policy and Practice (GAPP), and after a few years became convenor, and then worked with you [Cris Shore] to expand it into the organization Anthropology in Action and the journal with that title.

I was trying to get activities going and all the time trying to make connections with the people who had gone off into the jungle, outside of the ivory tower: they had created careers for themselves outside of academia yet still regarded themselves as anthropologists (Wright 2005). Quite a number of them were actually experiencing at first hand the changes that were occurring in the British welfare state under Mrs Thatcher. When we gathered 'practising anthropologists' in workshops, they described trying to engage with the shifting meanings of keywords in their everyday work. They were trying to understand the ideas (and ideology) embedded in seemingly innocent new administrative forms and procedures, just at the same time as they were having to fill them in and follow them, and they struggled to grasp how both language and technologies were part of changing systems of governance and emerging forms of power. They raised questions about language, meaning and power – issues at the core of anthropology. I felt it was important both to use their insights to shape the research agendas in the academy and to try and reconnect practising anthropologists with the next generation of PhD students who were concerned with these issues.

The thing that annoyed me – and still makes me cross – is this idea of 'pure' versus 'applied' anthropology. The whole language around the notion implies a 'pure anthropologist' as opposed to a 'polluted', no-longer anthropologist; I mean, you must be 'polluted' if you aren't pure, yeah? [smiles]. Tied to this notion is the assumption that 'applied' anthropology is somehow a *drain* on the discipline, which invokes not only an idea of hierarchy but also the image of anthropology going down the sewer. I *really* wanted to dislodge that stereotype, because I thought that at a moment of *enormous* social and political change, if there was anyone who could *really* grasp what was happening in the midst of the Thatcher era, it was the anthropologists who were working in the public sector and those who had firsthand experience in a day-to-day way of what was going on. They were sensing the shift in the language and seeing the tiny changes in procedures that were reshaping the conditions of people's existence. I wanted to draw on their insights to develop an academic research agenda.

I've devoted a terrific number of years trying to build a more constructive and creative relationship between people who work inside and outside of the academy, just as I try and work out how to do anthropology in a way that advances our theoretical understanding at the same time as it has practical implications. In particular, I'm interested in that 'public' of anthropologists and other interested people who struggle to take a critical and reflexive approach whilst they are embedded in day-to-day work as policy makers, service providers and community activists. I envisage a reciprocal relationship, where academic anthropologists learn from practitioners about current pressing issues that pertain to the core interests of the discipline and that need theoretical development; and where people involved in policy and practice draw from such research to enhance their ability to act as 'politically reflexive practitioners' (Wright 2004b).

Of course, practising anthropologists include not just those working in central and local government, agencies and nongovernmental organizations, but also those of us deciding day to day how to practice our profession in universities – in our teaching, our research and our contribution to society. I initially learnt from my fieldwork in Iran how important it is at a time of transformation to take a politically reflexive approach to the minutiae of day-to-day actions, so as to determine in each instance how best to act on existing constraints and shape the future of our organizations and professional activities.

References

Nelson, N, and S. Wright, eds. 1995. *Power and Participatory Development: Theory and Practice*. London: Intermediate Technology Publications.

Shore, C. and S. Wright, eds. 1997. *Anthropology of Policy: Critical Perspectives on Governance and Power*, EASA Series. London: Routledge.

———. 2000. 'Coercive Accountability: The Rise of Audit Culture in Higher Education'. In *Audit Culture: Anthropological Studies in Accountability, Ethics and the Academy*, EASA Series, ed. M. Strathern, 57–89. London: Routledge.

———. 2011. 'Conceptualising Policy: Technologies of Governance and the Politics of Visibility'. In *Policy Worlds: Anthropology and the Anatomy of Contemporary Power*, EASA Series, eds. C. Shore, S. Wright and D. Peró, 1–26. Oxford: Berghahn.

Wright, S. 1992. 'Rural Community Development: What Sort of Social Change?'. *Journal of Rural Studies* 8: 15–28. Reprinted in *The Sociology of Rural Communities*, ed. G. Crow, Cheltenham: Edward Elgar, 1996.

———. 1994. '"Culture" in Anthropology and Organizational Studies'. In *Anthropology of Organizations*, ed. S. Wright, 1–34. London: Routledge.

———. 1995. 'Anthropology: Still the "Uncomfortable" Discipline?'. In *The Future of Anthropology: Its Relevance to the Contemporary World*, eds. C. Shore and A. Ahmed, 65–93. London: Athlone Press.

———. 1998. 'Politicisation of Culture'. *Anthropology Today* 14(1): 7–15.

———. 2004a. 'Markets, Corporations, Consumers? New Landscapes in Higher Education'. *LATISS Learning and Teaching in the Social Sciences* 1(2): 71–93.

———. 2004b. 'Politically Reflexive Practitioners'. In *Current Policies and Practices in European Social Anthropology Education*, EASA series, eds. D. Drackle and I. Edgar, 34–52. Oxford: Berghahn.

———. 2005. 'Machetes into a Jungle? A History of Anthropology in Policy and Practice, 1981–2000'. In *Applications of Anthropology*, ASA series, ed. S. Pink, 27–54. Oxford: Berghahn.

Wright, S. and J. W. Ørberg. 2008. 'Autonomy and Control: Danish University Reform in the Context of Modern Governance'. *Learning and Teaching: International Journal of Higher Education in the Social Sciences* 1(1): 27–57.

———. 2009. 'Prometheus (on the) Rebound? Freedom and the Danish Steering System'. In *International Perspectives on the Governance of Higher Education*, ed. J. Huisman, 69–87. London: Routledge.

Wright, S. and S. Reinhold. 2011. '"Studying Through": A Strategy for Studying Political Transformations. Or Sex, Lies and British Politics'. In *Policy Worlds: Anthropology and the Anatomy of Contemporary Power*, EASA Series, eds. C. Shore, S. Wright and D. Però, 86–104. Oxford: Berghahn.

Notes

1. These themes are being developed in a book being written by Susan Wright, Stephen Carney, John Krejsler, Gritt Bykærholm Nielsen and Jakob Williams Ørberg entitled *Enacting the University: Danish University Reform in an International Perspective*, to be published by Springer.

Marilyn Strathern

Date of Birth: 1941

Place of Birth: North Wales. Grew up in Kent.

PhD: University of Cambridge, 1968. Published in 1972 as Women In Between, London: Academic Press.

Fieldwork: Papua New Guinea, United Kingdom

Current affiliation: Professor Emeritus at Cambridge University

Positions held: Professor Strathern's first research position was as a research fellow at the New Guinea Research Unit of the Australian National University, in 1970. She went on to hold posts as a fellow at Girton College (1976–83) and Trinity College, Cambridge University (1984–85); professor of social anthropology at Manchester University (1985–93); and, from 1993 until her retirement in 2008, as the William Wyse Professor of Social Anthropology, at Cambridge University. She was also Mistress of Girton College from 1998 to 2009. Her numerous awards and distinctions include receiving the Rivers Memorial Medal of the Royal Anthropological Institute (1976); election as a fellow of the British Academy (1987); the Huxley Memorial Medal, RAI 2004, and the Viking Fund Medal, Wenner Gren Foundation, 2003. She was knighted in 2001.

Major works
- 2005. *Kinship, Law and the Unexpected: Relatives Are Often a Surprise.* Cambridge: Cambridge University Press.
- 2000, editor. *Audit Cultures: Anthropological Studies in Accountability, Ethics and the Academy.* London: Routledge.
- 1999. *Property, Substance and Effect: Anthropological Essays on Persons and Things.* London: Athlone.
- 1992. *After Nature: English Kinship in the Late Twentieth Century.* Cambridge: Cambridge University Press.
- 1992. *Reproducing the Future: Essays on Anthropology, Kinship, and the New Reproductive Technologies.* Manchester: Manchester University Press.
- 1991. *Partial Connections.* Savage, MD: Rowman and Littlefield.
- 1988. *The Gender of the Gift: Problems with Women and Problems with Society in Melanesia.* Berkeley: University of California Press.
- 1981. *Kinship at the Core: An Anthropology of Elmdon, a Village in North-west Essex in the Nineteen-sixties.* Cambridge: Cambridge University Press.
- 1980, co-editor with C. MacCormack. *Nature, Culture and Gender.* Cambridge: Cambridge University Press.

Chapter 12

GENDER IDEOLOGY, PROPERTY RELATIONS AND MELANESIA
The Field of 'M'
Marilyn Strathern

The concept of 'property' has been an enduring theme running throughout your work, both in the context of intellectual property and gender in Papua New Guinea and reproductive technologies in Euro-American societies. In a recent essay you argue that anthropologists should not simply shift away from the dominant concept of property to focus on ownership and 'appropriation'. Rather, we should look instead at the work that these concepts perform in relation to each other (Strathern 2011; see also Strang and Busse 2011). Can you expand on these ideas?

I'm probably one of the few people around who's always had an abiding interest in property (see Strathern 1999). Much of my work on the Highlands of Papua New Guinea is actually about delineating an alternative vocabulary to the vocabulary of property. That is, avoiding the concept makes its contours evident. I have always been intrigued by the collection of interests around items that are transactable, 'sellable' and dispersible. I wanted to complicate the notion of property itself. I felt it would be a shame if the notion of property then became reified or treated as unproblematic. Instead, the essay explored the concepts of 'borrowing', 'sharing', and 'stealing' when put *in relation* with property and ownership (Strathern 2011). It demonstrated how conceptions of property underpin many social situations, for example, in everyday routines such as queuing, or in ideas about fairness, belonging and sharing in boarding schools. Property-based vocabularies may also be used to express different modes of sociality. For example, in some situations stealing is more about causing 'injury' to another person than about taking away their ownership rights. These debates about property and stealing may also reference the appropriation of certain kinds of personhood itself, as in the case of educational institutions that seek to mould their children in a particular way.

Let's go back to the start of your encounter with anthropology. When you were growing up in the United Kingdom, anthropology wasn't on the school curriculum. So how did you first discover it, and what was the nature of that encounter?

I grew up in a particular part of the United Kingdom, namely, Kent. Kent had been a Roman suburb, and I spent my teenage weekends digging, as there were a lot of Roman sites, local historical associations and so forth, and I became very interested in archaeology. I don't like thinking back to that particular period of adolescence, because I was very pompous, you have to know; I was very, very serious. My mother said I never smiled from the age of thirteen to nineteen, or something like that. I'm afraid I thought that there wasn't enough substance in archaeology and I was looking for something more. At school I did history for one of my A levels and we read Rousseau. Suddenly the notion of 'society' grabbed me. I somehow knew, but I don't know how, that anthropology was the study of society. Then, when I had the opportunity of the Cambridge degree, which [in the first year] combines archaeology *and* anthropology, I thought this was absolutely perfect; it would allow me to indulge my passion for archaeology but then go on and be serious and do anthropology. Of course, I was eighteen years old and that now sounds really pompous!

Later, I was completely hooked after reading *The Nuer*, which I read while digging on one of Barry Cunliffe's digs – at Fishbourne, in Sussex. I became completely hooked by ethnographic detail. When I read Evans-Pritchard's description of the bells on the cattle, I knew that *this* was what I wanted to do. It was the order of the descriptions and the details that grabbed me.

I remember the complete *certainty* with which I knew that social anthropology was what I wanted to pursue. I was slightly amazed that my parents hadn't picked this up. When my mother asked what I was going to do when I left university, I was really startled that it wasn't completely self-evident that I was going to go on to do fieldwork and pursue the subject further. But as I judged this to be the right subject, they were happy to support me. I was also lucky enough to get the funding and to be accepted. I'm afraid the rest rolls out very conventionally. I was a completely conventional academic, supported by the system and the resources that were available then, for which I'm very grateful.

So from Rousseau you got the idea of society, and from Evans-Pritchard, the ethnographer's eye for detail. You always had an interest in observing the micro details of social life. Like Jane Austen, perhaps, were you attracted to fine detail as a youngster?

Oh, I couldn't claim that. I think that would be claiming too much! [*laughing*]

Reflecting back on this, now that anthropology has become your profession, how has your thinking about anthropology changed?

I think I've been turned around by the various revolutions in thinking. Coming back to the UK in the mid 1970s from Papua New Guinea, where I had lived for quite a while, I found that suddenly everybody was talking about Marxist anthropology. Coterminous with that, of course, was the growth of feminist anthropology. That was a very potent mix, and it really turned my thinking around to the extent that, in a sense, *The Gender of the Gift* rewrites *Women In Between*.[1] I came back to an altered picture, and I was very influenced by both those developments. I found the reflexive turn less interesting, less rich. I mean, it's endlessly interesting, of course, to reflect on the way one creates and makes one's subject matter, but it didn't have the social breadth that Marxism and feminism had together or quite the same possibilities for social analysis. I hope my work reflects some of the changes that have occurred.

But since then I've been on a roller coaster, or a swing, or some sort of fairground mischief, all of which was really started off by a phone call. I was in Manchester. I can depict it now: the fifth floor of the Roscoe Building, big windows from which you can see Manchester's wonderful sky. I was standing by the radiator with my hand on it, because it wasn't really warm, and there came a phone call from Frances Price. It must have been around 1987. And Frances asked, did anthropology have a view on egg donation between sisters? Well, as far as I knew, nobody among my colleagues in anthropology had *any* view on egg donation between sisters, or even knew what it was about, or whatever – and that was my introduction to new reproductive technologies. And that led me to becoming intellectually engaged with what was happening within *this* country [i.e. Britain] in terms of certain developments (see Strathern 1992). That was really quite important for the way *my* anthropology developed. I don't know about anybody else's.

Beyond Marxism and feminism – and debates over new reproductive technologies – what other earlier influences shaped your anthropology?

If you want to go back to the very early influences, being taught by both Edmund Leach and Meyer Fortes had a huge impact on me. There was never anything linear about the way they taught. There was a constant dialogue going on between them, and that was very invigorating for a student. I suppose, as well as the feminist and Marxist interchange, my book *The Gender of the Gift* was also very influenced by symbolic anthropology, particularly [by] the work of Roy Wagner.

Tell us about your decision to do fieldwork in Papua New Guinea. What inspired you to go there?

That was a bit of mischief between myself and Andrew Strathern – I got married just before going to the field and we were going out as a couple – because the Cambridge department at that point was dominated by Africanists. Reo Fortune, who had worked in Papua New Guinea, offered a non-Africanist glimpse of the world. It seemed that somewhere other than Africa would be interesting. We had originally thought of going to a site that we then learned had experienced recent volcanic activity, so we could not go there. The Highlands had just been 'opened up' after the Second World War. Early explorations, which had been closed down completely, were possible again. When we left, it was 1963, because Andrew, who was a year ahead of me, had waited while I completed my degree, well, this was really only ten years since the opening of the Highlands, and the very first ethnographies were emerging. It just seemed very exciting – and it was beautiful, stunning.

But also quite challenging, I would imagine, doing fieldwork in the Highlands?

It's far more challenging now. Back then, the people there were trying out the idea of peace, trying out what it would be like not to fight. This was a new proposition that the administration was promulgating. The

Gender Ideology, Property Relations and Melanesia

Illustration 11. Temporary accommodation for the visiting anthropologist, Kelua, Mt Hagen, 1964. (Photo courtesy of the author)

number of administrative personnel there was miniscule, so pacification didn't occur by force. It occurred by people thinking, 'Well okay, we've been told not to fight. I wonder what happens next? Business perhaps?' It was very peaceful. You could walk around. People were curious, interested. There was very little fear. It's not like this at all now.

Many ethnographers experience a key moment during fieldwork of the kind that Clifford Geertz has immortalized in his description of the Balinese cockfight: a moment of discovery where you gain some key insight that changes your assumptions about the society. Let's call it an 'aha moment'. Did you experience any of those moments in the field?

Well, one such moment was the first time we saw two men carrying pearl shells – mounted on heavy resin boards and strung [on poles] rather like pigs – that were to become so dominant in our thinking about exchange. But something else that really was an 'aha' moment – and I knew it at the time – was when I started to investigate divorce rates in the Highlands.

My initial project, which was devised by my supervisor, was going to be on the impact of sibling order on the success of cash cropping. In the 1960s, anthropologists were very interested in descent groups. There was a lot of debate about the strength and weakness of descent group ties as opposed to conjugal ties. That was the way one thought in those days.

I was aware that in the Highlands there was a lot of talk about divorce and dispute settlement and that many disputes arose over marital relations. People were also inventing their own dispute-settlement system in imitation of the official courts, and there was a whole arena of unofficial courts. Basically, what I was witnessing was one of the reactions to colonization and the imposition of new legal forms. And what I observed time and again was that these unofficial courts were really dominated by problems over *women*: i.e. women running away from their husbands or women trying to bring complaints. You would come across situations where everybody would be sitting round and there'd be a woman accused of something and the men would be saying, 'No, it's nothing to do with me. It's to do with that woman'.

I thought this was going to be the topic of my dissertation and one thing that I had better do is actually find out what the divorce rate was. John Barnes had published an early version of his influential

Illustration 12. Marilyn Strathern with women and children at the edge of a ceremonial ground in Mbukl, Mt Hagen, 1964. (Photo courtesy of the author)

formula for working out divorce rates. For some miraculous reason I had brought it with me. Now, these people don't live in villages but are travelling around, so you have to travel everywhere too. Sometimes you'd arrive at a house which was all closed up. So it took some months before I had a fairly complete survey of marital histories. I used John Barnes's formula and worked out the divorce rate and compared it with two other Highland societies that I had the material for. We had taken some literature on this with us – I must have had some kind of prescience about that – and it was very clear that there was nothing interesting at all about the Hagan divorce rate. It was neither particularly high nor particularly low.

Although I could have still gone ahead and done something about the relative strength of the conjugal bond or whatever, that actually turned into an 'aha' moment, as I suddenly realized what I was looking at [slapping the side of her face] was not divorce, it was *talk* about divorce. I realized that I was actually looking at what I later came to call an ideology, and that allowed me to go from considering relations between men and women to the way they *talked* about them. This was really 'gender', except that the term 'gender' wasn't there yet; that word didn't occur until after I'd written my first book. *Women In Between*, which is all about patterns of divorce, doesn't have the word gender in it. (That book came out in 1972, and Oakley's book *Sex, Gender and Society* came out the same year. So I can date the arrival of gender in the British anthropological vocabulary to that period, to 1972!)

I had, as it were, discovered both gender and ideology. I suddenly realized that what I was dealing with was a preoccupation with – and people talking about – divorce. They were talking about relations between men and women, men *blaming* women for this and that. The brothers-in-law would be in alliance and it would be the woman who had to be blamed. Quite clearly there was a conceptual, rhetorical system going on here, and that – *that's* what got me into the field of gender (i.e. see MacCormack and Strathern 1980; Strathern 1987). It really was a significant moment.

Was this the discovery of a kind of a meta-organizing principle?

Absolutely. That's right. It also meant that when feminist scholarship got off the ground, I was receptive to it and I had the vocabulary I needed (such as sex-roles), because, as I said, even the very term 'gender' hadn't been coined as yet.

Were you described as a 'feminist anthropologist' in those days?

Yes, from the mid-seventies onwards. But of course when that first book, *Women In Between*, came out, it's extraordinary to think of now, but because it had 'women' in the title, it didn't sell. Nor was it reviewed. Incidentally, I used to peak into the pages of the journals to see whether or not the book was going to be reviewed, and it never was [smiling and shrugging]. Books with women in the title didn't sell in the very early seventies. But that was just on the cusp, because three or four years later, of course, the situation was completely different.

Let's continue this theme of things learnt in the field, because this is very useful for anyone who is thinking about anthropology. It is a personal encounter, and we often learn more from our mistakes than we do from our successes. What particular mistakes or blunders were key learning experiences for you?

At the outset I made a lot blunders in interpersonal relations. We just did a lot of things wrong to begin with, particularly because in Papua New Guinea there's a complex material nexus between setting up a relationship and the flow and exchange of goods – and that has to be constantly negotiated. Managing relationships when there is so much at stake is a constant source of anxiety. But there was another moment that was the most chastening for me. And if my first story sounded a bit smug – the independent invention of gender ideology or something like that – my second story is much more humbling.

I was later attached to what was then called the New Guinea Research Unit, which was part of ANU [Australian National University], and one of the things I did for the New Guinea Research Unit was a study of the local court system, because I was always interested in legal anthropology (Strathern 1972a). I was really interested in these unofficial courts that had caught my imagination ten years previously, when I was working on 'the role' of women. I was particularly interested in them as an institutional form. This was the 1970s, on the eve of independence. I wrote up a study of these unofficial courts and was very much a defender of the unpaid magistrates who, it seemed to me, had taken on a lot of the burden of colonial governance insofar as they tried to interpret what the administration wanted. They tried to settle local disputes but of course were seen by the government as taking things into their own hands in an illegal way. On the eve of independence, the Papua New Guinea Law Reform Commission was trying to create the constitution and put into place the framework for legal administration, and they were sorting out how to implement lower-level magistrates' courts (which were not the same as the unofficial courts). What I was writing fed into that debate. I was a great advocate of the need to formally recognize what these people were doing, not only informally but also (according to the admnistration)'illegally'. And although I had a point, I *completely* underestimated the power dynamics of what was going on. In a situation where formal power was absent, these unofficial settlers of disputes appeared simply to have the public good in mind. They had their own interests of course, but it seemed that they were basically trying to get people to sort out their problems. But when the new magistrates' courts were set up and the counterparts of these unofficial dispute settlers were appointed and given powers to impose fines and to send people to the higher courts and so forth, the situation changed completely. These people often became petty tyrants, imposing the highest penalties, and so on.

That was really quite a chastening experience. It wasn't that my original work was wrong or off key, or that I could have predicted anything different, it was just that it revealed my own partiality. My view simply fell short; there was just far more going on than what my little summaries had attempted to show.

What is the broader lesson here, the moral of this story?

It has to be: Beware of your own biases, beware of your assumptions and also beware of the limits of investigation. Beware the limits of knowledge-gathering and knowledge production. I don't think I'd even say that it was wrong to have done it, or wrong to have given advice, it's simply that one has to be wary, because analytical solutions aren't necessarily practical solutions. In the course of my analysis, I did what I'm sure most people do these days – engage a range of practitioners in order to produce recommendations. But rather naively I thought that the analysis itself suggested a form of recommendation, or a form of policy, and of course that's not true. The conversion of analysis into policy is, in fact, very tricky. I think that's the key point here.

What do you see as the most exciting developments within the discipline? I say this with a sense of irony, because in a sense, you yourself have set many of the new agendas within the discipline. But what issues particularly excite you, and what do you see as the most interesting areas between anthropology and other disciplines?

I certainly think that one key issue is the whole area that we dub 'technology'. In fact, it is very interesting what we call 'technology' and what we don't. For example, nowadays you probably wouldn't label an ordinary drinking glass as an item of technology. But given the role that *thinking* about technology plays in our lives, not to mention the manipulation of information technology and so forth, I think this is an area to which anthropology must remain absolutely alert.

I appreciate your own work [Cris Shore's] has been very germane here, an intervention in academic reflection on the processes of knowledge production in institutional contexts. It is important to focus on the world of universities and what we do by promulgating knowledge. I think anthropologists have something to say about the values involved here and the way knowledge is being produced in an environment increasingly shaped by requirements to 'perform' in teaching and research whilst also passing on knowledge to a younger generation (Strathern 2000). I don't know whether that is exciting or not, but it's incredibly important.

That notion of being reflexive about our own institutional existence brings me to another question. Regarding the future of anthropology, what is your vision for the discipline? Given the current conditions of academic existence, what particular challenges will we face?

Your comment about the conditions of academic existence really touches quite a raw nerve, as I'm now at the stage of thinking a lot about the lives that younger academics have – what they have to manage, the amount of information they have to deal with, the administrative forms to which they have to conform. It's not anthropological life but academic life that is actually quite difficult and really does produce certain stresses and strains. Rather than seeing this as a problem for anthropology, I think that this is perhaps a huge resource for anthropology to draw on. By the very nature of wanting to find out how things look from other points of view – whatever those other points of view are, wherever in the world they occur – we are interested in occupying other people's shoes and our own at the same time. And that submission to the knowledge systems or world systems that other people occupy, whether it is down the road or across the sea, is a tremendous source of personal nourishment. I think that anthropologists are *lucky* in the way that historians or scholars of English literature are not, in this particular regard, insofar as they are intimately tied to the mechanics of knowledge reproduction with no escape. Well, they can escape into their texts or they can escape into their particular discoveries, but anthropologists have lives outside of their own conditions of reproduction. That's because, where our hosts are gracious and kind enough, we talk to other people who stand on a different terrain. In terms of sustaining people as persons, as human beings, those encounters with other people are a resource that in the end will save the anthropologist as a person.

Although I may have turned my ethnographic material about Mount Hagen into an artefact of my own devising – 'this is field M', you know, is it Melanesia or is it Marilyn? – the material didn't *begin* there. It began with people with very different preoccupations, and I'm just so grateful for the opportunity of being able to *think* myself elsewhere. I think anthropologists have something there that they should be pretty grateful for.

One thing that anthropologists are sometimes accused of being is 'too academic'. What contribution do you think your work has made to wider public debate beyond the academy, and is that an important aspect of the work of an anthropologist?

Can I first of all *defend* the academic? Mary Douglas once said of me – and I don't think she was being entirely kind – that I'm 'an anthropologist's anthropologist'. If I defend the academic, it is because there is a point to academia, and that is why we defend universities. The point of academia is precisely to explore the kinds of narratives, analyses, theories and so forth by which we can best illuminate our material. However, the person who puts the treasure in the chest isn't necessarily the person who's going to take the treasure out. And if things of great value are locked up in there, then that's a great pity. I feel very strongly that we have to get things right first and foremost as scholars. We have a job to do and that job is to understand the world to the very best of our ability. That actually is a major task. It is not something trivial. Moreover, it's a collective task. We belong to a discipline. One can be consulted as a representative of a discipline, but it's a collective, not a solitary, task. If I could go back to my previous point about my own naivety in thinking that an analysis is a sufficient basis on which to make a policy recommendation, I now don't think it is. Policy making is a whole other area. It is not another discipline, but it is another social arena. And academics are not necessarily the best people to mobilize the pragmatic or utilitarian value of knowledge. But having said that, we also have a social conscience. There is no doubt, especially in the UK as compared, say, with France, that there is a marked interest in pragmatism and the *utility* of knowledge, which displaces the aesthetics of knowledge. So I belong to a culture that's interested in the utility of knowledge, and I have a social conscience bred of that culture. And of course, there are times when one wants to be helpful, but we need to know whom we are helping. In the story I told about the dispute settlers it was of course powerful male dispute settlers that I was thinking about at that time, and I wasn't really thinking about other categories of persons. So there are all kinds of hidden political choices that arise when we *activate* our knowledge.

However, and if I can be a little bit smug again, I had a sabbatical year in 1999 and spent a wonderful time reading up on intellectual property rights and being completely enchanted by this new discourse. What compelled me in this direction was the fact that at the same time as the Convention on Biodiversity, and explicit international attention to the protection of indigenous knowledge throughout the 1990s, the World Trade Organization was trying to extend both patent and copyright jurisdiction to as many developing countries as possible. What that meant is that 'technology rich' countries that export to 'technology poor' countries wanted protection for their inventions. So they had an interest in a place like Papua New Guinea having its own patenting jurisdiction which they could lock into. On the one hand, the World Trade Organization and the World Intellectual Property Organization were concerned to extend intellectual property rights ['IPR'] legislation to create jurisdictions wherever they could, because places that were not then located within any IPR jurisdiction (such as China) could copy whatever they wanted. At the same time, across the developing world people were sitting up and saying, 'Oh right, okay! So there's *value* in designs, is there? We can now talk about authorship of our material goods, can we? Have we finally found an international instrument that validates what we call our culture and its protection – the protection of indigenous knowledge?' These things were happening in parallel.

Looking around me and seeing in the UK a number of very interesting people who had worked in Papua New Guinea, it seemed to me that it would be interesting to study the way intellectual property was being talked about in PNG [Papua New Guinea]. And so that was the study that I did with Eric Hirsch and a number of other UK-based Melanesianists (Strathern and Hirsch 2004). Our project *had* to involve Papua New Guinean scholars too, as without them it would have been completely futile. We brought on board a wonderful Papua New Guinean lawyer who came over to Cambridge, and after a few weeks there he looked at me and said, 'I'm not an anthropologist, but it's about relationships, isn't it'. What soon became clear to us was that there was a small handful of people in PNG who were concerned with these things, not an elite, but a select number of Papua New Guinean academics. Papua New Guinea was also up to its eyes in NGOs, consultants and experts telling them what to do. They didn't *need* anyone to tell them what to do in matters of cultural protection. But, and it dawned on us more slowly, what it seemed our PNG colleagues would find useful would be to have an intellectual space opened up so that they could think through things that they already knew but wouldn't otherwise have had the space to articulate. I refer here to the constraints of the international legal and administrative language of the time and to hesitations about articulating issues about local knowledge in local terms. It seemed to me that the value of the work that we did was to expand the horizon of thinking upon which these particular scholars felt they could draw. It offered a kind of intellectual liberation, perhaps. Insofar as they were sympathetic to what we were doing – and they included a Papua New Guinean anthropologist who was head of the Cultural Commission – I felt that this was actually the way to make a contribution. This is the kind of contribution which will leave no trace, because that was never the point. Writing a handbook or producing recommendations or being didactic in any sense was never the point. Rather, the contribution will have simply disappeared into the thoughts and the trajectories of other people who will take the ideas and experiences forward with them and do with them whatever they want. I felt, actually, this wasn't a bad way to go [laughing].

References

MacCormack, C., and M. Strathern, M. (eds). 1980. *Nature, Culture and Gender.* Cambridge: Cambridge University Press.
Strang, V., and M. Busse, M., eds. 2011. *Ownership and Appropriation.* Oxford/New York: Berg.
Strathern, M. 1972a. *Official and Unofficial Courts: Legal Assumptions and Expectations in a Highlands Community.* Port Moresby: New Guinea Research Unit, Australian National University.
———. 1972b. *Women In Between: Female Roles in a Male World, Mount Hagen, New Guinea.* Lanham, MD: Rowman and Littlefield.
———. 1987. *Dealing with Inequality: Analysing Gender Relations in Melanesia and Beyond.* Cambridge: Cambridge University Press.
———. 1988. *The Gender of the Gift: Problems with Women and Problems with Society in Melanesia.* Berkeley: University of California Press.
———. 1992. *Reproducing the Future: Essays on Anthropology, Kinship, and the New Reproductive Technologies.* Manchester: Manchester University Press.
———. 1999. *Property, Substance and Effect: Anthropological Essays on Persons and Things.* London: Athlone.

———, ed. 2000. *Audit Cultures: Anthropological Studies in Accountability, Ethics and the Academy.* London: Routledge.
———. 2011. 'Sharing, stealing and borrowing simultaneously'. In *Ownership and Appropriation,* eds. V. Strang and M. Busse, 23–41. Oxford/ New York: Berg.
Strathern, M. and E. Hirsch, eds. 2004. *Transactions and Creations: Property Debates and the Stimulus of Melanesia.* Oxford: Berghahn.

Notes

1. In her first book, *Women In Between* (1972b), Strathern focused on what were then called sex roles, in Mount Hagen, New Guinea. Her later work, *The Gender of the Gift* (1988), used Melanesianist ethnography to examine the assumptions about gender that underpin much of Western scholarship.

Conclusion

LOOKING AHEAD
Past Connections and Future Directions

Cris Shore and Susanna Trnka

Contributions from the Periphery: Challenging the Core

The questions we posed at the outset of this book were what 'what is the nature of anthropological knowledge production' and what contribution can anthropology in the 'peripheries' make to the discipline at large? June Nash (2001), in her seminal essay, has highlighted how 'peripheral vision' plays a key role in opening up new ways of identifying and analyzing patterns and processes at work in the core, including post-colonial labour relations, migration, commodity production and forms of anti-capitalist resistance. More important, she shows how core and periphery are interconnected through these processes and how 'peripheral vision' sheds light on phenomena that are hitherto unseen or misrecognized. Indeed, it has often been observed that capitalist democracies commit their worst excesses outside of their national borders. The outsourcing of factory production to the cheaper, unregulated industrial zones of third world countries has become a defining feature of the organization of advanced capitalist economies (Lim 1983; Pearson 1998). Yet precisely because these zones are located in supposedly 'remote' sites outside the normal purview of Western media, those excesses are easily ignored until some 'exposé' brings international opprobrium – which is usually short lived. For example, Apple recently came into the limelight for various 'unfair labour' practices at its Chinese factories, including the use of under-age labour, improper disposal of hazardous waste, and excessive overtime being forced on its workers (Nuttall 2012). While such conditions are often depicted by many industrialists and journalists as aberrations from the norms and standards of international labour law, anthropologists have long shown how these are far from abnormal and, indeed, often fundamental to the workings of Western capitalism (Nash 1979; Taussig 1980; Ong 1987; Bonacich and Appelbaum 2000; Ingraham 1999).

These works provide a useful starting point for reflecting on the wider question of what perspectives from the periphery have to offer the discipline. Peripheral vision, however, offers useful insights not only on the uses and abuses of sweatshop labour, but on a variety of socio-political conditions, including how capitalist economies are being reconstituted in an age of late modernity. Many countries that were previously defined from the metropolitan centres as peripheral to the global economy have emerged as the new winners in the competitive world economy. These include not only Brazil, Russia, India and China (the developing 'BRIC' countries') but also other previously marginalized colonial outposts such as Australia, Indonesia and South Africa. The traditional habit of looking to the core G5 (or G7) countries, particularly the United States, for the model of successful economic development has been radically challenged in recent years, particularly with the global financial meltdown of 2008 and the euro zone crisis of 2011 (Graeber 2011). Today, as Comaroff and Comaroff note (2011), many of the economic conditions thought to be characteristic of third world societies feature prominently in the metropolitan core. The peripheries thus offer a unique vantage point for grasping some of the profound global shifts that are redefining the contemporary world, and for understanding the effects of this global shake-up.

Another key area for an anthropology informed by the peripheries, we suggest, is the analysis of the increasingly intrusive and expansive normative ordering associated with neoliberal forms of governance (Larner and Walters 2004). The governmentalization, medicalization and financialization of society are global phenomena whose effects operate differently across various sites and scales. Among the defining features of these global processes are regulation and regularization; harmonization and uniformity; a fetishization of technology and commercialization; new forms of governance based on the setting of benchmarks, targets and standards; and the battery of calculative practices aimed at realigning the behaviours of those who fall short of these norms. In the domain of health and well-being, this is evidenced in the proliferation of diagnostic categories and treatments for illnesses that hitherto did not exist (Martin 2009; Rose 2003, 2007). In education it is seen in the rise of national standards that define school curricula and levels of achievement and in the advance of regimes of audit and accountability in higher education (Shore and Wright 1999; Strathern 2000; Brenneis et al 2005). Elsewhere it is manifest in the dramatic spread of financial thinking and in the pecuniary imperatives that eclipse other systems for attributing value (Hart 2000; Unger and Rawlings 2008). As former colonies of the great European powers, the peripheries were often used as laboratories for trialling the practices of capitalism (Gledhill 2000; Mbembe 2003). Today, these peripheral locations are emerging sites for a critical reappraisal of the processes of global capital.

But there are many other key processes and developments on the periphery – and the work of anthropologists to understand them – that raise critical challenges to the normative assumptions of the metropolitan centres. One of these is the demand for post-colonial redress and compensation for historical injustices. Australia and New Zealand are among countries at the forefront of controversies over post-colonial restoration and reconciliation (Lawn 2008; Mookherjee et al 2009). In Australia, the Labour government under Kevin Rudd took the historic step in 2008 of apologizing to Australia's Aboriginal people for the crimes of forced assimilation and the 'stolen generations' of children forcibly removed from their families. In New Zealand, the Treaty of Waitangi has been deployed as the basis of a new post-colonial constitutional partnership between settler and indigenous population. Since the establishment of the Waitangi Treaty tribunal in 1975, there have been over 2,000 claims made for restitution and financial compensation, which, by 2010, had resulted in settlements with a value of over a 958 million New Zealand dollars (OTS 2010: 11). Compared to the situation of first-nation peoples in Canada and the United States, these are major developments towards recognition of the responsibilities of contemporary governments for the damage and suffering inflicted by the laws and policies of their predecessors. As our contributors' stories illustrate, anthropology has a major role to play in the outcomes of these challenges.

A final facet of anthropology's contribution from the periphery is in the field of ownership and the repatriation of cultural artefacts. The issue of indigenous groups' repatriation of cultural objects and trophies stolen by Western collectors or appropriated by metropolitan museums has led to a major rethinking of the politics of cultural representation and the responsibilities of museums as custodians of other people's culture (Busse 2008). One example is the controversial 1984 *Te Maori* Exhibition at New York's Metropolitan Museum of Art, which awakened among Maori an awareness of the international artistic value attached to their *taonga* (treasures) and concern over the representation of their culture in museums (Karp and Lavine 1991: 2). The result of such challenges is twofold: not only have they changed how we ascertain ownership rights over material objects, resulting in some museums having to return materials that were acquired unethically, but they have also precipitated a shift in understandings of where expert knowledge lies. No longer do Western scholars automatically have the last word. Instead, community consultations over museum displays are now common, and indigenous peoples are now vested with increasing authority over the display and use of cultural artefacts.

Our aim in this epilogue is to highlight a few key areas where events in the 'peripheries' – and the anthropologists who study them have – have dislodged some of the axiomatic certainties and unquestioned assumptions of the metropolitan centres. In a similar vein, Jean and John Comaroff, in their recent book, *Theory from the South: Or, How Euro-America Is Evolving Toward Africa* (2011), underline the theoretical contributions that the global 'south' can make to understanding the dynamics that are reshaping contemporary economy and society in the metropolitan centres of the developed north. Turning the usual order of analysis on its head, they draw attention to the ways in which the experiences of the Northern Hemisphere – including financial crisis, privatization, the demise of the public sector, ethnic conflict, urban unrest, corruption and maladministration – are now 'evolving southward, so to speak, in both positive and problematic ways' (Comaroff 2011). Certainly, theory developed in the south may contribute to understanding broader debates around democracy, law, national borders, labour and capital, liberalism and multiculturalism and other concerns (see also Mbembe 2012; Ferguson 2012). However, to claim that the south offers a model of the evolutionary trajectory of where the north might be heading is questionable. We would argue instead that peripheries offer valuable vantage points for perceiving the processes that are reshaping *both* the global north and south, in mutually constitutive ways. If the idea of 'peripheral vision' offers a useful way to perceive patterns of globalization (Nash 2001), that concept might be extended – or pluralized – to examine how actors in the peripheries negotiate and engage with those global processes, including the myriad ways that globalization is performed and *imagined*. But we also need to go beyond the term 'globalization' to unpack the variety of different scales on which technological, economic, geo-political, epidemiological and socio-cultural processes are traversing national borders and reconstituting the relationship between north and south.

Social imaginaries are, by definition, characterized by their inherently creative – and even liberatory – potential (Appadurai 1996; Crapanzano 2004). At the same time, however, social understandings of what is – and is not – conceivable are moulded by socio-political and economic conditions and constraints (Pieterse and Parkeh 1995; Trnka 2011; Haukanes and Trnka, in press). Slavoj Žižek famously wrote that 'it seems easier to imagine the "end of the world" than a far more modest change in the mode of production, as if liberal capitalism is the "real"' (Žižek 1994:1). Perhaps a good site for reimagining the 'real' of contemporary neoliberal capitalism is from the peripheries. Indeed, critical scholars such as Frantz Fanon, Paolo Freire, Stuart Hall and Amartya Sen have demonstrated how being located in the 'margins' creates a necessary distance for recasting conventional understandings in areas from psychology, psychiatry and education to economics, politics and development. The creative juxtaposition of differently located points of view is something, moreover, with which most anthropologists are well acquainted, as using the margins to question and unsettle normative orders is one of the central tenets of the production of anthropological knowledge.

The Challenge of Anthropology: Questioning Received Wisdom

Raymond Firth once famously described anthropology as the 'uncomfortable discipline' renowned for its inquisitiveness as well as for 'challenging [and] questioning established positions and proclaimed values, peering into underlying interests, and if not destroying fictions and empty phrases ... at least exposing them' (Firth, cited in Wright 1995: 65).

Questioning axiomatic assumptions and generating 'inconvenient truths' has arguably been pivotal to the anthropological project ever since the discipline's foundation. As the contributions to this book show, anthropology continues to have a major role to play in countering some of the hegemonic assumptions that underpin both lay perspectives and expert narratives. Indeed, as Besterson and Gusterson (2005) have shown, the discipline is particularly adept at analyzing the discourses of politicians and policy makers, not only in showing why many contemporary pundits are 'wrong', but also in tracing the socio-cultural and economic effects of their decisions.

Despite major changes in the nature and scope of anthropological research since the 1970s, including opening up to new areas of enquiry – from tourism, technology and global- commodity supply chains to visual culture, aesthetics, and emergent subjectivities – anthropology is still a discipline rooted in the study of people in their own socio-cultural contexts, with its primary method remaining grounded in observations and analyses of everyday social relations and cultural processes. 'The essence of anthropology', as Metge observes, 'is that it's people to people, or as Maori put it, *kanohi ki kanohi* – face to face.' Graburn concurs: '[T]he magic of anthropology ... is to know people as *people*, not just as numbers or representative samples.' Knowing people in such an intimate way demands being sensitive to the complexity and contradictions of human social behaviour, recognizing the disjunctures between what people say and what they actually do and revealing the often unarticulated dynamics that drive human behaviour and social relations.

Yet while anthropology remains committed to a method that is largely empirical, it is emphatically not *empiricist.* What it brings to the analysis of how other people view and organize their social worlds are multiple theoretical perspectives and a constant awareness that people's experiences and interpretations are shaped by larger social forces and historical processes not of their own making. One way to capture that fluidity and complexity is by highlighting the connections and movements between the local and the global. However, some anthropologists point out that many cultural processes occupy an intermediate space that is neither strictly 'global' nor 'local', one that Pinney describes as 'more than local, less than global'. One continuing challenge for anthropology, therefore, is to construct an analytical language that allows us to break out of the dichotomy between localism and universality to focus on *transversal* phenomena that necessarily transcend local boundaries and interconnect various social and technological fields. Examples here might include banking and international finance, medical technologies, policy assemblages, new religious movements, migration and human trafficking or popular protests and social activism such as the anti-globalization and 'Occupy Wall Street' movements. All of these entail multi-stranded, richly articulated matrices of relations that extend beyond their local manifestations. Anthropology's contribution is both to elucidate these processes themselves and to examine how they play out in people's daily lives.

Another of anthropology's fundamental contributions is its capacity to open up spaces for critical thinking in ways that not many disciplines can. Virtually all of our contributors have noted the dramatic effects of having their taken-for-granted viewpoints de-centred as a result of conducting fieldwork in unfamiliar contexts and the deep insights this can bring, those truly unsettling and revealing 'eureka' moments that lend themselves to epistemological reflexivity. But it is not just 'out there' in the field that this transformative intellectual work takes place. It can also happen in the classroom and through academic debate. Indeed, being exposed to anthropological ideas and concepts can have transformative effects for students. '[E]ach year', says Graburn, 'I take the unformed minds of fifteen hundred or so of California's future leaders and I teach them a *totally new view* of the world and humanity, which will affect them for the rest of their lives.' Graburn's reflections epitomize one of the principal aims of liberal higher education: to enlarge students' perspectives and give them the skills that enable critical and independent thinking.

No less profound is anthropology's capacity, as Strathern puts it, to create scholarly knowledge and 'expand the horizon of thinking' in the academy. While some might criticize this for being too 'ivory tower' and elitist, Strathern makes two important points: first, that every society needs a place that is conducive to independent research and scholarship that is not necessarily of immediate instrumental utility, and second, that the future beneficiaries of knowledge cannot be known in the present, or to use her metaphor, the 'person who puts the treasure in the chest' is usually not the one who reaps the rewards in the years to come.

As many of our contributors have shown, part of the process of rethinking neoliberal capitalism and its effects upon the world is to consider how it is reshaping our own conditions of existence and the production of academic knowledge – or of what today *counts* as valid academic knowledge (Shore 2010; Wright and Rabo 2010; Shore and McLauchlan 2012). Our authors' accounts underscore that anthropology remains a highly iconoclastic and eclectic endeavour, with many of its most profound insights being generated through serendipity rather than excessive planning. Many anthropologists find that they go into the field to study one thing but come out writing their thesis or book on something quite different. Against a background of an ever-more instrumental and prescriptive higher-education sector, anthropology demonstrates the continuing necessity for open-ended enquiries and an empirical approach that emphasizes the importance of personal relations in the production of knowledge. Programmatic and output-focused research is not necessarily the best way to generate insight into the human condition. Anthropology, as Firth acknowledged, is still the 'uncomfortable discipline' whose challenging and critical perspectives arise from the unexpected and contingent nature of the ethnographic encounter and teaches us this about ourselves and others.

References

Appadurai, A. 1996. *Modernity at Large: Cultural Dimensions of Globalization*. Minneapolis: University of Minnesota Press.
Besteron, C., and Gusterson, H. 2005. *Why America's Top Pundits Are Wrong: Anthropologists Talk Back*. Berkeley: University of California Press.
Bonacich, E., and R. P. Appelbaum. 2000. *Behind the Label: Inequality in the Los Angeles Apparel Industry*. Berkeley: University of California Press.
Brenneis, D., C. Shore, and S. Wright. 2005. 'Getting the Measure of Academia: Universities and the Politics of Accountability'. *Anthropology in Action*, 1: 1–10.
Busse, M. 2008. 'Museums and the Things in Them Should be Alive'. *International Journal of Cultural Property* 15: 189–200.
Comaroff, J. 2011. 'Theory from the South: or, How Europe is Evolving Towards Africa', Keynote lecture, Australian Anthropological Society conference, Perth (July), http://www.anthropologywa.org/iuaes_aas_asaanz_conference2011/0023.html.
Comaroff, J., and J. Comaroff. 2011. *Theory from the South: Or, How Europe is Evolving Toward Africa*. Boulder, CO: Paradigm Publishers
Crapanzano, V. 2004. *Imaginative Horizons: An Essay in Literary-philosophical Anthropology*. Chicago: University of Chicago Press.
Ferguson, J. 2012. 'Theory from the Comaroffs, or How to Know the World Up, Down, Backwards and Forwards', Theorizing the Contemporary forum, *Cultural Anthropology*, http://www.culanth.org/?q=node/502 [accessed 20-12-2012]
Gledhill, J. 2000. *Power and Its Disguises: Anthropological Perspectives on Politics*. London: Pluto.
Graeber, D. 2011. *Debt: The First 5,000 Years*. New York: Melville House.
Haukanes, H., and S. Trnka. In press. 'Recasting Futures and Pasts: An Introduction'. In *Recasting Futures and Pasts: Imagination and Memory across Generations in Post-socialist Europe*. Special issue of *Focaal: Journal of Global and Historical Anthropology*.
Hart, K., 2000. *The Memory Bank: Money in an Unequal World*. London: Profile Books.
Ingraham, C. 1999. *White Weddings: Romancing Heterosexuality in Popular Culture*. London/New York: Routledge.
Karp, I., and S. Lavine. 1991. 'Introduction: Museums and Multiculturalism'. In *Exhibiting Cultures: The Poetics and Politics of Museum Display*, eds. I. Karp and S. Lavine, 1–10. Washington: Smithsonian Institute.

Larner, W., and W. Walters, eds. 2004. *Global Governmentality: Governing International Spaces*. London/New York: Routledge.

Lawn, J. 2008. 'Settler Society and Postcolonial Apologies in Australia and New Zealand'. *Sites: New Series* 5(1): 20–40.

Lim, L. Y. C. 1983. 'Capitalism, Imperialism, and Patriarchy: The Dilemma of Third-world Women Workers in Multinational Factories'. In *Women, Men and the International Division of Labour*, eds. J. Nash and M. P. Fernandez-Kelly, 70–93. Albany, NY: SUNY Press.

Martin, E. 2009. *Bipolar Expeditions: Mania and Depression in American Culture*. Princeton: Princeton University Press.

Mbembe, A. 2003. 'Necropolitics'. *Public Culture* 15(1): 11–40.

———. 2012. 'Theory from the Antipodes. Notes on John & Jean Comaroff's TFS', Theorizing the Contemporary forum, *Cultural Anthropology*, http://www.culanth.org/?q=node/502 [accessed 20-12-2012]

Mookherjee, N., N. Rapport, L. Josephides, G. Hage, L. R. Todd and G. Cowlishaw. 2009. 'The Ethics of Apology: A Set of Commentaries', *Critique of Anthropology* 29(3): 345–66.

Nash, J. 2001. 'Globalization and the Cultivation of Peripheral Vision'. *Anthropology Today* 17(4): 15–22.

———. 1979. *We Eat the Mines and the Mines Eat Us: Dependency and Exploitation in Bolivian Tin Mines*. New York: Columbia University Press.

Nuttall, C. 2012. *Financial Times*, 'Apple Chief Defends Factory Conditions', 14 February. http://www.ft.com/intl/cms/s/2/a914607c-575d-11e1-869b-00144feabdc0.html#axzz1mUinxsbx. Last accessed 16 February 2012.

Ong, A. 1987. *Spirits of Resistance and Capitalist Discipline: Factory Women in Malaysia*. Albany, NY: SUNY Press.

OTS (Office of Treaty Settlements). 2010. *Four Monthly Report* (November 2009 – February 2010), http://nz01.terabyte.co.nz/ots/DocumentLibrary/FourMonthlyReportNov09toFeb10_final.pdf

Pearson, R. 1998. 'Nimble Fingers Revisited: Reflections on Women and Third World Industrialization in the Late Twentieth Century'. In *Feminist Visions of Development: Gender Analysis and Policy*, eds. C. Jackson and R. Pearson, 171–89. London/New York: Routledge.

Pieterse, J. N. and B. Parkeh, eds. 1995. *The Decolonization of Imagination: Culture, Knowledge and Power*. London: Zed Books.

Rose, N. 2007. *The Politics of Life Itself*. Princeton: Princeton University Press.

———. 2003. 'Neurochemical Selves'. *Society*. 41(1): 46–59.

Shore, C. 2010. 'Beyond the Multiversity: Neoliberalism and the Rise of the Schizophrenic University'. *Social Anthropology* 18(1): 15–29.

Shore, C. and McLauchlan, L. 2012.'"Third Mission" Activities and Academic Entrepreneurs: Commercialization and the remaking of the university'. *Social Anthropology / Anthropologie Sociale*, 20 (3): 267–286.

Shore, C., and S. Wright. 1999. 'Audit Culture and Anthropology: Neo-Liberalism in British Higher Education'. *Journal of the Royal Anthropological Institute* 5(4): 557–75.

Strathern, M. 2000, ed. *Audit Cultures: Anthropological Studies in Accountability, Ethics and the Academy.* London/New York: Routledge.

Taussig, M. 1980. *The Devil and Commodity Fetishism in South America.* Chapel Hill: University of North Carolina Press.

Trnka, S. 2011. 'Specters of Uncertainty: Violence, Humor, and the Uncanny in Indo-Fijian Communities Following the May 2000 Fiji Coup'. *Ethos* 39(3): 331–48.

Unger, B., and G. Rawlings. 2008. 'Competing for Criminal Money'. *Global Business and Economics Review* 10(3): 331–52.

Wright, S. 1995. 'Anthropology: Still the Uncomfortable Discipline?'. In *The Future of Anthropology*, eds. A. Ahmed and C. Shore, 65–93. London: Athlone.

Wright, S., and A. Rabo. 2010. 'Introduction: Anthropologies of University Reform'. *Social Anthropology* 18(1): 1–14.

Žižek, S. 1994. 'The Spectre of Ideology'. In *Mapping Ideology*, ed. S. Žižek, 1–33. London: Verso.

INDEX

Page numbers in **bold** indicate full chapters in this book by the respective authors.

Aboriginal Land Rights (Northern Territory) Act 1976, 111
Aboriginal people: apology to, 197, 249; art, 21, 27, 127–28, 131, 132–33, 134–35, 138; assimilationist policies, 41–42, 146; child-rearing, 106; and Christianity, 144–45; Cowlishaw's work, 94–95, 97–106; culture, 20, 21, 23, 94–95, 101, 102–4, 106, 115–16, 119, 120–22, 143, 178; gender relations, 97, 99; impact of requirements for improving health and material circumstances, 119, 121–22; intermarriage with non-Aboriginal people, 119; and introduced plants and animals, 142–43; Jackson's work, 52–53; land and native title, 18, 20, 21, 24, 102–4, 119–21, 127, 128, 131, 137, 143, 145, 149, 151, 178; languages, 116–17, 133; perceptions of Aboriginality as connected only to the past, 102–3; Morphy's work, 127–28, 130, 131–35, 136, 137–38; Peterson's work, 110–11, 112–14, 115–22; Piddington's articles on Karadjeri people, 26–27, 40–41, 79; post-colonial restoration and reconciliation, 249; relations with anthropologists, 26, 99–100, 119–20, 147–49; relations with state, and experiences with non-Aboriginal people, 98–99, 100, 101, 102, 104–6, 119–22, 127–28, 135, 146, 147; rights, 18, 20, 21, 24, 102–4, 105, 110, 119–21, 127, 128, 131, 137, 145; 'ritual manager' in Central Australian ceremonial life, 115–16; social activism, 146, 147; 'teaching the children their culture', 94–95, 103; Trigger's work, 26, 142–45, 147–52, 155–56; in urban areas, 20, 94, 97, 102–4. *See also* Darug people; Garawa people; Torres Strait Islanders; Wik people; Yanyuwa people; Yolngu people
Abrahams, Ray, 201
'accidental anthropologist', 9, 10, 50–51, 52, 145, 161, 162, 188, 199–200, 215
'action anthropology', 183
Adler, Judy, 204
Adorno, Theodor W., 45
advocacy, 21, 24–25, 40–41, 119, 151
Africa, 43, 44, 53, 138, 189, 190, 201, 236. *See also* Congo; Ghana; Sierra Leone; South Africa; West Africa
Alaska, 178–79
American Anthropological Association, 24, 51
American Field Service scholarship, 59
American Kinship Project, 184
Amoy (Xiamen), 179
Andersen, Raoul, 204
Anderson, Lenin, 150
Annals of Tourism Research, 188
'anthropological imagination', 15
anthropologists: anthropologist-as-hero, 8; employment, 89–90; indigenous, 89, 190–91; institutional constraints, 26–28, 54, 76, 130–31; perception of

subversion, 190; public opinion and stereotypes, 7–8. *See also* fieldwork encounters; historical influences on anthropologists; personal influences on anthropologists; public sphere, anthropologists in; scholarly influences on anthropologists

anthropologists' reasons for coming to anthropology, 8–15; Anne Salmond, 58–60; Christopher Pinney, 161–66; David Trigger, 145–47; Gillian Cowlishaw, 95–97; Howard Morphy, 128–31; Joan Metge, 77–80; Marilyn Strathern, 234–35; Michael Jackson, 37–38, 41–44, 50; Nelson Graburn, 179–83; Nicolas Peterson, 111–13; Nigel Rapport, 199–202; Susan Wright, 215–21. *See also* 'accidental anthropologist'

anthropologists' thinking about anthropology, 20–21; Anne Salmond, 70; David Trigger, 151–52; Joan Metge, 87–88; Marilyn Strathern, 235–36; Michael Jackson, 41–44; Nelson Graburn, 183–85; Nicolas Peterson, 113

anthropology: anchorage in traditional cultural forms, 102–4; biological (physical), 10, 12–13, 129, 201; cosmopolitan, 19, 22, 199, 208, 209, 210–11; 'critical anthropology', 190; diversity of approach, 88, 166–67, 172; encompassing humanity, 67, 69, 70, 71, 87–88; 'existential', 19, 45; feminist, 16, 235, 236, 239–40; focus on individuals, 19, 48, 198, 204, 207, 208–11; focus on universal dimensions, 19, 48, 106, 172; future of, 50, 70, 71–72, 90, 106–7, 122–23, 155–56, 189–91, 211–12, 242–43; generational shifts, 3, 4, 16–17, 89–90; global and local levels, 18, 138, 172–74, 209, 252; as 'handmaiden of colonialism', 64–66, 72; human subjects with agency, 13–14, 19, 78–79, 113; image and identity, 7–9, 154; innovations and new directions, 1, 17, 18–20, 69, 88–90, 118–19, 136–37, 138, 155–56, 171–74, 241–42; interfaces with other disciplines, 66–67, 69, 89, 102, 145, 151, 166, 190, 207, 210, 211, 226; legal, 240–41; professional practice, 1, 17, 28; public recognition, 7–8; questioning received wisdom, 251–54; social and contextual changes, 1, 3, 4, 18, 41–43; study of the human mind, 14, 43, 45; symbolic, 236; transformative effects, 253; 'uncomfortable discipline', 251, 254; as a vocation, 8–9. *See also* 'action anthropology'; applied anthropology; cultural anthropology; fieldwork encounters; knowledge production; research; social anthropology; visual anthropology

Anthropology in Action, 228

Antipodes, 4–7, 24. *See also* Australia; New Zealand

apologies, 5, 197–98

Apple, labour practices in Chinese factories, 247–48

applied anthropology, 5, 20, 24, 118–22, 123, 129, 131, 138, 143, 145, 150–52, 154, 156, 182, 191; *versus* 'pure' anthropology, 228. *See also* public sphere, anthropologists in

appropriation, 5, 21, 22, 75, 94, 127–28, 198, 199. *See also* ownership

archaeology, 10, 12–13, 37–38, 77, 78, 200, 234

archival concerns, 137, 150, 155–56, 164–65, 186

Arctic, 181–82, 183, 185–86

Arendt, Hannah, 48–49

Arnhem Land, Australia, 97, 99, 101, 110–11, 113–14, 115, 127–28, 131, 132–33. *See also* Goinjimbi (Bulman), Australia

art: Aboriginal people, 21, 27, 127–28, 131, 132–33, 134–35, 138; anthropology of, 131–32;

commercialization of indigenous art, 18, 20, 179, 188–89
Asia. *See* South Asia; Southeast Asia
Association of Social Anthropologists of Aotearoa/New Zealand, 90
Auckland, New Zealand, 38, 63, 76, 77–78, 85, 95
Auckland Teachers' Training College, 43, 95, 96
Auckland University, 26, 37, 40–41, 43, 44, 59–60, 70, 76, 79, 189
Auckland War Memorial Museum, 76, 78–79
audio recordings, 150, 155–56
Australia: applied anthropology, 24; concepts of 'nativeness' and 'nature', 142–44; economy, 248; government apology to Aboriginal people, 197; indigenous issues compared to New Zealand and Canada, 142, 249; restoration and reconciliation, 249; social anthropology discipline, 4–7; universities, government regulations and requirements, 27. *See also* Aboriginal people; New South Wales; Northern Territory; periphery and peripheral visions; Queensland; Victoria
Australian Institute of Aboriginal [and Torres Strait Islander] Studies, 112, 131, 134, 147
Australian National Research Council, 27
Australian National University (ANU), 27, 130–31, 134; New Guinea Research Unit, 240
autobiography, 2, 3
Awatere, Donna, 59, 64

Baader-Meinhof Gang, 202–3
Baffin Island, 182, 186–87
Bakhtiari people, 13, 216
Baluba people, 42–43
Barber, Marcus, 137
Barnes, John, 132, 238–39
Barth, Fredrik, 13
Bartlett, Frederic, *The Study of Society*, 180

Baxter, Paul, 202
Beckett, Jeremy, 144–45
beginnings, distinguished from origins, 47–48
Ben-Gurion University of the Negev, 205–6
Benjamin, Walter, 165
Berkeley, California, 187–88
Berkeley, University of California, 182, 183, 190
Best, Elsdon, 58, 77
Bhopal, 163
Biggs, Bruce, 59, 62
Bilsborough, Alan, 201
Binney, Judith, 89
biological (physical) anthropology, 10, 12–13, 129, 201
Bloomington, Indiana, 51, 54
Blue Mud Bay native title claim, Australia, 21, 137
Bombay, 161
Borneo, 144
Borroloola, Australia, 148
Bourke, Australia, 101, 104–6
Brazil, 183, 190, 248
BRIC countries, 248
Briggs, Jean, 204
Brisbane, Australia, 143, 146–47
Bristol, England, 199
Britain, 4, 19, 27, 81, 111, 114, 179–80, 184, 197, 198, 199–200, 202, 206, 209, 218–20, 221–23, 225, 228, 236, 243
British Museum, 130, 133
Brookes, David, 13
Brooks, David, 215–16
Buck, Sir Peter (Te Rangi Hiroa), 58, 76, 83
Bulman (Goinjimbi), Australia, 98–99, 100
Bulmer, Ralph, 59
Bunten, Alex, 178–79
Buyi people, 192

'calendar art', 164
Cambridge University, 13, 44, 45, 65, 66, 68, 113, 114–15, 179, 180, 183–84, 189, 200–1, 202, 209, 234, 236, 244
Camfoo, Tex and Nelly, 99–100
Campbell, Donald, 183
Campbell, John Logan, 77

Canada, 142, 178–79, 181–82, 185–86, 188–89, 191, 204–5, 249
Cape York Peninsula, 146
capitalism, 6, 106–7, 163, 247–48, 249, 251, 253
Captain James Cook Research Fellowship, 76, 86
Cardiff, Wales, 199
Carnegie Foundation, 183
Carnegie Social Science Research Fellowship, 76
Carter, Angela, 47
Central Land Council, Alice Springs, 52
Ceylon (Sri Lanka), 161, 179–80
Charles Sturt University, 100–1
Chase, Athol, 146
Chatwin, Bruce, *The Song Lines*, 53
Chicago, 160, 181, 182–83, 184–85
Chicago University, 182–83, 184–85, 189
Childe, Gordon, *Man Makes Himself*, 37
childhood, 106
China, 95, 138, 179, 191, 192–93, 244, 247–48
Chomsky, Noam, 62
Choukoutien (Peking Man), 192
Christianity, 14, 53, 77, 78, 119, 144–45
Chuuk, Micronesia, 16
citizenship, 6
civil society, 101, 211
Clarke, Annie, 137
Cleveland, England, 219, 221–23
clichés, use in city talking-relationships, 205
Clifton College, England, 200
Codrington, Robert Henry, *The Melanesians*, 166
Cohen, Anthony, 202
Cohen, Erik, 188
Colombia, 2
colonialism, 6, 12, 14, 17, 23, 39–40, 64, 147, 190, 217, 238, 240
Comaroff, Jean and John, *Theory from the South*, 248, 250
community: and collective belonging, 209–10, 211;
neoliberal transformation, Britain, 220, 222
community action, 220, 229
comparative connections, 15–16, 66, 71, 89, 137, 142, 172
Congo, 42–43
context, cultural, 15, 16
Cook, James, 61, 66–67
Cooperative Cross-cultural Study of Ethnocentrism, 183
Copenhagen University, 51, 54
cosmopolitan anthropology, 19, 22, 199, 208, 209, 210–11
Cowlishaw, Gillian, 9, 11, 16, 18, 20, 23, **92–107**; *Blackfellas, Whitefellas and the Hidden Injuries of Race*, 105–6; *The City's Outback*, 97; 'Culture as Therapy', 94–95; *Love Against the Law*, 100; *Rednecks, Eggheads and Blackfellas*, 98–99
Cree Naskapi, 183
'critical anthropology', 190
critical thinking, 253
Croker Island case, 111
cross-cultural communication, 20, 82–83, 84, 85, 87, 123, 150–51
cross-fertilization in academia, 5
C-SAP, 221
cultural anthropology, 4, 15, 172
cultural artefacts, 249–50
cultural dynamics, 184
cultural ecology, 16, 114
cultural genocide, 5, 21
cultural geography, 145
cultural relativism, 24, 169
cultural survival, 21
culture: change resulting from interventions by anthropologists, 25; collective belonging and personal existence, 209–10, 211–12; concepts, 22; context, 15, 16; and economy, 119; material culture, 21, 129, 130, 133, 138, 167, 173; multiple perspectives, 22–23; political nature, 23, 211, 212; as a repertoire of possibilities, 45; representation of other cultures, 18, 22–23, 28, 62–66; 'teaching the children their culture', 94–95; and tourism, 178–79. *See also under*

Index

Aboriginal people; indigenous peoples; Māori
Cunliffe, David, 234

Dalit people, 24, 169, 170–71
Darug people, 94
Davis, Natalie Zemon, 69
democracy, 205–6, 219, 247, 250
Denmark, 221, 226–27
Department of Northern Affairs (Canada), 181
Derrida, Jacques, 172
development, international, 24, 190, 219, 224–25
Deveson, Pip, 127
Dewey, John, 46
discourse, anthropological, 16–17
divorce patterns and talk, Papua New Guinea, 237–39
Dominion Museum, Wellington, 58, 61
Dominy, Michele, 145
Doomadgee, Australia, 144, 148–49
Douglas, Mary, 80, 129, 243
Duff, Roger, 37
Dunlop, Ian, 127, 133
Durham University, 215–16
Durkheim, Émile, 121, 167

East Asia, 144
East Cape, New Zealand, 20
East Coast, New Zealand, 61, 66
Eastern Arctic Patrol, 182, 185
Eastern Canadian Indians, 183
ecological restoration, 144
Economic and Social Research Fund (ESRC), 27, 130
economy, relationship to culture, 119
education, neoliberal policies, 249
Eggan, Fred, 182, 183, 185
empiricism, 17, 46, 47, 97, 167, 170, 252, 253
Engels, Frederick, *Communist Manifesto*, 200
Enlightenment heritage, 72, 209, 211
'enunciative authority', 160–61
epistemology, 1, 137, 253
Eruera, Taura, 64
ethics, 2, 24–26, 75, 118, 156; of apology, 197–98

ethnocentrism, 183
ethnography, 2, 9, 20, 21, 23, 27, 28, 42, 50, 58, 59, 69, 97, 101, 102, 137, 149–50, 164, 172, 174, 184, 209, 210, 235. *See also* fieldwork encounters
ethnology, 215–17
Europe, 138, 144, 161, 191
European Association of Social Anthropology, 191
Evans-Pritchard, E.E., 14, 79, 166, 234, 235
'existential anthropology', 19, 45

Fagg, Bernard, 216
Fallers, Lloyd, 182
Far North, New Zealand, 76, 77
Fawlkner, Patrick, 137
Feld, Steve, 166
feminist anthropology, 16, 235, 236, 239–40
fieldwork encounters, 2, 3, 7, 14, 17, 47; anthropologist as pupil, 117; in anthropologist's own country, 67–68, 75, 76, 79, 97, 99, 100–1, 118–19, 153, 190, 202–4, 218–19; career-long association with same place, 162–66, 168–70; conversion of analysis into policy, 241, 243; engagement with other ways of being, 1, 8, 9, 10–12, 17–18, 22, 28, 70, 71, 102, 117–18, 122–23, 209, 210, 242–43, 251, 254; ethnographic methodology, 3, 7, 17, 25, 26, 47, 97 149–51, 153, 210, 219–20, 254; expansion of field sites and research methods, 17; important or revelatory moments, 47, 84–87, 99–100, 115–16, 134–35, 147–49, 168–69, 185–87, 221–25, 227–28, 237–39, 253; mistakes of anthropologists, 10, 48–49, 100–1, 116–17, 240–41; negative experiences, 26, 64, 68, 75, 86–87, 89, 97, 99–100, 136, 147, 148, 223; personal involvement of anthropologists with informants and communities, 12–14, 24–26, 40–41, 60–61, 63, 64–65,

66, 67, 68, 88, 97, 117, 135, 136, 169, 191, 203–4, 218, 252; Piddington's teaching, 81; protection and defence of fieldworkers by informants, 25–26, 68, 86, 87, 100, 148–49; protection of informants, 25, 218; and realignment of anthropologists' identities, 12, 42, 71; sense of discomfort about, 97; and serendipity, 10, 253; training, 81, 114–15, 146–47. *See also* ethnography; film and video; knowledge production; photography; research
film and video, 127, 133–34, 135, 150, 155–56, 170–71, 172–73
financialization of society, 248, 249
Firth, Raymond, 5, 79–80, 88, 184, 251
Fishbourne, Sussex, 234
Fisher, Vic, 76
folktales, 47–48, 77
Forde, Darryl, 129; *Habitat, Economy and Society*, 137
Foresters' Masonic Lodge, 39
Forge, Anthony, 133
forgiveness, 48–49
Forster, E.M., 207
Fortes, Meyer, 79, 88, 114–15, 236
Fortune, Reo, 236
Foucault, Michel, 17, 19, 22, 220
Fox, Jim, 114
France, 43, 188, 191, 243
Fried, Jack, 181
Friedrich, Paul, 185
Frobisher Bay (Iqaluit), 182
functionalism, 16, 43, 79, 80, 113, 114

G5 (or G7) countries, 248
Gandhi, Mahatma, 179
Garawa people, 148–49, 150
Geertz, Clifford, 2, 17, 47, 169, 172, 182, 183, 210, 226, 237
gender: arrival of term in anthropological vocabulary, 239; socially constructed nature of Western dichotomies, 18; Strathern's work, 239; and study of kinship systems, 189; in traditional Aboriginal society, 97–98; in traditional Hindu society, 18
'gender ideology', 19
generational shifts in anthropology, 3, 4, 16–17, 89–90
Genovese, Eugene, 144–45
Germany, 191
Ghana, 54
Gisborne, 12, 58–59, 61, 67
global and local levels in anthropology, 18, 138, 172–74, 209, 252
globalization, 123, 190, 201, 248–49; academia, 5; competitive world economy, 248; and cultural diversity, 138; focus on sameness and difference, 211–12; peripheral vantage points, 6, 250–51
Gluckman, Max, 45, 80, 202
Goffman, Erving, 62
'going native', 2, 7
Goinjimbi (Bulman), Australia, 98–99, 100
Golson, Jack, 37–38
Good, Kenneth, 2
Goodenough, Ward, 62
Goody, Jack, 44, 183
governance: Britain, transformation during Thatcher era, 22, 219–20, 221–23; neoliberal forms, 248; and rural communities in Iran and England, 217–18, 219, 222–25
Graburn, Nelson, 4, 9, 10, 12, 13, 16, 18, 19–20, 21, **176–94**, 253; *Ethnic and Tourist Arts*, 189; *To Pay, Pray and Play*, 188
Gramsci, Antonio, 17, 144
Greece, 43
Green, Roger, 59
Greenwood, Martin, 185
Group for Anthropology in Policy and Practice (GAPP), 228
Guanxi autonomous region, China, 192
Guilin, China, 192–93
Guinea Bissau, 54

Hamilton, Alexander, *The Federalist Papers*, 200
harmonization and uniformity, 248

Index 263

Harvard University, 46–47, 51–52, 181
Hastrup, Kirsten, 51
Head, Lesley, 145
Hertzfeld, Michael, 15, 51
Hiatt, Lester, 97, 99
Higgs, Eric, 200
Hinduism, 18, 160–61, 164
Hirsch, Eric, 244
historical influences on anthropologists, 3, 13, 39–40, 58, 60–61, 66–67, 77, 96, 225, 234
history, relationship to anthropology, 66–67, 69, 89, 102, 166, 215, 217, 226, 242
Hohepa, Pat, 5, 64
Holocaust, 147, 197
Homans, George C., 184–85
Honigmann, John, 186
hospital porters, Rapport's research, 198, 206–7
Howard University, 166
Howell, William, *Mankind So Far*, 37
Hudson Strait, 181, 182
Hugh-Jones, Stephen, 13
human rights, 24, 209, 210
Humanist Society, 201
humanities, 69
Hurd, Douglas, 222
Husserl, Edmund, 46
Hymes, Dell, 62

identity: cultural, 209–10, 211–12; national, 206–7; symbolic differences, 209, 211; at work, 206–7
Ilisapi Kululak people, 182
India, 18, 24, 138, 161–66, 168–71, 248
Indiana University, Bloomington, 51, 54
indigenous peoples, 5, 20; activism, 17, 18; anthropologists, 89, 190–91; commercialization of culture, 18, 20, 21, 178–79, 188–89; in a multicultural society, 94, 101, 103; multiple cultural perspectives, 22–23; ownership and repatriation of cultural artefacts, 249–50; perspectives, 6, 20; rights, 5, 20, 21; and tourism, 178–79, 188–89. *See also* Aboriginal people; Inuit, Canadian; Māori; Native Americans
individualism, 207; possessive, 21, 72; Thatcher's 'enterprising individual,' 19, 22, 219–20, 221–22
individuality: anthropological focus on individuals, 19, 48, 198, 204, 207, 208–11; Anyone, 208, 209, 210; individual as manifestation of the human, 199, 208, 209, 210, 211–12; individual world-views within a cultural community, 203–4; individuals, and communitarian assumptions of political apologies, 197–98; political and moral justice (emancipation), 207–8, 209, 210–11; representation, 207. *See also* self, concepts of
Indonesia, 142, 144, 248
industrial sociology, 162–63, 164
Inglewood, Taranaki, 37, 38–39
Institute of Aboriginal [and Torres Strait Islander] Studies. *See* Australian Institute of Aboriginal [and Torres Strait Islander] Studies
Institute of Community Studies, London, 111–12
intellectual property rights, 244–45
intellectuals, public, 2, 3
International Academy for the Study of Tourism meeting, Zakopane, Poland, 188
Inuit, Canadian, 18, 178–79, 181–82, 185–86, 188–89, 249; shrimp industry, 21, 191
Inuktituk language, 185
Iran, 18, 25, 216, 219, 223–25; forced settlement of nomadic people, 217–18; revolution, 18, 25, 218
Ishimori, Shuzo, 188
Islam, 107, 209, 211
Israel, 18, 147, 201–2, 205–6

Jackson, Michael, 5, 9, 10, 11, 12, 13, 14, 16, 18, 19, 26–27, **34–55**, 208; *The Accidental*

Anthropologist, 10, 50–51, 52; *At Home in the World*, 52–53; *Life Within Limits*, 53; *Paths Toward a Clearing*, 51; *The Politics of Storytelling*, 52
Jafari, Jafar, 188
James, William, 46
Japan, 187, 188
Japanese language, 187–88
Jay, John, *The Federalist Papers*, 200
Jewish people: American immigrants to Israel, 205–6; apologies to, 197; Brisbane, Australia, 146–47; Britain, 200; expansion of settlements in Israeli-occupied territories, 18
Jinzhongshan agricultural valley, China, 192
Jones, Pei Te Hurinui, 87

Kaa, Hone, 59
Kabbery, Phyllis, 129, 136
Kant, Immanuel, 198, 209
Kapferer, Bruce, 5
Karadjeri people, 26–27, 40, 79
Kasai Province, Congo, 42, 43
Katherine, Australia, 98, 99
Kaua, Peggy, 61
Kawharu, Margaret, 89
Kawharu, Sir Hugh, 5, 6, 44, 51, 64
Keen, Ian, 132
Keesing, Roger, 5, 114
Keita, Seydou, 165
Kent, England, 234
Kernot, Bernie, 80
kibbutz life, 201–2
Killoran, Pat, 146
Kimmirut (Lake Harbour NWT), 182, 186–87
Kingi, Wiremu, 39
kinship systems, 16, 119, 121, 132–33, 146, 183, 184–85, 186, 189
Kluckhohn, Clyde, 129
knowledge production, 2, 15–18, 20–21; and anthropological location, 4–7; 'emancipatory knowledge', 190; and government policy, 27–28, 242; importance of personal relations, 1, 13–14, 253; key contributors, 18–20; limits on, 241; and rethinking of neoliberal capitalism, 253; using margins to question and unsettle normative orders, 6, 14, 251. *See also* fieldwork encounters; research
kōhanga reo, 86–87
Kotare, Northland, New Zealand, 82–83, 85
Kuranko people, Sierra Leone, 34, 44, 49–50, 54
Kyoto, Japan, 188

labour relations and practices: and outsourcing of production to third world countries, 247–48; post-colonial, 247; rayon factory, India, 162–63
Labov, William, 62
Langton, Marcia, 145
Lapland, 112, 115
Latour, Bruno, 167, 171–72, 173
Laughton, Horiana, 86
Leach, Edmund, 13, 65, 180, 181, 183–84, 201, 236; 'Jinghpaw Kinship Terminology', 183; *Political Systems of Highland Burma*, 184
Leacock, Seth, 182
legal anthropology, 240–41
Leopoldville, Congo, 43
LeVine, Bob, 183
Lévi-Strauss, Claude, 9, 14, 45, 48, 51, 80, 132, 185; *Les Structures Élémentaires de la Parenté*, 43
Lewis, I.M., 129
Leyton, Elliot, 204, 205
linguistics, 61–62, 70, 133
Linton, Ralph, 184, 186, 201
Lips, Julius, 166
Lithuania, 200
local and global levels in anthropology, 18, 138, 172–74, 209, 252
Loizos, Peter, 162
London, 12, 40, 42, 76, 111–12, 128–30, 133, 179
London School of Economics, 76, 79, 161–62, 166, 167, 202
Luangiua, 61–62
Lucht, Hans, 54
Luluabourg, Congo, 42

Mabo v. Queensland, 110
MacCormack, Carol, 201
MacDougall, David and Judith, 134
Macfarlane, Alan, 201
Madison, James, *The Federalist Papers*, 200
Magee, Bryan, 167
Mahuta, Robert (Bob), 5, 64
Mair, Lucy, *Marriage*, 162
Malaya, 179
Malaysia, 142, 144
Malinowski, Bronislaw, 7, 79, 89, 166, 180
Malouf, David, 143–44
Malwa, India, 168–69
mana, 66, 68, 78
Manchester, 235
Manchester University, 202, 206
Māori: anthropologists, 190; archaeologists' research, 37–38; art, 189; culture, 5, 11, 22–23, 62, 64–65, 82–83; education, 5, 86–87; first meetings with *Pākehā*, 20, 66–67, 89; influence of anthropology on Māori leaders, 5–6, 64; inter-tribal warfare, 40; knowledge systems, 66, 75; land rights, 5, 6, 18, 21, 24, 39–40, 60, 64, 65, 75, 249; and literacy, 44; *mana*, 66, 68, 78; Metge's work, 20, 75, 76, 79, 80, 81–87; post-colonial restoration and reconciliation, 249; relations with anthropologists, 25–26, 64, 68, 75, 86–87, 89; relations with *Pākehā*, 63–64, 66–67, 75, 78, 80, 82–83, 84, 86, 87, 89; renaissance, 5, 59, 60, 64, 87; representation of culture in museums, 250; Salmond's work, 20, 62–69, 70, 71, 89; social activism, 5, 6, 18, 26, 59–60, 64, 65, 87; *tapu* (taboo), 22, 65, 66, 68; and tourism, 179; urban migration, 80, 81–82, 86; welfare, 43; *whakamaa*, 85. *See also te reo Māori* (Māori language); Treaty of Waitangi
Māori, early influence on anthropologists, 11–12; Anne Salmond, 58–61; Joan Metge, 77, 78, 80; Michael Jackson, 38–40

Māori Women's Welfare League, 86
Marcel, Gabriel, 52
Marriott, McKim, 174, 183
Martin, David, 145
Marx, Emanuel, 205
Marx, Karl, *Communist Manifesto*, 200
Marxism, 16, 121, 146, 235, 236. *See also* neo-Marxism
Massey University, 46, 51
Matamata, New Zealand, 77
material culture, 21, 129, 130, 133, 138, 167, 173
Maymuru, Narritjin, 131
McDonald, James, 58, 61
McGill University, 181, 184, 185
McLuhan, Marshall, *The Gutenberg Galaxy*, 44
Mead, Margaret, 184
medicalization of society, 248–49
Mediterranean, 202
Meggitt, Mervyn, 115
Meja, Volker, 204
Melanesia, 174
Memorial University, St John's, 204–5
Merleau-Ponty, Maurice, 45
Metge, Joan, 4, 11, 13–14, 16, 18, 20, 25–26, 27, **73–91,** 252; *The Māoris of New Zealand*, 83–84; *A New Māori Migration*, 81, 82
Metropolitan Museum of Modern Art, New York, 250
Mexico, 189
Miao people, 192
migration, 24, 54, 103, 143, 190, 247. *See also* rural–urban migration
Mikio, Kimura, 188
Mill, John Stuart, *On Liberty*, 200
Mitzpe Ramon, Israel, 205–6
modernity, 19, 170, 190, 201, 248
Montreal University, Canada Research Chair in Globalization, Citizenship and Justice, 206
Moon, Okpyo, 188
Morocco, 2, 205
Morphy, Frances, 115, 131, 132, 133, 135, 137
Morphy, Howard, 13, 16, 18, 20, 21, 27, 104, 115, **125–39**; *In Gentle Hands*, 127

Morrison, Stuart, 189
Motutapu Island, Auckland, 38
Mount Roskill, Auckland, 38
Mt Hagen, Papua New Guinea, 237, 238, 239, 243
Mulcock, Jane, 143
multicultural society: and concepts of 'nativeness', 143; and concepts of 'nature', 143; and indigenous peoples, 94, 101, 103; and theory developed in the south, 250
Muriwhenua claim, 77
Murngin. *See* Yolngu people
Muru-Lanning, Marama, 89
museums and museum collections, 138, 249–50
Myers, Fred, 115

Nader, Laura, 190
Nanda, Serena, 18
Nandy, Ashis, 169–70
Nash, June, 6, 247
Naskapi Cree, 183
National Council of Churches, Māori Section, 86
national identity, 206–7
National Museum of Ethnology, Japan, 188
National Science Foundation (US), 54, 184
Native Americans, 179, 183, 201, 216, 249
'nativeness' concepts, 142–45
'nature', 143, 144
Nazism, 211
Needham, Rodney, 45, 184–85
Negev Desert, 205–6
neo-colonialism, 178
neo-Darwinism, 172
neoliberalism, 19, 22, 27, 106–7, 219–20, 221–23, 226, 228, 253; analysis informed by the peripheries, 6, 247–48, 251
neo-Marxism, 114
neo-pragmatism, 46
New South Wales, Australia, 94, 97, 98, 100–1, 104–5
New Zealand: applied anthropology, 24; colonialism, 23; concepts of 'nativeness' and 'nature', 144; indigenous issues compared to Australia and Canada, 142, 249; multiple forms of indigeneity, 145; social anthropology discipline, 4–7; universities, government regulations and requirements, 27. *See also* Māori; periphery and peripheral visions; and names of individual cities, places and institutions
New Zealand Historic Places Trust, 70
Newfoundland, 204–5
Nga Tamatoa, 64
Ngata, Lady Lorna, 61
Ngata, Sir Apirana, 61, 83
Ngāti Maru, 39
Ngāti Porou, 59
Ngeru, Eddie, 38
Nkomo, Joshua, 43
North America, 144, 145, 160, 168, 191, 205, 216
Northern Coordination and Research Centre (NCRC), 181, 182
Northern Territory, Australia, 21, 98–100, 101, 110–11, 112, 120–21, 137, 151. *See also* Arnhem Land, Australia
north–south divide, 250–51
Nuer, 14, 217, 234
Nunavut Territory, 182

Oakland Buddhist Church, 187–88
Oakley, Ann, *Sex, Gender and Society*, 239
Opie, Iona and Peter, *The Classic Fairy Tales*, 47
oppression. *See* war, violence and political oppression
oral history, 63, 66, 69
Orientalism, 17
origins, distinguished from beginnings, 47–48
Ortner, Sherry, 183
Osaka, Japan, 188
Otakiri, New Zealand, 95, 96, 106
otherness, encountering, 1, 8, 9, 10–12, 17–18, 22, 28, 70, 71, 95, 96, 98, 209, 210, 242–43, 251, 254
outsourcing of factory production, 247–48
ownership, 5, 21, 128, 198; Aboriginal people, 98, 127;

'borrowing', 'sharing', and 'stealing', 16, 233–34; Māori knowledge, 22, 198–99, 211; self-ownership, 22, 198–99, 211. *See also* appropriation; property
Oxfam, 128
Oxford University, 215, 216–17, 225

Pacific Art Association conference, Wellington, New Zealand, 188
Paine, Robert, 204
Papua New Guinea, 18, 19, 22–23, 37, 114, 201, 233–34, 235, 236–39, 240–41, 244–45
Papua New Guinea Law Reform Commission, 240–41
Park, George, 204
Parker, Wiremu, 84, 87
Parsons, Talcott, 129
Paul, Robert, 183
Pawson, Andy, 62
Pearson, Noel, 145
Pennsylvania University, 62
People's Union for Civil Liberties (India), *Gas Chamber on the Chambal*, 162–63
periphery and peripheral visions, 4–7, 11, 14, 28, 247, 248–51
personal influences on anthropologists, 3, 10–12; Anne Salmond, 60–61; Christopher Pinney, 161, 162, 170; Gillian Cowlishaw, 95–96; Howard Morphy, 128–29; Joan Metge, 77–78, 80; Marilyn Strathern, 235–36; Michael Jackson, 39–40; Nelson Graburn, 179–80; Nicolas Peterson, 111–13; Nigel Rapport, 200, 201–2
Perth, 143
Peters, Emrys, 202
Peterson, Nicolas, 12, 16, 18, 21, 24, **108–24**, 134, 137
photography: as fieldwork method, 132, 133, 166, 168, 173–74; Indian small-town photographic practice, 164–65, 173; as metaphor for knowledge protocols of anthropology, 166; and visual memory, 187
physical (biological) anthropology, 10, 12–13, 129, 201

Piddington, Ralph, 13, 26–27, 40–41, 59, 76, 78, 81, 89
Pinney, Christopher, 4, 11, 17, 18, 20, 24, **158–75**, 252; *Camera Indica*, 168, 173; 'Epistemo-patrimony: Speaking and Owning in the Indian Diaspora', 160–61
Plato, definition of knowledge, 15
poetry, 52
Poland, 188, 200
policy: anthropology of, 222–23, 226, 227, 251–52; conversion of fieldwork analysis into policy, 241, 243
political issues, anthropologists' engagement with, 14, 24–25, 251
political oppression. *See* war, violence and political oppression
political science, 190, 200, 226, 227
possessive individualism, 21, 72
post-colonialism, 5, 6, 12, 18, 21, 23, 71, 145, 166, 247, 249; restoration and reconciliation, 5, 249
post-modernism, 17, 88
Pouwer, Jan, 51, 76, 80
Poverty Bay, New Zealand, 66–67
Powdermaker, Hortense, 190
power: anthropological concern with, 16, 19, 107, 152, 153, 190, 228; and apology, 197; cultural perspectives, 22–23, 241; and gender, 19; institutions as subjects of, 226; and race relations, 144; and self-ownership, 199
pragmatism, 46
Price, Frances, 235
Proll, Astrid, 202–3
promise, 49
property: concepts of 'borrowing', 'sharing', and 'stealing', 16, 233–34; intellectual property rights, 244–45; vocabularies, 233–34. *See also* appropriation; ownership
public opinion about anthropology, 7–8, 154
public sphere, anthropologists in: Aboriginal art, 138; attempts to break down social barriers, 52–53, 63–64; defence of academia,

243, 253; industry, 149, 150, 151, 152; intellectual property rights, Papua New Guinea, 244–45; Inuit shrimp industry, 21, 191; land claims, 21, 24, 77, 102–3, 110–11, 119–21, 137, 149, 150–52, 154, 191; museums, 138; Native American education and self-empowerment, 183; policy work, 20, 24–25, 90, 122, 153–54, 227, 243–44, 251–52; public intellectuals, 2, 3; relationships between anthropologists and practitioners, 227–29; science community, 70; teaching, 2–3, 191; tourism-development projects in China, 192–93; university politics, 70; writing and speaking, 52–53, 62–64, 70–71, 104–6, 155, 171
Pukekohe, Auckland, 77–78, 80
Punjabi, Suresh, 165

qualitative research methods, 149
quantitative research methods, 149, 190
Queensland, Australia, 144, 146, 147–49. *See also* Brisbane, Australia
Queensland University, 145–46

Rabinow, Paul, 2, 183
racism, 20; Australia, 98–99, 104–6, 146; New Zealand, 39, 63–64, 78, 80, 82
Rappaport, Roy, *Pigs for the Ancestors*, 114
Rapport, Nigel, 4, 10, 12, 13, 17, 18, 19, 22, **195–212**
reflexivity, 2, 3, 14, 28, 137, 225, 229, 235, 253
representation of other cultures, 22–23, 28, 62–66
reproductive technologies, 235–36
research: Anne Salmond, 61–68; Christopher Pinney, 169–70; commercialization, 27; David Trigger, 142–45, 149–51; Gillian Cowlishaw, 97–99; Howard Morphy, 131–34; institutional regimes and contexts, 26–28,

54; Joan Metge, 76–77; Michael Jackson, 44–46, 54; Nelson Graburn, 187–89; Nicolas Peterson, 113–14; Nigel Rapport, 198, 202–8; shifting of focus in response to events on the ground, 17; Susan Wright, 226–27. *See also* fieldwork encounters; knowledge production
Rhodesia, 112, 115
Richards, Audrey, 79, 88
Ricoeur, Paul, 47–48
Rimaldi, Max, 45
Rivers, W.H.R., 166
Romania, 200
Rousseau, Jean-Jacques, 14, 234, 235
Rowlands, Mike, 173
Royal Anthropological Institute (RAI), London, 129–30
Royal Commission into Aboriginal Land Rights, 110, 111, 120
rural communities, and government decision-making: England, 219, 222–23; Iran, 217–18, 223–25
rural–urban migration: Aboriginal people, 94, 97, 102–4; Britain, 81; India, 162–63; Kuranko people, 54; Māori, 80, 81–82, 86; theories, 81–82
Russia, 95, 178, 205, 248

Sahlins, M., 21, 114
Salluit (Sugluk), 182, 185–86
Salmond, Anne, 5, 9, 11, 12, 13, 16, 18, 20, 22, **56–72**, 89; *Amiria: The Life Story of a Maori Woman*, 63; *Eruera: Teachings of a Maori Elder*, 64–65; *Hui: A Study of Maori Ceremonial Gatherings*, 62; 'Theoretical Landscapes', 66; *Two Worlds: First Meetings between Maori and Europeans, 1692-1772*, 66; *Between Worlds: Early Exchanges between Maori and Europeans, 1773-1815*, 67
Sami people, 112
San people, 142
Sandall, Roger, 112–13
Sartre, Jean-Paul, 45, 96
Schneider, David, 182, 183, 184–85, 189

scholarly influences on anthropologists, 3, 12–13, 14, 16–17; Anne Salmond, 60, 62, 65; Christopher Pinney, 162, 166–67; David Trigger, 144–47; Gillian Cowlishaw, 95–97; Howard Morphy, 128–30; Joan Metge, 79–80, 81–82, 84, 88; Marilyn Strathern, 234, 235, 236; Michael Jackson, 37–38, 43, 45–46; Nelson Graburn, 180–83, 184–85, 189; Nicolas Peterson, 114; Nigel Rapport, 200–1, 202, 204–5; Susan Wright, 215–17
Schwartz, Ron, 204
Scobie, Dick, 78–79
Scottishness, research on, 206
self, concepts of, 19, 22, 198–99; diversity within and between selves, 204; ontology of selfhood, 19, 22, 199, 207, 208, 209
self-ownership, 22, 198–99, 211
Sen, Amartya, 53
Sharples, Pita, 5, 59, 64
Shore, C., 18, 25, 27, 221, 223, 226, 228, 242, 249, 253
Sider, Gerry, 144
Sidibé, Malcik, 165
Sierra Leone, 18, 44, 48–49, 52, 53
Singapore, 95, 179
Singer, Milton, 183
Sitka Native Corporation, Alaska, 178–79
Smith, Valene, *Hosts and Guests*, 189
social activism, 2–3, 41, 252; Aboriginal people, 146; indigenous peoples, 17, 18; Māori, 5, 6, 18, 26, 59–60, 64, 65, 87
social anthropology, 15, 40, 76, 129, 200, 201, 234–35; Australia and New Zealand, differences from Britain, 4–7; British tradition, 4; cross-cultural fieldwork as defining feature, 7; practice of, 2–3
social conscience, 243–44
social issues, anthropologists' engagement with, 1, 14, 21, 24–25, 26–27, 234
social justice, 6, 14, 15, 41, 77

sociality, 44, 95, 113, 119, 222, 234
sociolinguistics, 62, 66
sociology, 190
Solomon Islands, 62
South Africa, 142, 144, 179, 248
South America, 142
South Asia, 172, 173, 189
Southeast Asia, 179
south–north divide, 250–51
Spanish Inquisition, 211
Spencer, Stanley, 207
Sri Lanka (Ceylon), 161, 179–80
St Andrews University, 206; Centre for Cosmopolitan Studies, 208
St John's, Newfoundland, 204–5
stereotypes: of Aboriginal people, 105–6; about Africa, 53; of anthropologists, 7–8, 154; and discourses of collective belonging, 209–10
Stirling, Amiria, 59, 60, 61, 62, 63, 66, 67, 68, 71
Stirling, Eruera, 59, 60–1, 62, 63, 64–65, 66, 67, 68, 71
Strathern, Andrew, 236
Strathern, Marilyn, 9, 12–13, 14, 16, 18, 19, 22–23, 27–28, 65, 167, 171–72, 174, 198, 206, **231–46**, 249, 253; *The Gender of the Gift*, 235, 236; *Women in Between*, 235, 239, 240
structural functionalism, 16, 79, 80, 113, 114
structuralism, 16, 43, 51, 80
subjectivity, 19, 46–47
Sugluk (Salluit), 182, 185–86
'supply chain capitalism', 6
Sussex University, 219
Sutton, Peter, 145
Sydney, Australia, 23, 40, 94, 97, 103
Sydney University, 51, 99, 144
symbolic anthropology, 236

talking-relationships in cities, 205
Tanner, Adrian, 204
tapu (taboo), 22, 65, 66, 68
Taranaki, New Zealand, 37, 38–40, 39–40
Taussig, Michael, 5, 162, 163
Tax, Sol, 182, 183

Te Hau, Matiu, 82, 87
Te Kuri a Paoa (Young Nick's Head), Gisborne, 12, 61
Te Māori exhibition, Metropolitan Museum of Modern Art, 250
Te Rangi Hiroa (Sir Peter Buck), 58, 76, 83
te reo Māori (Māori language), 5
Te Whānau-ā-Apanui, 59
teaching, 2–3, 13, 16; Anne Salmond, 68–69; Jack Golson, 37–38; Joan Metge, 76, 79; Michael Jackson, 50; Nelson Graburn, 191; Ralph Piddington, 13, 40, 59, 79, 81
technology, and anthropology, 137, 241–42
Thatcher, Margaret, 19, 22, 219–20, 221–22, 228
'Third Stream' activities in universities, 27
third world countries and societies, 129, 131, 247–48
Thompson, E.P., 162, 163
Thomson, Donald, 115
Tioke, Tawhao, 84, 87
Tlingit people, 179
Torres Strait Islanders, 144–45
tourism, 178, 189; China, 192–93; and commercialization of indigenous culture, 20, 21, 178–79, 188–89; indirect, 189; Japanese domestic, 188; medical, 190; 'reproductive', 190; 'roots', 189
Tourism Research Institute/NGO, Guilin, China, 192–93
Treaty of Waitangi, 6, 60, 249
Tregear, Edward, 77
Trigger, David, 14, 17, 18, 24, 26, **140–57**
Trnka, Susanna, 25, 251
Trobriand Islands, 7
Trotsky, Leon, 162
Tuhoe, 84, 89
Turkey, 181, 190
Turner, Victor, 45, 80
Turton, David, 202

Ucko, Peter, 129, 130, 131
Ujjain, India, 170
UNESCO, 179, 192

United Nations, 42; Social Affairs Department, 43
United States, 4, 24, 52, 59, 138, 184, 188, 189, 223, 248, 249. *See also* Native Americans
universities: audit culture, 18, 206, 221, 242, 249, 253–54; defence of academia, 243, 253; government policies, 26, 27–28, 54, 221, 226–27, 242, 249; self-owning institutions, 226–27
University College London (UCL), 129, 130, 134, 136, 138, 173
University of ... *See under* name of city or state, e.g. Cambridge University
urban migration. *See* rural–urban migration

Valentine, Vic, 185
Venezuela, 2
Victoria, Australia, 41
Victoria University, 51, 76, 77, 80, 84
Vigh, Henrik, 54
violence. *See* war, violence and political oppression
visual anthropology, 130, 134, 137, 167–68, 172–74. *See also* film and video; photography
visual memory, 187
Von Sturmer, John, 146

Wade, Peter, 2
Wagner, Roy, 236
Waitangi Tribunal, 40, 77
Waitara block, Taranaki, 39
Walker, Ranginui, 5, 64
Wanet, Yorkshire, 202–4, 205
Wannambi, Welwe, 134–35
war, violence and political oppression, 25, 107; violence in Newfoundland, 205; war in Sierra Leone, 49–50, 52
Warner, Lloyd, 79, 132
Weber, Max, 8, 121
welfare state, British, 219, 225, 228
Wellington, New Zealand, 43, 58
Wells, Edgar, 131
Werbner, Dick, 202
Wesley, Professor, 181
West Africa, 173

whakamaa, 85
Whitehead, Harriet, 183
Whyte, Susan Reynolds, 51
Wik people, 146
Williams, Nancy, 136
Willmott, Peter, 112
Winiata, Maharaia, 86
Witkiewicz, Stanislaw, 166
Wolf, Eric, 10
Wollogorang, Gerald, 150
Woodward, A.E., 110, 135
World Intellectual Property Organization, 244
World Trade Organization, 244
Wright, Susan, 9, 13, 16, 18, 19, 22, 25, 27, **213–30**, 249, 251, 253
writing, anthropological, 1, 2, 3, 20, 119, 136, 207, 209; about Africa, 53; Anne Salmond, 62–64, 66, 70–71; David Trigger, 155; Gillian Cowlishaw, 104–6; Joan Metge, 76–77, 81, 83; Michael Jackson, 46–47, 52–53. *See also* titles of books under names of contributors to this book

Xavier High School, Chuuk, Micronesia, 16

Yalman, Nur, 181
Yamashita, Shinji, 188
Yang Shengmin, 192
Yanomami people, 2
Yanyuwa people, 157n.1
Yap, 184
Yarmirr case, 111
Yatsushiro, Toshio, 181, 185
Yirrkala, Australia, 131, 133
Yolngu people, 127–28, 131, 132–33, 134–35, 138
Young, Michael, 112
Young Nick's Head (Te Kuri a Paoa), Gisborne, 12, 61

Zaslavsky, Victor, 204
Zhang Xiaosong, 192